S0-BRV-192

Race and Kinship in a Midwestern Town

BLACKS IN THE NEW WORLD: *August Meier, Series Editor*

A list of books in the series appears at the end of this volume.

Race and Kinship in a Midwestern Town:

The Black Experience in Monroe, Michigan, 1900–1915

James E. DeVries

University of Illinois Press
Urbana and Chicago

Publication of this work was supported in part by a grant from the Andrew W. Mellon Foundation.

This book is printed on acid-free paper.

Library of Congress Cataloging in Publication Data

DeVries, James E., 1941–
Race and kinship in a Midwestern town.

(Blacks in the New World)
Includes index.
1. Afro-Americans—Michigan—Monroe—Social conditions. 2. Afro-American families—Michigan—Monroe. 3. Monroe (Mich.)—Race relations. 4. Monroe (Mich.)—Social conditions. I. Title. II. Series.
F574.M7D48 1984 305.8'96073'077432 83-6508
ISBN 0-252-01084-1

To Sharon for her patience

Contents

Preface

From a demographic standpoint, it is clear that most Americans, Negro and white, lived in rural settings until the second decade of the twentieth century. Yet for the most part, the black experience in the first years of the current century has been related and interpreted against the backdrop of the southern plantation and of northward migration and urbanization. While these are certainly important themes, the lives of blacks particularly in small towns and agrarian areas outside the South have remained unnoticed and uninvestigated by the professional historian. Frankly, little is generally known about the Afro-American past in those environments. This inquiry is addressed to that gap in historical understanding and knowledge.

Monroe, Michigan, the focus of this study, was similar to the hundreds of other small communities in the Midwest where "handfuls" of blacks lived, worked, and raised their families. Always present, but few in number, the Negroes in Monroe did not establish or develop their own ethnic enclave until the 1920s. Before then local Afro-Americans were destined to carry on their lives in an overwhelmingly white milieu. How did they fare?

In an effort to answer that query, the problem has been addressed from both a white and a black perspective. In fact, on the subject of racism, this chronicle is as much about Caucasians as Negroes. How did whites "learn" about blacks in a setting where an Afro-American subculture was nonexistent? Of course, few, if any, of Monroe's white majority had any real understanding or grasp of black perspectives or cultural practices, yet it is certain that many of her "finest" regarded themselves as knowledgeable in this area. How did this transpire? Tracing the development of white racist folk thought in Monroe provides a partial explanation. Insights from the historians and interpreters of popular culture are refracted against actual events in the city to show the presence and development of racial stereotypes. A careful investigation of such folk expressions as Negro minstrelsy, as played in the community, the proliferation of racist ideas in large city and Monroe newspapers, and the memories of Monroe citizens provide the keys that unlock this process of perverse socialization.

More important are the ways in which racist ideas constrained black life chances and affected the lives of all Negroes who dwelled in or passed through Monroe in the first fifteen years of the twentieth century. What social, occupational, economic, and residential opportunities were open to Afro-Americans in Monroe? A combined cliometric and anthropological approach, which develops data from the decennial manuscript censuses, Monroe city directories, and other sources, delineates black life chances in these respects. Perhaps the most important finding in this regard was the presence and persistence of several "favored" Negro families in Monroe. Indeed, a careful reconstitution of several black family trees reveals that the *only* Afro-Americans who achieved economic and property mobility during these years were those who could trace their roots in the community to the Reconstruction era or before.

While on the surface it would appear that these people were not barred from participating in the American Dream in the community, it is certain that their very real accomplishments were due primarily to individual tenacity and to the continued presence of several black mutual support kinship networks, rather than to any inherent openness in the city's class structure. To be sure, several of Monroe's Negro "native sons" were able to avoid unemployment, purchase homes, and provide their children with secondary education—achievements that eluded many whites. Nonetheless, even these hard-won successes, as viewed from the vantage point of the late twentieth century, seem ephemeral. Ultimately, only those Afro-Americans who could cross the color line would remain in the community and unfetter themselves in their quest for mobility. As for the others, they would die or move on to other environs. Today, no individual or family claiming a black identity in Monroe can trace his or their origins in the community to the pre–World War I era.

On a more intimate note, this investigation is essentially about black identity in Monroe. Who were these people? How were they regarded in the community? How did they view themselves? The concepts of role theorists and social psychologists are particularly useful in establishing a framework to discuss these human dilemmas. The problems Negroes faced in creating and establishing individual identities in Monroe are seen as reflecting both racism and the viability of Afro-American family networks. Certainly, identity for the city's native blacks was always ambiguous. On the other hand, some did acquire personal identities with redeeming qualitites—primarily because they were "known." How they perceived this predicament can only be inferred from their actions and the few personal statements that have survived. The investigation of the difficulties they faced in maintaining individual identities in a hostile environment provides the necessary strand—the common theme—that holds this study together.

Much of the material and data used in this history is nontraditional in nature and local in origin. County vital and probate records, cemetery listings, Monroe city registers of electors, tax assessment rolls, maps, church minutes, and business ledgers and account books, when added to information in the city directories and federal population schedules, permitted the reconstitution of black family trees and kinship networks. Much of the "story" of these people's lives was reconstructed from references in local newspapers. Each publisher of the various Monroe presses during this time period supplied his readers with gossipy "news about town" columns, and each of the Negroes treated biographically was mentioned on numerous occasions as "doing this or that." Although much of the foregoing kinds of data has survived for the several decades preceding the turn of the century, the selection, for close scrutiny, of the era between 1900 and 1915 was not arbitrary but was made with much forethought. Put simply, this was the earliest period in Monroe's past for which the memories of its living citizens were still accessible. An important portion of the narrative is based on oral history sources; indeed, there were enough reminiscences to render living texture and dimension to the written and printed documents.

Because it draws from so many disciplines and the basic data originates from and reflects so many different sources, the organization of this study moves back and forth across various levels and dimensions of the human experience. The ideas of social psychologist Erving Goffman and intellectual historian George Fredrickson, and the insights of social anthropologists, were invaluable in this task. Specifically, the introduction provides the reader with a general portrait of Monroe in 1900. The first chapter demonstrates the presence of several black kinship networks in the city and answers questions regarding Negro occupational opportunity, residential patternings, institutional integration, and political involvement. Chapters 2 and 3 explain the development of racist stereotypes in the white community and their impact on the lives of blacks. Biography is utilized in the final chapter to portray the quality of life experienced by selected Monroe Negroes. In the conclusion the phenomenon of "passing" is discussed. In essence this account moves from Monroe to a national, back to a local, and then to an individual frame of reference. The goal was to depict in as complete a manner as possible the prevailing atmosphere of life for Afro-Americans in Monroe in the first years of the twentieth century.

A basic assumption throughout this inquiry is that Monroe's values, behavioral norms, and cultural understandings were national in nature. While her actual history was unique, the mind-set of Monroe's inhabitants was not. The mobility of people moving in and out of the city, for short or long duration, combined with an effective nationwide mass media of newspapers, periodicals, magazines, books, and entertainment forms, ensured that Monroe's citizens shared the thoughts and perceptions of most Americans. The community was not isolated. The crucial social and cultural processes affecting blacks in Monroe were national in scope. The city's experience reflected, in microcosm, forces and ideas at work throughout the country. Consequently, the black experience in Monroe provides a lens through which a national theme, racism, can be clearly viewed.

At the least, the local setting of Monroe has furnished a sufficient backdrop for examining and illuminating some of the enduring issues in Afro-American history. The manner in which these questions are addressed and answered will determine the success of this study. This narrative endeavors to provide some movement toward understanding and interpreting the lives of the thousands of "faceless" Afro-Americans living in the many small Midwestern communities at the turn of the twentieth century.

Invariably, when one embarks on the road to publication, numerous debts are incurred in the process. I spent more than a few hours ferretting-out some rather obscure portions of Monroe history in the Detroit Public Library-Burton Historical Collections, the University of Michigan, Bentley Library-Michigan Historical Collections, and the Toledo Public Library-Local History Department. The staffs at each of these institutions were helpful and facilitated my quest for Monroe data. The Monroe County Library System and the *Monroe Evening News* graciously shared all their pertinent holdings. I also appreciate the access given me by the

County of Monroe to vital and probate records. A debt of gratitude is owed to Charles Verhoeven, Jr., for permitting me to look over his extensive Monroe manuscript holdings. Special thanks in this regard are due to the Monroe County Historical Museum. Through many productive and delightful afternoons, archivist Patricia Hudson provided essential assistance in unearthing material pertaining to my topic.

The manuscript has been read by many individuals at various stages of development. As a doctoral dissertation, it was carefully perused and edited by my chairman, the late Lester F. Schmidt, my thesis advisor, C. Warren Vander Hill, and Whitney Gordon. Several of my colleagues at Monroe County Community College, including David Moore, John Holladay, Robert Merkel, Grant Strickland, and Gerald Welch, aided and encouraged me at this level. As I proceeded through the several rewrites moving toward publication, two of my friends were particularly solicitous. Dennis Au and Donna Hicks read through the manuscript several times. Most important to the fruition of this book was my editor, August Meier. His discerning judgments and suggestions not only prevented numerous errors but added depth to the interpretation. I am especially thankful that he persevered with me over a several-year period.

Also deserving recognition for their conscientious and proficient typing and word processing are Judy Hileman and Lori Meader. Deserving credit for the many hours of darkroom work that went into the photos and maps in this volume are Ron Goulet and Dennis Au. The indexing task was accomplished through many hours of time investment by Patricia Hudson and is most appreciated. In addition, I would like to thank my copy editor Ann Prisland Thorpe for the meticulous attention she paid to the final manuscript. Finally, I would like to acknowledge the Board of Trustees of Monroe County Community College for extending me a leave without which this project would not have been completed.

INTRODUCTION

Monroe, Michigan, 1900–1915

> For a number of years the second oldest city in Michigan has been enjoying an era of prosperity which has been very gratifying to her public-spirited citizens, and a surprise to the few pessimists who still tarry within her borders, always ready to raise the calamity howl, with or without provocation. The unprecedented growth of the past four years has not partaken of the "boom" or mushroom order, but has rather an element of substantiality which becomes apparent when one takes note of the character of buildings which have been erected during that period.
>
> *City Directory, Monroe, Michigan, 1905*

> The old town of Monroe, which, in its existence of more than a century, has kept the even tenor of its way undisturbed by "booms," is beginning to attract the attention of manufacturers as being from its eligible location and general advantages especially adapted to various industrial enterprises.
>
> "Monroe, Mich.," *Detroit Free Press,* 25 Oct. 1891

Monroe, Michigan? To the student of American history, Monroe may be recalled as the site of the "Massacre of the River Raisin" in the War of 1812 or as George Armstrong Custer's boyhood home. Nothing else seems to distinguish its past from that of hundreds of other contemporary small midwestern towns. Located on the western shores of Lake Erie near the mouth of the River Raisin, about twenty miles north of Toledo, Ohio, and thirty-five miles south of Detroit, Monroe was first settled in the 1780s by people of French descent. The community was called Frenchtown until July 1817 when it was renamed in honor of the nation's fifth president, who was visiting the area at the time.

Destined to remain a small rural community during its first century of existence, Monroe was little more than a way station between Detroit and Toledo in the closing decades of the nineteenth century.[1] Its population stabilized near 5,000 in 1870, and no appreciable change would occur until after 1900. While it would neither become a large metropolis nor compete commercially with its big-city neighbors to the north and south, forces were beginning to work in Monroe in 1890 which would transform it from a farming hamlet to an urban community in the next quarter-century. The following descriptions and assessments of Monroe in the period between 1890 and 1915 will give an overview of some of the more important changes in the community at that time. It was against this backdrop that local Negroes carried on their lives.

Monroe in 1890 was not without its charm. Stately elms lined the residential streets, and spacious lawns and flower gardens encircled large antebellum homes.[2] Lake Erie, the River Raisin, and the extensive marsh lands provided aquatic recreation possibilities which were absent in most small cities. Monroe's bucolic qualities attracted many visitors, and the town was generally regarded as a desirable place of residence.

Except for a few brick and cedar-block streets surrounding Loranger Square, where the county courthouse was located, and Front Street, which was paved from the center of the town, west to the Père Marquette railroad station—a distance of more than a mile—Monroe's avenues were dirt.[3] The city's hired driver could be seen every weekday, first dragging and then sprinkling the streets behind his team of horses. In the evening, gaslights illuminated the business section, but the wooden sidewalks running past the town's homes were easily visible only on moonlit nights. Citizens still got their water for domestic purposes from wells on their property, and only the affluent had water closets in their homes. A few businesses had telephones, but most of the townspeople had not yet discovered the invention's usefulness.

In essence, Monroe was a "farmer's" town. A goodly portion of its economy revolved around trade from the outlying agricultural district, and the town's business section contained several of all the "necessary" stores. Patrons could choose from a wide selection of retail establishments. The business listings for the *Monroe City Directory* of 1892–93 included three clothiers, six dry goods and millinery businesses, nineteen grocers, and twenty saloons.[4]

Its basic transportation system, which included three major railroad trunk lines and a Lake Erie port, had remained essentially unchanged since the Civil War. Monroe's primary industry in 1890, the nursery business, was first organized in the late 1840s. Known nationally as a nursery center since that time, Monroe had acquired the appellation of "The Floral City." The two largest firms, the Monroe Nursery and Greening Brothers' River Raisin Valley Nurseries, shipped thousands of trees and plants by rail each year to destinations throughout the country. Each company employed large sales and clerical staffs and sizable field crews.

While members of virtually every racial and nationality group lived in Monroe at one time or another, its basic ethnic makeup in 1890 was French, English, and German. The French people remained dominant until the 1830s, when incoming English began to take control of the politics and commerce of the community. Germans began to migrate to Monroe in appreciable numbers in the late 1840s and by post–Civil War days made up a sizable minority in the city. These nationalities were reflected in the existence of the various churches of Monroe. Each group was identified with one of the Roman Catholic parishes: St. Mary's was recognized as the "French" parish, St. Michael's as the "German," and St. John's as the "English and Irish." Both the Missouri and Wisconsin Lutheran synods had churches in the community, Trinity and Zion respectively, for their Protestant German members; Protestant English attended the First Presbyterian, St. Paul's Methodist, or Trinity Episcopal in the largest numbers. The Baptists also had a congregation in Monroe.[5]

Beginning in the 1890s, Monroe's character slowly began to change as the new technology in the form of electric lighting and citywide sanitation was introduced and telephones became instruments of general use. As a rule, "The Floral City" lagged ten or more years behind Toledo and Detroit in those areas. Before the turn of the century, the first public water mains and sewers were laid, a private electric lighting plant was built, and the city commenced a project to replace all the wooden sidewalks with concrete. Nothing, however, did more to alter Monroe's rural character than the development of the electric interurban railways. The extensive preparations of the 1890s for a Monroe-Toledo connection were finally realized in 1901, and the line was extended to Detroit two years later. The torn-up streets, new power house, rebuilt bridges, and numerous utility poles lining Monroe Street did much to create an urban atmosphere. Just as important was the easy access which the Detroit, Monroe and Toledo Short Line Railway gave Monroeites to their large urban neighbors. At the cost of a few cents, Monroe citizens could visit, shop, or even work in Toledo or Detroit. Monroe's population became more cosmopolitan in viewpoint as a result of these trips, and the town became a quasi suburb of its neighboring metropolises.

Also portentous was William Greening's purchase of the first automobile in Monroe in 1901.[6] At first a toy for the rich, by 1912 over one hundred autos were owned in the city.[7] The commitment to this new mode of transportation in Monroe was reflected in numerous ways: the owners of autos began building "snug little homes for their machines"[8]; the city council launched extensive and expensive projects to pave its more important thoroughfares, and new business enterprises emerged to manufacture, sell, and service the automobile. By 1915 the paved connections extending from Detroit to Toledo through Monroe were beginning to supersede the interurbans as the primary means of transportation between those cities.

To meet the needs of its burgeoning population, which had increased by over 50 percent since 1890, there was an appreciable growth in the number of retail establishments. The business directory for the 1892–93 *Monroe City Directory* was a mere two pages in length; a listing of establishments for the 1915–16 *City Directory* comprised ten pages. There were more businesses of every kind. Notable additions over the period included automobile-related businesses, electric supply companies, insurance agencies, plumbing shops, and telephone offices.[9]

While the nurseries continued to prosper, the industrial face of Monroe was altered greatly. Between 1900 and 1913 Monroe added a glass factory, a large office furniture company, a motor company, two canning factories, and a new paper mill to its list of industries. It would be a mistake, however, to conclude that Monroe's new factories determined the city's character. Rather, it was the enormous expansion in the native paper mill industry, which had its beginnings in the 1880s, that did so. If Monroe was a nursery town in 1890, it was a paper mill city in 1915, and a majority of the city's working class was employed by the paper mills in that year.

Among the city's growing populace was an ethnic group which was new to Monroe. In the early 1900s, men of Italian descent began coming to Monroe to work in the stone quarries and on construction projects. At first they were largely transient, working when there were jobs and then moving on when tasks were completed. By 1911, however, there were enough permanent residents from southern Italy in Monroe to muster a cornet band, and within two years they had formed a Christopher Columbus Mutual Aid

Society.[10] To the church structure of Monroe were added Evangelical and Christian Scientist congregations, but the Italian group would have to wait for its own parish until 1923, when St. Joseph's Catholic Church was founded.[11]

Afro-Americans do not appear to have fared as well as other ethnic groups during this time period. The formation of a true Afro-American community and subculture would have to wait until well into the third decade of the century. There would be no founding of a black church, nor would any Negro mutual improvement society be initiated.

It was in this setting that the American theme of "racism" was played out in Monroe. The goal of this study is to demonstrate the manner in which that theme affected and worked through the lives of Negro and white Monroe citizens during the first years of the twentieth century. In the process, as complete a statement as possible will be made regarding the black experience in Monroe, a small midwestern American city.

NOTES

1. The two basic histories of Monroe County are Talcott E. Wing, *History of Monroe County* (New York: Munsell, 1890), and John Bulkley, *History of Monroe County Michigan*, 2 vols. (Chicago: Lewis, 1913). Unfortunately, neither was of great value in writing this introduction since both lack balance and synthesis. As county histories go, however, Wing's must be rated with the best. It is a treasure chest of information. Bulkley's study, a "subscription" history, rehashes much of Wing's data and is of most value for the time period between 1890 and 1910. The information in this chapter was gleaned primarily from accounts in the local newspapers. Also of great usefulness were Michigan's annual factory inspection reports.

2. An excellent description of Monroe at this time period is contained in the reminiscence by David Elihu Winkworth, "From Lotus Beds to Umfolossi: An Autobiography of David Elihu Winkworth," unpublished manuscript, Monroe County Library, 1970, p. 14.

3. Landon Cooke, interviewed in his home at 404 North Macomb, Monroe, by Ben Tompkins, 16 Apr. 1977. At that time, Mr. Cooke, a lifelong resident of Monroe, was eighty-three. Mr. Tompkins was an undergraduate student in American history in 1977.

4. *Monroe City Directory 1892–93* (Monroe: Frank Wilder, 1892).

Other businesses listed were two bakeries, five stationery stores, six boot and shoe shops, four drugstores, four hardware establishments, three hotels, three notions stores, and four tailor shops. Because Monroe's city directories had a number of different publishers between 1860 and 1915, they often appeared under different titles. Hereafter, each will be cited by its correct title.

5. Ibid. Also see Wing, "History of the Churches of Monroe County," in *History of Monroe County*, pp. 498–523.

6. *Monroe Democrat,* 5 Sept. 1901, p. 5; *Monroe Record,* 5 Sept. 1901, p. 4.

7. *Record-Commercial,* 23 May 1912, p. 7. This newspaper was the Republican organ of the city of Monroe from 1904 until its sale to the *Monroe Evening News* in 1921.

8. *Monroe Democrat,* 29 Sept. 1911, p. 1.

9. *City Directory, Monroe, Michigan 1915–16* (Monroe: McMillan, 1915), pp. 147–56.

10. *Record-Commercial,* 20 Apr. 1911, p. 7, 9 Jan. 1913, p. 12. Unfortunately, a detailed analysis of the foreign population of Monroe between 1890 and 1915 is impossible. "Data on aliens are not shown for 1890, 1900 and 1910, because the information collected in those censuses was restricted to males 21 years of age and older." *Historical Statistics of the United States Colonial Times to 1957* (Washington, D.C.: U.S. Department of Commerce, 1961), p. 3.

11. *City Directory, Monroe, Michigan 1915–16,* p. 156.

1

Black Kinship Networks and the Afro-American Presence in Monroe, 1785–1915

> Twenty-one able bodied negroes passed through Monroe on Sunday last on their way to the Quaker Settlement in Oakland.
>
> *Michigan Sentinel,*
> 21 Oct. 1825

> "Bill" Cobb, an expert shoe polish manipulator from Flint, is permanently located at Charles Verhoeven's barber shop and is prepared to shine up your foot gear with as resplendent a lustre as that of his own dusky countenance.
>
> *Monroe Democrat,*
> 16 Sept. 1910

The oral tradition of Monroe of the 1950s has it that Aaron Bromley, who arrived in the city sometime in the 1860s, was Monroe's first Negro.[1] Older folks reminiscing today recall that his son, James, was the intial Afro-American resident. People just beyond middle age suggest that the Covingtons and Caines, who arrived shortly after World War I or in the early 1920s, and who were among the founders of Monroe's current black community, are the city's earliest black inhabitants. And so goes the spoken past: each generation can only review accurately what it has experienced, and people misrepresent what their forebears have told them. None of the surviving oral history is accurate on the question of the "first" Afro-American in Monroe. In fact, the black tradition not only runs back to the period of original European settlement in the late eighteenth century, but some of the "white" people in town today are descendants of a mulatto family that had its Monroe beginnings in the territorial period, and the local roots of several Negro families of the early twentieth century ran deep—to the Civil War era and before.

While it is not within the purview of this study to investigate in depth the white-Negro tradition in Monroe before 1900, the fact that most Afro-Americans of that era had extensive nineteenth-century backgrounds means that recreating a black demographic past for the community is an important task. Retrieving hard data about the lives of Afro-Americans from the distant past has been the bane of those historians interested in the black experience, and what has survived from the Negro past in Monroe provides no exception to that generalization.[2] This is certainly true of the early population structure of the area. Indeed, it is impossible to pin down precisely the year in which Negroes were first present in the River Raisin region. Shifting boundaries and changes in governmental jurisdiction in the first decades of settlement there make meaningful interpretations of existing demographic data difficult and render comparison with later census information extremely troublesome.[3]

Nonetheless, indirect evidence exists for placing Negroes in the vicinity of what would later be the city of Monroe from the time of first European settlement in the mid-1780s. Frenchtown, the first permanent white community in the area, was colonized in large part by French Canadians from Detroit. A survey of the roll of inhabitants in Detroit in 1779 and again in 1782 when compared with a tax list of people in Sargent Township on the River Raisin in 1802 reads like a genealogist's paradise.[4] Several of the same people appear in all three enumerations, and a large percentage of individuals in the 1802 list bear identical surnames to those in Detroit some two decades earlier. While the 1802 enumeration gives no indication of Negro presence in Frenchtown, several individuals in the listing had been slaveholders in Detroit twenty years earlier.[5] It does not seem unreasonable to suspect that some of these citizens took their human property with them when they migrated to the River Raisin in the 1780s and 1790s.

Additional indirect evidence indicates that some Afro-Americans were in the River Raisin region in 1805. A piece of correspondence from that year establishes a link between an owner of considerable portions of real estate on the River Raisin, Jacques Lasselle, and a Negro family. The letter, dated 5 June 1805, threatened Lasselle, a citizen of Detroit, with legal suit if he refused to release from slavery the wife and children of a black man, Anthony Smith.[6] It is not unlikely that Lasselle was accompanied on his journeys to Frenchtown by his slaves.

The conjecture assuming Negro presence in the Frenchtown area during its first years of existence changes to certainty by 1810. In that year, the third decennial census of the United States placed nine "other free persons except Indians not taxed" and four slaves in the civil district of Erie, Wayne County, Michigan Territory.[7] Portions of this Erie civil district would become Monroe County in 1817. In 1874, an "aged colored man" residing in Monroe recalled that he had been counted as a slave in an 1812 census of the taxable inhabitants of Wayne County. The farm on which he resided during that enumeration would later be within Monroe city limits.[8] Finally, a close connection between the Monroe environs and Afro-American presence is established by a manumission document dating from 1818. On 28 December 1818, a Frenchman named Lajiness freed "John, a blackman" at the River Raisin.[9]

In the years before the incorporation of Monroe as a city in 1837, Negroes continued to appear in the region. The federal census of 1820 showed nine blacks living within Monroe County.[10] Edward Ellis, editor of the village's *Michigan Sentinel,* commented in 1825 on the passage of a group of Negroes through Monroe on their way to an Oakland County Quaker settlement.[11] Two years later, the same newspaper, in reporting Michigan's first special territorial census, showed thirteen colored inhabitants in the county.[12] The federal enumeration for 1830 indicated an increase of five Afro-Americans.[13] While none of the special territorial censuses (1827, 1834, and 1837) includes a breakdown by race for the village of Monroe, the 1834 tabulation showed the county as having thirty-seven "free colored persons" and two slaves as residents.[14] At least two individuals of African descent, who had a passing residency in the community during this formative period, would eventually achieve national fame. William Wells Brown, noted Negro abolitionist, playwright, and novelist, related his experience as a barber in the village of Monroe in 1835 in his book, *Clotel* (1853).[15] Landscape artist Robert S. Duncanson spent his adolescent and early adult years in the community.[16] Despite the presence of this and other information on Monroe's early blacks, it is impossible to set a precise figure for the village's or city's Afro-American population before 1840. Not until the sixth decennial census of the United States in 1840 can one begin to draw a historical profile of Negro demography in the city of Monroe. Table 1, constructed from the state and decennial censuses and the Monroe *City Directory* of 1904,

Table 1[17]

Afro-American Population of the City of Monroe 1840–1930

Date	Total Population	Afro-American Population	Percentage
1840	1,703	36	2.11
1845	2,455[a]	—	—
1850	2,813	38	1.35
1854	3,889	43	1.11
1860	3,895[b]	21	0.54
1864	4,214	26	0.62
1870	5,086	42	0.83
1874	5,782	29	0.50
1880	4,930	44[c]	0.89
1884	5,242	38	0.72
1890	5,258	32	0.61
1894	5,613	29	0.52
1900	5,043	27	0.54
1904	6,128	15[d]	0.24
1910	6,893	16[e]	0.23
1920	11,573	26	0.22
1930	18,110	379	2.09

[a] None of the extant data from the 1845 state census reflects a breakdown by race for the population of Monroe. *The Manual of Legislature, 1847* (Detroit: Bogg and Harmon, 1847), p. 33, gives a population of 2,496 for the city of Monroe.

[b] Figures in *Population of the United States in 1860* (Washington, D.C.: U.S. Government Printing Office, 1864), p. 243, reveal a population of 3,892 for the city of Monroe.

[c] The official breakdown in statistics of the *Population of the United States at the Tenth Census, 1880* (Washington, D.C.: U.S. Government Printing Office, 1882) 1 : 183, showed a Negro population of forty-one. A careful review of the population manuscripts indicate an additional three. *Population Schedule of the Tenth Census of the United States, 1880* Roll #596 *Michigan* vol. 18 *Monroe (part) and Montcalm (part) Counties*, p. 540.

[d] The 1904 Michigan state census shows only eight Afro-Americans living in the city. *Census of the State of Michigan, 1904, Population* (Lansing: Wynkoop Crawford, 1906)1: 165–66. When combined with material in the Monroe city directory for that year, however, a figure of at least fifteen was indicated. *The City Directory of Monroe, Michigan, 1904* (Monroe: Goodrich, 1904).

[e] The statistical abstract of the decennial census for Michigan in 1910 indicates a Negro population of three, but a careful perusal of the 1910 manuscript schedules themselves revealed sixteen. See *Thirteenth Census of the United States, 1910, Abstract of the Census with Supplement for Michigan* (Washington, D.C.: U.S. Government Printing Office, 1913), p. 622; *United States Thirteenth Census of Population, 1910* T624 Reel 664 *Michigan* vol. 62 *Monroe (part) and Menominee Counties*.

reflects the population history of blacks in Monroe from 1840 to 1930.

While the demographic picture revealed in these figures is useful for gaining a fairly accurate idea of the relative size of Monroe's black population, the official enumerations, particularly those in the twentieth century, were often in error and in other respects were not very useful in interpreting the experience of Afro-Americans in the community. A careful scrutiny of the manuscript censuses, for example, showed that some individuals' and some families' racial heritage "changed" over the years. Robert W. Duncanson was counted as a mulatto child in the 1860 census but was enumerated as a white household head in the 1880 schedules.[18] One family listed as "black" in the 1880 manuscript schedules for Monroe city was designated twenty years later as "white" in the Monroetown count.[19] A decade later, members of this family still resided in the township and were listed as mulatto.[20] Twelve individuals, from two different families, counted as "white" in the 1910 schedules, had been enumerated as Afro-Americans in the 1900 schedules.[21] The consequence of this ambiguity regarding racial heritage was an underreporting of Negroes in the city in the 1880 and 1910 federal censuses.

The 1904 Michigan state census shows similar weaknesses. Although no manuscript schedules for Monroe city have survived for that year, it is certain that there were more than the eight Afro-Americans enumerated. The Monroe *City Directory* for that year reveals eleven individuals with an African ancestor, and when this is added to information in the statistical abstract, it turns out that there were at least fifteen people with a documentable black racial heritage residing in the community.[22]

In another sense, a straightforward numerical analysis and presentation of the raw data in the various national and state censuses does not lend itself to an understanding of a most important human and historical process—the formation and maintenance of kinship structures in the community. Only a close examination of specific Negro surnames in the decennial censuses, local newspapers, county vital records, church records, Monroe city directories, tax assessment rolls, city registers of electors, oral reminiscences, probate proceedings, and other sources documents the presence of several black family networks in Monroe.[23] Much of what can be understood and explained about the Afro-American experience in Monroe can be grasped only in terms of these relatively permanent social structures. A large portion of the surviving information on Negroes in Monroe suggests this interpretation. In fact, it is primarily within the context of these interlocking kinship systems that much of the "countable" data in the population schedules and elsewhere makes sense.

To demonstrate the reality of these Afro-American kinship structures, the selection of an appropriate methodology is absolutely crucial. A detailed analysis of data in the decennial census population schedules, city directories, and elsewhere suggests an approach to this information that is quite different than has previously been taken by historians. While a straightforward numerical examination of this material, including the construction of detailed tables and figures, has been most notably taken by Katzman and Kusmer to delineate such important matters as black occupational opportunities, patterns of geographical mobility, and residential settlement in Detroit and Cleveland respectively, a similar approach does not lend itself to an adequate understanding of these processes in Monroe.[24] Because of the consistently small local black population, utilization of the model so effectively developed in other studies would only obscure these realities in the Monroe community. Put simply, there are not enough "numbers" from which to draw any meaningful statistical generalizations.

A careful breakdown of the "place of birth" of Monroe's black citizens in the decennial censuses between 1850 and 1910, for example, indicates no distinctive pattern of geographic mobility. The demographic base is simply inadequate for making any meaningful generalization about Afro-American migration to Monroe. Never, during these years, did the federal census marshals count more than forty-three Negroes in the community. Moreover, at no time during this period had the majority of the city's Afro-Americans journeyed from one single state or nation. Rather, they came in varying numbers and at different times from New York, Kentucky, Virginia, Ohio, Massachusetts, Pennsylvania, Indiana, Illinois, Maryland, Alabama, Georgia, Washington, D.C., England, Canada, and Santo Domingo.[25] There were never more than eleven individuals at any one time originating from a single geographic area outside Michigan.

Obviously, the "numbers" data do not lead automatically to any meaningful conclusion. However, if viewed in another manner, the basic information in the population schedules gives some support to a black kinship network thesis.[26] The rough outlines of several Monroe linkages are indicated in the census manuscripts. Indeed, the very lack of numbers is, ironically, a boon in this regard. A careful review of the census reveals the persistence of several family surnames for this time period. The Duncansons appear in all the records between 1840 and 1910, the Millers from 1860 to 1880, the Wickliffes from 1870 to 1880, the Bromleys from 1870 to 1910, the Fosters from 1880 to 1910, and the Johnsons in 1900 and 1910.[27] In addition, at least one other black kinship group, the Smiths, resided at various times in the city of Monroe or neighboring townships between 1830 and 1900. Indeed, what is remarkable is that beginning in 1860 these identifiable family groupings constituted the majority of the town's Afro-American population. The figures are as follows: 1860, 13 of 21; 1870, 31 of 42; 1880, 37 of 44; 1900, 18 of 27; and 1910, 10 of 16. What is certain is that a small number of black family groups had selected Monroe as their permanent residence in the nineteenth century.

Who were these people? Unfortunately, the total lack of the traditional kind of manuscript material historians have usually turned to when reconstructing the past means that little can be said about the intimacies of thought and habit in their private lives. None of these people seems to have left correspondence, diaries, or business records; indeed, not much beyond the mere existence of many of these individuals is known. Yet the continued appearance of the same family surnames on maps, in the decennial censuses, city directories, county vital records, cemetery listings, city assessment rolls, property deeds, voter registration rolls, probate records, church minutes, local newspapers, and other sources for much of the nineteenth and the early portion of the twentieth centuries suggests the persistence of several viable kinship structures.[28] A biographical and family time-line approach to the primary materials provides the most adequate framework for interpreting the experience of Afro-Americans in Monroe.

For each identifiable family group, an "approximate" family reconstruction has been diagramed and carefully documented (see Appendix). In these reconstitutions, certain assumptions have been made regarding "surnames" and network membership. For example, those individuals whose last name appears in the various records as Cox, and who are identifiable therein as Negro, are presumed related. The same holds true for Duncanson, Smith, and Miller. In the decennial censuses before 1880, where the kinship connection between individuals in a household is not specified, the basic relationships are taken to be, unless other sources prove otherwise, husband-wife and parent-child. In addition, it is presumed that the essential family type is consanguineal rather than nuclear in organization.[29] An Africanist rather than a Western conceptualization, in this case, facilitated the re-creation of Monroe's black mutual assistance networks, which included not only conjugal units but also affines and, in at least one instance, fictive kin. In that sense, the data give a reasonable impression and are a graphic representation of their presence. It would seem that much of the "black history" in Monroe is essentially the chronicle of the creation, evolution, and maintenance of these interlocking family systems.

One of the earliest and perhaps the largest Afro-American family network in Monroe was the Duncansons (see Appendix, Figure 1). In 1836, the clan leader, John Duncanson, a New York emigrant, purchased a portion of land in the Curtis and Wilson plat, which immediately bordered on the village. His seven children produced many Monroe natives in the succeeding years, and at least one individual bearing the Duncanson cognomen, a grandson, would claim the city as his home until he died in 1931. The Duncanson name appears in many of the existing nineteenth-century sources. More than a handful of Duncanson births, deaths, and nuptials are recorded in the county's vital records. The family apparently had a mixed racial heritage because some Duncansons are designated in these documents as mulatto or white. Several Duncanson estates were probated, and their names appear in church minutes, tax rolls, and voter registrations. The newspapers, in "mortuaries" and "news about town" columns, tell us the most about this rather large kinship structure. Their presence in the city was quite apparent. Although they no longer bear the surname, a seventh generation of Duncanson progeny still lives in the Monroe community.

Also currently claiming roots in Monroe are Foster family descendants (see Appendix, Figure 2). James W. Foster, a Canadian by birth, arrived with his family in the city in 1879. As with the Duncansons, the Foster name abounds in the sources, and there were also several Caucasians in the Foster lineage. The Foster kinship in Monroe was much smaller than the Duncansons, being restricted to a single core nuclear family with each succeeding generation. As will be seen, however, the Fosters more than made up for their small numbers when it came to involvement in the city's institutions.

The family group about which the most is known is the Wickliffe-Cox-Bromley network (see Appendix, Figure 3). At some point in the 1860s, many family members migrated from Kentucky to Monroe. Alexander Wickliffe and his wife, Minerva (née Cox), brought five children with them, and Marie Cox, Minerva's sister-in-law, arrived with her five children. Aaron Bromley, a native of Alabama, in marrying Ellen Cox in 1866 joined this lineage. The issue of the latter would persist in the community until at least 1930. These people turn up in the records in numerous places. In at least one instance, the "family ties" of these people extended beyond consanguines and affines. The Johnsons, the fictive kin in this grouping, began calling Monroe their home in 1881.[30] The surviving sources indicate that these Virginian emigrants retained strong ties with the Bromleys.

Unfortunately, the record is sketchy regarding what was perhaps Monroe's "oldest" African-American network. The Smiths (see Appendix, Figure 4) predated the Duncansons in the area. Although they may have been related to the Anthony Smith who complained about being held in bondage in 1805, they are first documented in Monroe County in the 1830 federal population schedules which record Stephen Smith, a "free colored person," as head of a household.[31] In the succeeding years some Smiths continued to live in the Monroe environs as the 1840, 1860, and 1900 census manuscripts reported family members residing in neighboring Raisinville Township. In 1850, Stephen Smith and his family farmed in nearby Monroe Township. The most persistent Smith on the Monroe city scene seems to have been the elderly Stephen. He witnessed a marriage between two Negro friends in the community in January 1869, appeared with his family in the 1870 Monroe city population schedules, and registered to vote there on 1 November 1870. He is also listed in the 1874–75 *Monroe City Directory* as a "(col'd)" laborer living in the First Ward on Cass Street.

Whether or not Stephen Smith and his descendants were related in some manner to another local black family group, the Millers, is not known (see Appendix, Figure 5), but a connection may be indicated in the 1880 decennial census which lists a John Smith as a nephew to the household head, Edward Miller. Miller, who had been born into slavery in Kentucky, came to Monroe via Canada shortly before the Civil War. The Monroe city directories for 1860–61 and 1874–75 and various Michigan gazetteers from 1863 to 1881 report him as a tailor living on Front Street. After his death in 1881, the records indicate that Mrs. Miller remained a resident of Monroe until at least 1889. Thus the family spanned at least three decades of existence in Monroe.

Never were all these people in the genealogical diagrams present in Monroe at the same instant. In essence, the schema depict each lineage through time. The situation was extremely fluid with individuals arriving and departing. Critical life-cycle events and the quest for mobility propelled people into and out of the community. Additionally, each succeeding decade witnessed network additions by birth and depletions by death, yet for most of the years before the turn of the century, these kinship structures remained viable. Between 1840 and 1900, as many as seventeen Duncansons can be documented as residing at one time in Monroe; between 1880 and 1900, six Fosters; between 1870 and 1900, eleven Bromleys; and between 1860 and 1880, seven Millers. Given the gaps in data, there were most likely more individuals present at various times.

Of course, it can be argued that sharing a family surname and having a "blood" connection with others does not necessarily place an individual in a support structure. Several kinds of evidence, however, suggest that for these families the ties were more than superficial. The household compositions of the Duncansons, Wickliffe-Cox-Bromleys, and Millers, in particular, point toward strong kinship bonds. Even though the federal population schedules before 1880 do not specify the relationships of household members, information in nineteenth-century Monroe County vital and probate records permits some judgment regarding internal family arrangements before that time. Marriage, death, and birth entries, of course, state precise genetic relationships, as does a listing of heirs in estate conveyances. As far as can be known, the people in the genealogies comprised ten different households during much of the latter part of the nineteenth century. The Duncansons lived in three separate homes, and the Wickliffe-Bromleys, if the Johnsons are taken into consideration, owned three housing units. Each of the other black Monroe families resided in a single dwelling. The households ranged in size from one to ten and took many different forms during this time period.

The family arrangements of the Duncansons for much of the nineteenth century reflect lines or chains of responsibility beyond the immediate nuclear family. In 1850, John Duncanson, the clan patriarch, headed an extended family which consisted of his spouse, four children, and two grandchildren. The other Duncanson household was nuclear; Simeon, his wife, and two children lived under one roof. The 1860 census showed the Duncansons with atypical household structures. The widower Simeon was the single head of his immediate family, and his sister Fanny, a spinster, managed the other Duncanson unit. Living with Fanny was another brother, Nathan, his three children, and three other youthful Duncansons of undetermined origin. By 1870, Simeon had found a second spouse and resided with her and his two youngest children by the first union. Fanny continued to provide a home for her brother, Nathan, and his issue. Ten years later, there were three Duncanson households. This time, however, three of John Dean's (John's youngest son) orphaned children were present: Eliza lived with her aunt

Fanny, uncle Nathan, and his children; Louisa and Rosa resided with Simeon, his wife, and his children by two marriages. Robert W. Duncanson, second son of Simeon, rented a home in the second ward with his wife, two children, and a boarder. By 1900, the Duncanson clan had passed into its fourth Monroe generation. Of the original New York emigrants, only Fanny remained alive. In that year, Fanny, her niece Eliza, and her nephew John C., comprised one family unit. Mary Hermann, a daughter of Simeon, her husband, Charles, and their five children made up the other Duncanson household. The 1910 census schedules showed the same basic structure except that Fanny had died, and Charlotte Hermann had married and had moved with her husband to a new Monroe residence.

The Millers, because of lack of data, present a less clear picture. In 1860, Edward and Mary Miller were a simple two-person household. The following census indicated the presence of bonds of mutual obligation beyond the nuclear unit. In 1870, their family had expanded to include two children, and they had living with them Mary and Annie Cooper, presumed to be Mrs. Miller's mother and sister respectively. In the 1880 census, the Miller family was extended and augmented. It consisted of Edward, Mary, their two children, a nephew, and Sarah Miller, a servant.

A great deal more involved was the changing composition of the Wickliffe-Cox-Bromley nexus. First appearing in the population schedules for Monroe in 1870, members of this extended group lived under a variety of arrangements. Four family members "lived in" as servants in the Monroe Young Ladies Seminary and Collegiate Institute, an elite finishing school.[32] Another relative, Joseph Wickliffe, worked as a day laborer for a farmer in the city. Finally, Aaron Bromley headed an extended subfamily. In a single dwelling, Mr. and Mrs. Bromley lived with their son, her mother, brother, and sister, and another family—which happened to be white. The 1880 schedules showed two Bromley units. This time, Aaron Bromley headed a simple nuclear family which consisted of his wife, Ellen, and their two sons, James and Noel. Alexander Wickliffe, his spouse, son, and married daughter made up the other household. Twenty years later, in 1900, the Bromley family was again extended in form. At that time Aaron, Ellen, their son Jim, Jim's wife, their son Aaron Alcayde, and two nephews lived under one roof. Finally, in 1910, the family was again nuclear in configuration. This time James, his wife, Elizabeth, and Aaron Alcayde comprised the unit. Alexander and Fanny Johnson, who are regarded as fictive kin in the Bromley reciprocity network, were an augmented family in 1900. In that year the household consisted of themselves and a boarder. A decade later, the widowed Fanny was living alone.

The Fosters had the simplest and clearest family composition. The 1880 census revealed a household comprised of James, Elizabeth, and their four children. Twenty years later, the Monroe Township schedules revealed a nuclear-augmented structure. In this census, three of their children and a boarder lived with the couple. The widow Elizabeth resided with two children and a servant at the same location in 1910.

While the Smiths had the earliest tenure in the Monroe environs, not a great deal is known about their changing family composition. The historical record is fragmentary on this point. Apparently, the elder Stephen headed two different households in the nineteenth century. The 1850 Monroe Township census listed an extended family of eight members, and the 1870 city enumeration showed a "new" and nuclear household consisting of three members. A portion of the intervening years, it would seem, were spent in Canada, where Stephen's youngest family member, Laura, had been born in 1857.

What is obvious from this brief analysis is that no single type of household configuration prevailed among Monroe's Afro-American families. While they might have preferred easier arrangements, various family tragedies and difficulties prevented most of the city's native blacks from retreating into simple conjugal units. Penury, illness, death, and other life-cycle events usually required a reshuffling of family alignments. The continued presence of the Bromleys, Duncansons, Millers, and Fosters indicates that they were successful in meeting these demands. More important, the various changes in family styles demonstrate the existence of shared understandings regarding responsibilities and mutual obligations. The Duncansons and Bromleys, in particular, expanded and contracted their households to meet the vicissitudes of time. Indeed this varying composition testifies to the viability of Monroe's Negro kinship networks.

Undoubtedly, the most precise and intimate understandings about family responsibilities can be gained by a careful reading of probate proceedings. At times new kinship connections and areas of obligation emerge. This is particularly true in the case of Phoebe Duncanson, who was committed to the state asylum for the mentally ill in 1890. The wife of Nathan, she appears in no other extant record connected with the Duncanson family. Rather, Nathan and "their" children show up in the household of Fanny Duncanson in the federal manuscript censuses of 1870 to 1880, and it is not until the latter year that Fanny and Nathan are noted as siblings. Phoebe appeared only in the 1860 shedules, and then as a twenty-two-year-old, unmarried, next-door neighbor of the Duncanson's, living with her widowed mother, Magdalina Grobb, and three younger siblings on Harrison Street. The Grobbs, who were German immigrants, were Caucasian. Phoebe, the 1890 court proceedings indicate, had a series of breakdowns through the years and spent much of her married life in the Monroe County house for the indigent and impaired. Fanny, who never married, devoted her life to managing a household for Nathan and his children. Significantly, it was not until Nathaniel's death that the Duncansons moved to have Phoebe declared legally insane.[33] The absence of an expected relationship of mutual obligation—husband and wife—in this instance, exposes and highlights a broader pattern of support. Obviously, the Duncansons depended upon one another.

In total, the Duncanson lineage went to probate four times in the nineteenth century and six times in the twentieth. In all but the foregoing instance, the proceedings followed the demise of a family member. In each case, family members moved in to take care of minors, claim an inheritance, or otherwise assist in the adjudication. The outcome in several of these determinations was not pleasing to the heirs or guardians. The committal of Phoebe was certainly a task no one relished. In other judgments, there seem to have been some recriminations between family members. For example, shortly after John Dean Duncanson was killed in a railway accident in Chicago in 1871, the court appointed Simeon, his brother, as guardian of "Dean's" children and administrator of his estate. Seven years later, Dean's widow, Margaret, petitioned to remove Simeon from that position because he had "neglected" the estate and "subjected" her and her children to "great trouble." In another proceeding, Charles Hermann, the spouse of Simeon's daughter Mary, deliberately left his children out of his will because they had "caused [him] to endure very unpleasant treatment and experience."[34]

Nevertheless, even these unhappy denouements attest to the existence, at some point in time, of a functioning network of cooperation. It would seem that the mere mentioning of the activity of various relatives in these transactions points to some level of commitment and responsibility and to the existence of certain expectations. Beyond a doubt, some of these individuals "believed" that their relations should have responded in a specified manner and counted on them to do so. In reality, it has never been unusual for families to "fall out" over inheritances and guardianship responsibilities. It is safe, therefore, to assume that the Duncanson network was functioning— at least before some of these dealings.

The various probates involving the Wickliffe-Cox-Bromleys offer additional insight into the maintenance of kinship structures.[35] Three of these cases concerned Wickliffe Fox, nephew of Aaron Bromley and grandson of Alexander Wickliffe. In 1892, when Fox was orphaned at the age of twelve, his mother's sister, Mary Dickinson, was made guardian and executrix of his estate. Until he reached the age of majority, various members of the kinship system were called on for support—and it was forthcoming. In 1896, his uncle, Joseph Holt Wickliffe, assumed guardianship, and in 1900 Fox was residing in Monroe in the household of another uncle, Aaron Bromley. Between 1900 and 1912, he apparently shuttled between relatives in Ann Arbor and Monroe before permanently settling in the latter year in Toledo.[36] It is certain that a somewhat diffuse but nevertheless significant support system was in operation for this family.

Most interesting, however, was the prominence of James Bromley in the conveyance of the estate of Mrs. Ellen "Fannie" Johnson, a nonrelation, in 1923. Although she had written a will dividing her property in equal portions between two nieces, one living in Washington, D.C., and the other in Appalachicola, Florida, the court determined that James Bromley would receive the balance of her estate after the settlement of claims having priority and that her nieces would receive nothing. Evidence and testimony presented to Judge Franke showed that Fannie's consanguines had, for the most part, ignored her during her final illness, and that James "Bromley took the old lady, who was helpless and in a very filthy condition into his own home and care[d] for her very thoroughly and kindly during the last weeks of her life."[37] Bromley's role in those dealings demonstrates that the shared obligations between some blacks in Monroe extended beyond blood ties. It would seem that a form of fictive kinship had evolved in this instance, and that the Johnsons had, to no small degree, been involved in the Bromley support network.

The location of Afro-American households in Monroe also provides corroborating evidence for a kinship network thesis. Even if family members lived in different homes, they still resided very close to one another—next door or within easy "shouting" distance. Data available in the state censuses, beginning in 1854 and continuing every ten years thereafter until 1904, and in the national decennial censuses from 1840 to 1880 and 1900 to 1910, make a breakdown of the black and white population in Monroe by ward possible for many of these years. Monroe had three different ward arrangements during this span of time. The last division which existed between 1870 and 1920 (see Map 1) showed four wards or precincts, three south and one north of the River Raisin.[38]

A brief review of the statistics in Table 2 shows that the city's Negro population lived predominantly in the First Ward between 1874 and 1910. If the choice of locale of residence was partially a reflection of wealth and income, it was also a manifestation of the presence of complex patterns of family responsibility and interaction. In large part, the figures in Table 2 represent people enmeshed in kin networks. First-ward inhabitants were mostly working class; the Duncansons, Bromleys, Wickliffes, Millers, Johnsons, and Smiths were not exceptions, but the proximity of their dwellings, in some instances, intimated more than monetary considerations. A close perusal of information on maps and in city directories reveals a clustering of relatives (see Map 2)[39] that cannot be entirely explained in terms of income. This is particularly true of the Duncansons, who owned portions of real estate in other sections of the community but chose to dwell across the street or down the block from one another for much of the nineteenth century. Similarly, when Alexander Wickliffe and his immediate family had accumulated enough resources to buy some land, they did not purchase "just anywhere." They bought a slice of their nephew's, Aaron Bromley's, lot and built a home there in 1871.[40] Between 1874 and 1880, when Aaron Bromley and his immediate family moved to the Fourth Ward to work for the Comptons, the Wickliffes continued to dwell at the family homestead on Cass Street.[41] The exact circumstances surrounding this arrangement cannot be ascertained, but Bromley did retain title to his property and had returned there by the 1890s. Various members of this kinship group continued to live next door to one another for the next two decades.

Specific and ongoing relationships between individuals and families cannot be inferred from residential propinquity alone, yet it is not unreasonable to assume that there was more than a passing acquaintance between some of these first-ward Afro-Americans who did not share a lineage. Undoubtedly, the nearness of the Johnsons to the Bromleys—a mere block and a half—played a part in the primary relationship that evolved between them. The Smiths, who lived "around the corner" from the Johnsons, also seem to have been involved, at some level, in the Wickliffe-Cox-Bromley network. In 1869, William Cox and Stephen Smith witnessed a marriage between Alexander Belmore and Mary Hill.[42] What is certain is that all of these people knew one another and probably rubbed

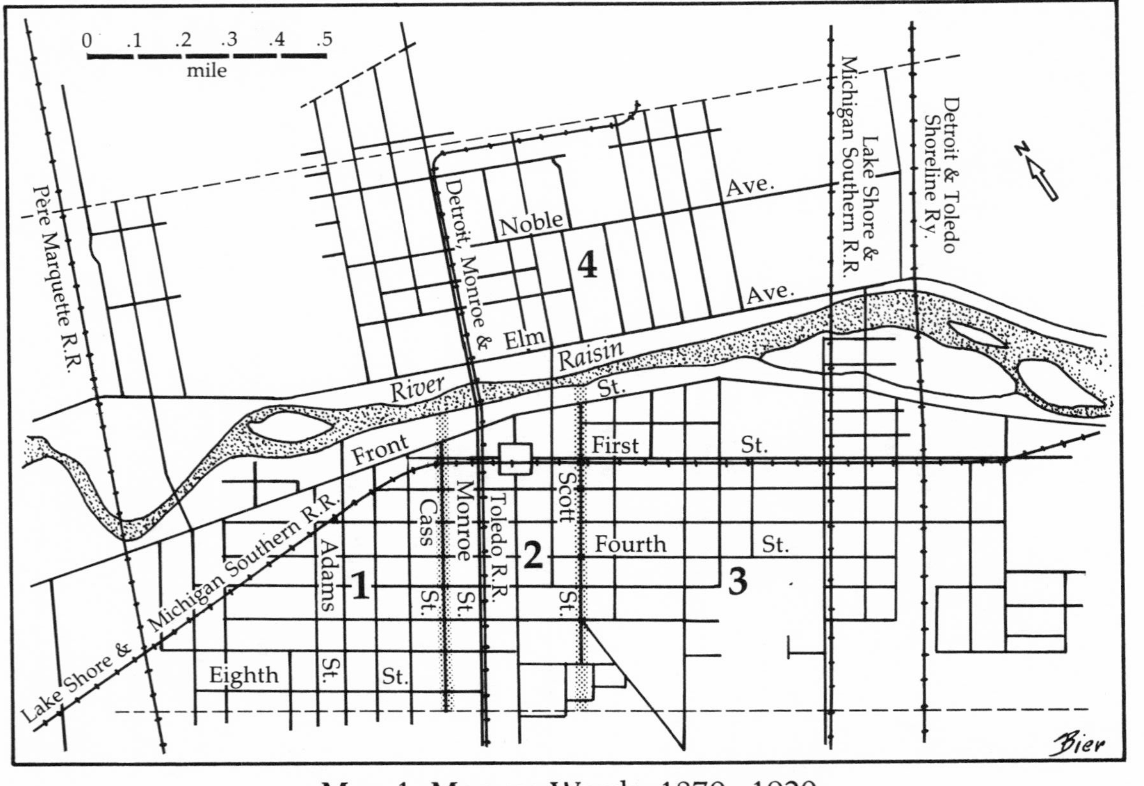

Map 1. Monroe Wards, 1870–1920

Table 2
Total and Afro-American Population of the City of Monroe by Wards 1874–1910

	1874			1880[a]	
	Total	*Negro*		*Total*	*Negro*
1st Ward	2,273	20	1st Ward	1,672	22
2nd Ward	1,014	6	2nd Ward	961	10
3rd Ward	1,634	—	3rd Ward	1,411	7
4th Ward	861	3	4th Ward	886	5
Monroe	5,872	29	Monroe	4,930	44
	1884			**1894[b]**	
	Total	*Negro*		*Total*	*Negro*
1st Ward	1,799	13	1st Ward	1,901	22
2nd Ward	1,008	14	2nd Ward	985	7
3rd Ward	1,481	10	3rd Ward	1,738	—
4th Ward	993	1	4th Ward	989	—
Monroe	5,281	38		5,613	29
	1900[c]			**1904**	
	Total	*Negro*		*Total*	*Negro*
1st Ward	1,742	23	1st Ward	1,953	7
2nd Ward	928	—	2nd Ward	1,043	4
3rd Ward	1,616	4	3rd Ward	2,010	—
4th Ward	757	—	4th Ward	1,122	4
Monroe	5,043	27	Monroe	6,128	15
	1910[d]				
	Total	*Negro*			
1st Ward	2,029	10			
2nd Ward	1,147	2			
3rd Ward	2,517	4			
4th Ward	1,146	—			
Monroe	6,893	16			

[a]The data on Negroes by ward are not available in any compilation. It was taken from *Population Schedules, 1880*, pp. 503–51.

[b]At present the Negro population statistics of Monroe by wards are not accessible for 1890 or 1920.

[c]These data were taken from National Archives Microfilm Publications, *United States 12th Census of Population, 1900* T623 Reel 733 *Michigan* vol. 55 *Monroe (part) and Montcalm (part) Counties*, pp. 221A-73B.

[d]See *United States 13 Census of Population, 1910* T624 Reel 664 *Michigan* vol. 62 *Monroe (part) and Menominee Counties*, Monroe City, First Ward sheets 3A, 3B, and 20B, Second Ward sheet 5B, and Third Ward sheet 21A.

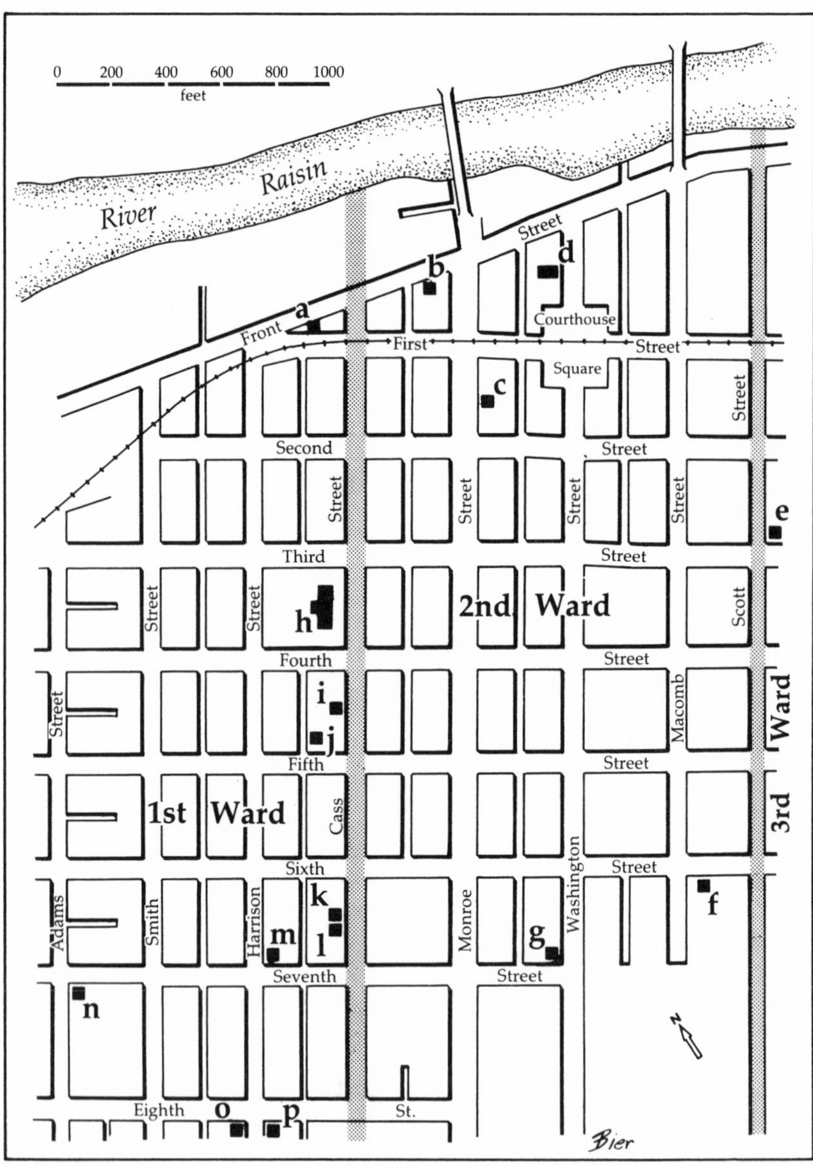

Map 2. Afro-American Residency and Business, 1870–1900

See facing page for notes to map.

shoulders daily. Close proximity created the basis for the creation of reciprocity networks.

To a large degree, the question of choice of neighborhood and property ownership revolved around the extent of employment opportunities. The Fosters, for example, could not have built their fine home in 1884 on Sixth Street in the Second Ward without a steady and substantial income. None of the first-ward Afro-American families could have persisted in the community without continuing access to the job market. The evidence that has sur-

---

[a] Site of various Bromley business ventures. Between 1899 and 1902, Jim Bromley ran his paint store from this location. He moved his restaurant to the corner of Cass and Front in 1911. See *Monroe Democrat*, 5 Oct. 1899, p. 5, 19 Sept. 1902, p. 8, and 24 Mar. 1911, p. 7; *City Directory, Monroe, Michigan, 1901*, (Monroe: Record Pub., 1901), p. 11.

[b] Ella and Mae Foster operated a confectionary store here between 1900 and 1902. See *Monroe Democrat*, 19 Oct. 1899, p. 5; *Monroe Record*, 27 Mar. 1912, p. 5; Business Directory portion of *City Directory, Monroe, Michigan, 1901*, pages unnumbered.

[c] Edward Miller's home and tailor establishment after 1874. See *Monroe City Directory, 1874–75*, (Detroit: Barch, Montgomery, 1874), p. 52.

[d] James Foster's livery establishment at 22 Washington Street, which he operated from 1879–93. See *Monroe Democrat*, 2 Nov. 1893, p. 1.

[e] The Foster home from 1881 to 1885. See Monroe County Deed Record, Liber 105, 18 Oct. 1881, p. 34; *Monroe Democrat*, 1 Oct. 1885, p. 1.

[f] The Foster home between 1885 and 1894. See *Monroe Democrat*, 10 Oct. 1885, p. 1.

[g] Robert W. Duncanson rented here in the 1880s. See *Population Schedules, 1880*, p. 540; *Monroe Democrat*, 14 Aug. 1884, p. 1.

[h] Boyd's Young Ladies Seminary and Collegiate Institute. The Wickliffes lived and worked there in the early 1870s. See Microcopy 593 *Population Schedules of the Ninth Census of the United States, 1870* Roll #691 *Michigan* vol. 17 *Monroe County*, p. 413.

[i] Stephen Smith and his family rented here in the 1870s. See *Monroe City Directory, 1874–75*, p. 64.

[j] Alexander and Fannie Johnson resided here. See *City Directory* of Monroe, Michigan, 1904 and thereafter.

[k] Alex Wickliffe purchased a portion of Bromley's lot in 1871. Monroe County Deed Record, Liber 73, 1 Mar. 1871, p. 623; *Monroe City Directory, 1874–75*, p. 70 and thereafter.

[l] Homestead of Aaron Bromley, purchased in 1864. See Monroe County Deed Record, Liber 61, 19 Oct. 1864, pp. 577–78. Members of this family would retain title to the property until 1955.

[m] The Hermanns lived here for more than two decades. See *Monroe City Directory, 1896–97* (Monroe: Billmire and Kiley, 1896), and thereafter.

[n] The widow of John Dean Duncanson and her family lodged here from 1871 until her death in 1879. See *Monroe City Directory, 1874–75*, p. 30.

[o] Part of the original Duncanson land purchase. See Monroe Deed Record, Liber Z, 8 Sept. 1836, p. 56. This was the home of Simeon and family until after his death in 1890.

[p] Part of the original Duncanson land purchase. Fannie and Nathaniel called this location home. Later, John A. resided here until 1931.

vived makes clear that individuals who were part of these kinship groups always had work.

The occupational structure that existed for male Afro-Americans in Monroe between 1850 and 1915 presents a more complex and ambiguous picture than has been offered by historians for two larger midwestern cities.[43] The information in the decennial census manuscripts and elsewhere regarding Negro employment needs to be carefully structured within a family network framework in order to avoid serious misconceptions. The construction of tables, listing black occupations by year, would not lend itself to an adequate understanding of these economic realities in Monroe. Stated simply, the utilization of this model would overstate the number of skilled positions held by blacks and obscure a most significant social process—the relatively unencumbered access that members of these special families seem to have had to occupations in the community.

A detailed analysis of the occupational data in the Monroe city directories and population schedules between 1850 and 1915 indicates that of the 114 jobs listed in all the sources combined for male Afro-Americans, fifty-seven, exactly half, were skilled, professional, or proprietary positions.[44] These included the following occupations: physician, musician, livery stable operator, eating-house proprietor, farmer, carpenter, joiner, painter, tailor, stationary engineer, clerk, and decorator. An "obvious" but erroneous conclusion would be that the Monroe community had an open job structure for blacks in general. A close look at these "favored" fifty-seven positions reveals that only fifteen individuals were involved, thirteen of whom were members of these identified kinship networks. The same people appear time after time in the sources. John Duncanson shows up as an "engineer" twelve times; Simeon Duncanson as a painter in five places; Edward Miller as a tailor in five; James Bromley as a painter, "eating-house proprietor," or business partner in twelve instances; and his son, Alcayde Bromley, as a musician, music teacher, or piano tuner five times.

Not every adult male member of these networks held an advantaged position. Nathan Duncanson appears as a day laborer in the 1870 and 1880 population schedules, and Aaron Bromley, Alexander Wickliffe, Joseph Wickliffe, Wesley Joyce (Bromley's nephew), and Stephen Smith, when listed, also have similar job designations. Men from these families were recorded as having lower status occupations twenty-nine times through the years. It is important to note that none of these native sons appears to have suffered from un- or underemployment. Each found a secure and permanent place in the community's job structure.

Much less information has survived for female Negro work patterns in Monroe.[45] The federal census marshals recorded female employment in a haphazard fashion for most of these years, and it cannot be known from some of the job descriptions, e.g. "keeping house," whether or not an individual was gainfully employed. The city directories for Monroe also contained sexual biases. Females, unless widows, household heads, or entrepreneurs, were often left out. For the most part, the data that have survived show that Negro women in Monroe worked as cooks, housekeepers, domestic servants, and laundresses. They appear to have suffered from the same occupational limitations and disadvantages as their white counterparts. A few Monroe black women, though, did have skilled proprietary or professional positions in this era. In all but one instance, they were part of the identified kinship groupings. In 1870, Edward Miller's wife's mother and sister worked as tailors.[46] From 1899 to 1902, two Foster sisters, Ella and Mae, operated a candy store at 9 West Front Street.[47] Their older sister, Myrtle, and Ida Hermann (a Duncanson) appear to have been teachers.[48]

On a more subtle level, the economic experience of these lineages revolved around credit and service exchange. The records of several businesses indicate that the Duncansons, Fosters, and Bromleys were enmeshed in the total economic life of the community. John D., Nathaniel, and Simeon Duncanson each had an established line of credit at Steiner's Hardware Store, where they purchased their paint supplies between 1865 and 1871. G. F. Grant kept an accounting of his transactions with Simeon from 1862 to 1865. In return for a setting of table aprons, a gold ring, and a watch and its repair, Simeon "painted" for Grant. F. Schwingschlegt, an interior decorator, instructed Sebastian Lauer, Monroe's leading retail merchant, to credit John Duncanson with "five dollars and change" from his account for service rendered in 1884.[49] It is apparent that the Duncansons were involved in the town's barter system.

James W. Foster received similar recognition. In 1896 and 1898 he bought "on account" some ice cream from Munch's Cigar Store, Tavern Bus Stop, and Hotel. The Fosters also received credit from Dr. Amos Long, dentist, and from the Record Publishing Company.[50] Jim Bromley used his word to purchase "letters and cards" from the Record Publishing Company in 1900 and beer from Johan A. Kirschner between 1900 and 1915.[51] Members of these families were known and trusted by the townspeople. The merchants and professionals understood that they would eventually get their money. The level of recognition enjoyed by these people sometimes extended to the sharing of entrepreneurial burdens. In more than one instance, business partnerships were formed between Negroes and whites. John Gamblin and Robert S. Duncanson worked together as painters and glaziers in 1838. The firm of Duncanson and Westerman operated two paint shops in 1886 and Jim Bromley had white partners in the 1890s.[52] Clearly, these black kinships had pecuniary advantages in the Monroe community that did not extend to strangers—black or white.

The institutional commitment of Monroe's blacks in the nineteenth century reflected both the importance of family and the absence of an Afro-American subculture. Since there was no black church in the city, Monroe's Negroes, generally speaking, attended either Baptist or Methodist services. It would seem that religious affiliation was primarily a manifestation of patterns of family interaction and not a reflection of race. The church-going individuals of the Duncanson clan belonged to the Baptist church. Fanny Duncanson was a charter member of the First Baptist Church and her several brothers' children, Lucius, Robert, Mamie, Louisa, Mary Lucy, and Robert were baptized there. The Hermanns, a fourth generation of Duncansons, figured prominently in Baptist records, too. The Baptists also claimed the loyalty and efforts of the Fosters. James W. Foster and wife were "received in letters from the Baptist Church at Amherstberg, Ontario" in 1879. Each of their children related their Christian experience at the Washington Street location. The elder Fosters remained "faithful to the end." Sister Mary Dickinson (née Wickliffe) transferred her membership from Ann Arbor in 1892 when she returned to Monroe to assume the guardianship of her nephew, Wickliffe Fox.[53]

Apparently the Millers, Wickliffes, and Bromleys chose to practice their religion in the city's Methodist Episcopal church. Aaron and Ellen Bromley and their affines, Minerva and Alexander Wickliffe, were parishioners throughout their lives.[54] Edward Miller was buried from St. Paul's M. E. Church and his nephew, John Smith, was its sexton.[55] The Johnsons offer a more muddled picture in this regard. They were Methodist parishioners between 1883 and 1886 and attended "sabbath evening before church" classes with the Bromleys during this time period. It seems, however, that Alexander Johnson was unable to settle on a lifelong commitment to any particular institution. In 1897 he joined the Baptist church, and when he died in 1904 he was a member and sexton of the town's Presbyterian church.[56]

The part that Afro-Americans played in the city's political life is more uncertain. No Monroe Negro between 1870, when equal suffrage became a reality in Michigan, and 1915 ran for, held, or was appointed to political office in the city. There is no evidence that politics performed an ameliorative function for Monroe's black people.[57] In fact, white males were not anxious to see voting rights extended to Afro-Americans. On three occasions in the nineteenth century, Michigan voters were given the opportunity to cast their ballots on an equal suffrage amendment to the state consititution. In 1850 and 1868 they turned down the proposal, but it was passed in November 1870 by a narrow margin.[58] In each instance, Monroe voted against the measure.

Since the Fifteenth Amendment became part of the U.S. Consititution on 30 March 1870, the November vote in Michigan was superfluous. Ironically, in the fall of 1870, blacks across the state enrolled to vote for the presidential election, and one of the measures they cast their ballots for was male Negro enfranchisement! On 5 November 1870, Aaron Bromley, Simeon and Nathan Duncanson, Edward Miller, Stephen Smith, and Alex Wickliffe recorded their names on the city register of electors. The election took place three days later. In the following years, other first-ward Afro-Americans would register to vote as they arrived in the community or came of age. All the adult males in the genealogies appear to have taken their right to vote seriously when residing in Monroe. Even James Foster, a Canadian by birth, participated in the city's electoral process.[59] Foster and the Bromleys were Republican supporters, but the loyalties of Monroe's Negroes were not totally with the party of Lincoln.[60] Stephen Smith was a Democrat, and at least one of the Duncansons played a highly visible and active role in that party. In 1884 the *Monroe Democrat* noted the raising of a democratic pole in the front of the residence of Robert W. Duncanson. Two years later, the same newspaper observed that he was sergeant-at-arms of the executive committee of the Young Men's Democratic Club.[61]

The hundreds of "bits and pieces" of information that exist in numerous places in Monroe's historical record do not reveal much when viewed separately. When placed together, however, the rough outlines of several viable mutual-assistance black kinship groupings take form. Even the naming practices of the various networks implied linkages of responsibility and obligation.[62] A quick perusal of the genealogies shows that the lineage principle of naming children after fathers was followed in several instances. There were four generations of Aaron Bromleys, two Stephen Smiths, and two John and Robert Duncansons in a direct line. Other family bonds of affection and alliance were recognized at christenings. There were four John and six Robert Duncansons in four generations. The clan's matriarch, Lucy, had her name recalled with two grandchildren, Mary Lucy and Lucius B., and a great grandson, another Lucius B. The Foster surname appeared as a given name in the third generation with "Foster" Schmitt. In another family, the Wickliffe cognomen was remembered when Wickliffe Fox and John Wickliffe Bromley were named. Noel Cox's relationship to the Bromleys was recognized through three generations: a nephew was called Noel, and a great-nephew, Leo Noel. Finally, Aaron Alcayde Bromley named a son after his brother, Leo, who had died in childhood. In each instance, the recalling of given names through several generations testifies to the strength of these units. There is little doubt but that in the final quarter of the nineteenth century each of these families functioned as a viable social system in the community. As a rule, only those Afro-Americans who were members of these networks experienced some measure of success. Much of the evidence about the black past in Monroe relates to these kinships.

At any given time, of course, there were other Afro-Americans residing in or passing through the city. Perhaps there were even other black family networks, but the historical record is sketchy regarding people who "appear" to have been transient. While little of substance can be determined regarding their lives, it is important to demonstrate that there was more than a small amount of Afro-American movement in and out of Monroe. The impression that needs to be conveyed is that throughout much of the nineteenth and early part of the twentieth centuries, "new" Negroes were arriving perhaps as often as weekly in the city, remaining for a short time, and then moving on to the next community. A close review of the existing sources confirms a mobile black population. A careful scrutiny of Negro names in the federal censuses between 1850 and 1900, for example, points to this fact. In this instance, it is assumed that if an Afro-American surname is listed in only one schedule and is not connected with an identifiable kinship network, these people had not selected Monroe as a place of permanent habitation.[63] This line of reasoning shows that the years between 1850 and 1860 witnessed the largest population turnover. In that decade, twenty-six of the thirty-eight individuals counted had cognomens no longer appearing in subsequent censuses. Only eight of the twenty-one Afro-Americans appearing in the 1860 enumeration were without long-standing local family linkages. Eleven of the forty-two in the 1870 and seven of the forty-one in the 1880 schedules seem to have moved their families from Monroe between censuses. The 1900 manuscripts indicate that only four of the twenty-seven had ephemeral Monroe residency. All sixteen of the persons counted in the 1910 census had long-standing individual or family connections with the city.[64]

Of course, there were some members of the black minority who lived in or passed through Monroe between census years and who, consequently, were not counted in any of the federal enumerations. The vital records of Monroe County are important sources in bringing some of these folk to light. The early marriage records in particular contain entries for several Afro-Americans whose names appear in no other source as Monroe city residents. The Civil War enlistment records for blacks list several Monroe recruits noted nowhere else. Various state and city directories also list "unenumerated" Negroes. The one remaining political party enrollment log contains an Afro-American not appearing in any of the censuses.[65] Accounts in the Monroe newspapers also disclose the existence of many of these "other" Afro-Americans.[66] At times, for example, the only source indicating a Negro's tenure in the city was a mortuary notice. The racial heritage of individuals who had committed a crime, violated a community norm, or been involved in something interesting or unusual was often noted in a local "brevity" column. Given the haphazard quality of record keeping and news reporting, it is reasonable to assume that there were more itinerant blacks who walked the streets of Monroe and lived there for a short time than can be identified. The existing sources understate this reality.

What happened to these wandering souls cannot be known. In a fashion, however, their experience did impinge on the lives of Monroe's "native" Afro-Americans. The manner in which these "others" were depicted in the newspapers hints at a social process every bit as important as the evolution of kinship networks. The development and articulation of an elaborate nationwide white racial ideology in the late nineteenth and early twentieth centuries determined the quality of life, in large part, for all blacks. The experience of Afro-Americans in the city of Monroe cannot be properly understood outside of this context. What white men thought about blacks, in general, did make a difference. Kinship networks provided a measure of shelter for Negroes from the most obvious consequences of racism in Monroe. As a survival strategy, the "family" ensured some blacks a modicum of mobility and economic security, yet no individual identified as Afro-American was completely immune from verbal assault or innuendo regarding his color. As the final chapter will demonstrate, life was not easy for Monroe's Negro citizens. There were numerous instances when the racial heritage of long-time residents was viewed as a barrier to full acceptability by the white community. Ostracism, at some level, was an experience shared by all those who claimed an African ancestor.

NOTES

1. See Mrs. Edmund Childs, interview with W. C. Sterling, 8 Oct. 1956, and with Mr. and Mrs. Albert Heck, 18 Dec. 1956, in "Recollections of Life in Monroe County, Michigan, 1956–62" (Monroe: Monroe County Library Board, unpublished), pp. 26, 261.

2. This is undoubtedly the reason why a systematic study of the Negro experience in the Midwest before the Progressive Era has not been a popular area of investigation for historians. Undoubtedly, the best studies of this kind are David M. Katzman's *Before the Ghetto: Black Detroit in the Nineteenth Century* (Urbana: University of Illinois Press, 1973), Kenneth L. Kusmer's *A Ghetto Takes Shape: Black Cleveland, 1870–1930* (Urbana: University of Illinois Press, 1976), and David A. Gerber's *Black Ohio and the Color Line 1860–1915* (Urbana: University of Illinois Press, 1976). While many other Michigan areas claimed a number of Negroes as inhabitants throughout the nineteenth century, a systematic study of the black experience in such communities has yet to be undertaken. Willis Dunbar in his book *How It Was in Hartford: Small Town Life in Mid-America, 1900–1920* (Grand Rapids, Mich.: William B. Eerdmans, 1968) makes passing references to Negroes in Hartford (see p. 35). The most ambitious work to date is Melvin Banner, *The Black Pioneer in Michigan,* vol. 1 *Flint and Genesee County* (Midland, Mich.: Pendell, 1973). Using such sources as the census manuscript schedules, city directories, and oral histories, Banner tells us about the occupations, institutions, and life experiences of various Negroes in the Flint area. Although the research is excellent, a meaningful synthesis is absent as he does not attempt to make a unified and coherent statement regarding race relations in Flint or Genesee County.

3. The governmental jurisdictions incorporating the geographical area which would become the city of Monroe underwent many

transitions between 1785 and 1837. Frenchtown, the first white settlement in the immediate area, was founded on the River Raisin in 1785. Two years later, it was within the confines of the newly created Northwest Territory. When Wayne County was formed in 1796, Frenchtown became part of that unit's Sargent Township. In 1805 when Congress created the territory of Michigan, the community was in the Erie civil district of Wayne County. After much of Frenchtown was destroyed by the British and Indians in 1813, a new village, which would later be Monroe, was started on the south side of the River Raisin. After President Monroe's visit to the territory in 1817, Monroe County was organized, with the village of Monroe as the county seat. At this point in time, the new jurisdiction included all of what would later be Lenawee County (1822) and disputed border lands in Ohio. When Monroe township government was formed in 1818, the village became part of the township of Monroe. In 1827, the Monroe community was incorporated as a village by the territory, but remained in Monroe Township. The county lost the contested border lands in Ohio when Michigan gained statehood in 1837. In that year, the new state legislature incorporated Monroe as a city, separating it from township government. See Talcott E. Wing, *History of Monroe County* (New York: Munsell, 1890), pp. 41–45; George E. Lang, *Monroe County Briefly* (Monroe: McMillan, 1917), pp. 24, 26, 30; Willis F. Dunbar, *Michigan: A History of the Wolverine State*, rev. ed., George S. May (Grand Rapids, Mich.: William B. Eerdmans, 1980), pp. 211, 251–56.

4. Between 1877 and 1929, the state of Michigan published under various titles forty volumes of primary historical materials and essays relating to the state's early history. These books are generally cited as the *Michigan Pioneer and Historical Collections*, hereafter cited under the abbreviated title *MPHC*. For the Sargent Township tax list see *MPHC* 8 (1886): 536–39. For the 1779 and 1782 lists of Detroit citizens see ibid., 10 (1888): 311–27, 601–13. Additional years for which there are population data for Detroit are 1778 and 1780. See ibid., p. 446 for 1780 and ibid., 9 (1887): 496 for 1778. The information for these last two years, 1778 and 1780, does not include names of individuals. For the experience of Negroes before Michigan became a territory, consult Norman McRae, "Early Blacks in Michigan, 1743–1800," *Detroit in Perspective* 2 (Spring 1976): 159–88.

5. While the Detroit "censuses" for 1779 and 1782 do not classify inhabitants by race, and it is likely that some of the people held in bondage were Indians, it is a certain historical fact that not a small number of Negroes were kept in slavery by Detroit citizens before

and during the territorial period. See J. A. Girardin, "Slavery in Detroit," paper read before the Detroit Pioneer Society, 27 Sept. 1872, *MPHC* 1 (1877): 415–17.

6. A. J. Hull to Jaques Lasselle, 5 June 1805, Solomon Sibley Papers, Burton Historical Collections, Detroit, Mich. Interesting to note is the fact that one Antoine LaSalle of Monroe County had four Negroes living in his household in 1820. Microcopy 33 *Population Schedules of the Fourth Census of the United States, 1820* Roll #56 *Michigan Territorial Census*.

7. *Aggregate Amount of Persons within the United States in the Year 1810* (Washington, D.C.: U.S. Census Office, 1811), p. 88. Also see *MPHC* 36 (1908): 235.

8. "Early History," *Monroe Commercial,* 26 Mar. 1874, p. 1.

9. Manumission document freeing "John, a blackman" by a Frenchman Lajiness at the River Raisin, 18 Dec. 1818, State Archives, Michigan History Division, Lansing, Mich.

10. *Population Schedules, 1820*. While the official totals indicated eight blacks, a careful reading of the manuscript showed nine.

11. *Michigan Sentinel,* 21 Oct. 1825, p. 3.

12. *Michigan Sentinel,* 15 Sept. 1827, p. 3.

13. Microcopy 19 *Population Schedules of the Fifth Census of the United States, 1830* Roll #69 *Michigan Territorial Census*.

14. Clarence Edwin Carter, comp. and ed., *The Territorial Papers of the United States,* vol. 12: *The Territory of Michigan 1829–1837* (Washington, D.C.: U.S. Government Printing Office, 1945), p. 1020. In this enumeration, Monroe County had the dubious distinction of having two of the three slaves in peninsular Michigan. The other chattel resided in Jackson County.

15. William Wells Brown, *Clotel: or The President's Daughter: A Narrative of Slave Life in the United States* (London: Partridge and Oakey, 1853), pp. 39–42. The first American novel by a black, *Clotel* is a fictional account of a supposed mulatto daughter of Thomas Jefferson. The book, however, does contain some autobiographical material. Brown's foremost biographer, William E. Farrison, regards the 1835 Monroe experience, which was also related in the same words in Brown's *Three Years in Europe* (London, 1852), as actual. See William E. Farrison, *William Wells Brown: Author and Reformer* (Chicago: University of Chicago Press, 1969), pp. 63–66. Unfortunately, barbers did not advertise in the Monroe newspapers during this time period, and a thorough investigation of the village's *Michigan Sentinel* failed to confirm Brown's presence there in 1835.

16. At some time, apparently after 1830, Robert S. Duncanson migrated from New York to Monroe with John and Lucy Duncanson. Unfortunately, the precise family relationship between Robert S. and the Monroe Duncansons is not known; it is taken here to be immediate and primary. Despite the fact that a precise genealogy cannot be documented, there does seem to be enough circumstantial evidence to reasonably conclude that he was the fourth child of John and Lucy. For example, while only six of the seven Duncanson children can be accounted for in the existing records, Robert's birthdate makes it possible for him to be the other sibling. At the least, it is fairly certain that he did spend the majority of the 1830s living in Monroe. For a year, beginning in April 1838, the *Monroe Gazette* advertised a new firm, "John Gamblin and R. Duncanson, Painters and Glaziers," in the city. There was no other R. Duncanson at that time. A Monroe background is also suggested by the title of one of his paintings, "Battleground of the River Raisin." After the early 1840s, Duncanson claimed Cincinnati as his home. In the years before his death, he would often travel to Detroit to exhibit his works or paint commissions. On those trips, he would at times stop over in Monroe, presumably to visit relatives. When he died in 1872, his remains were brought to Monroe for burial. At that time, the *Monroe Commercial* claimed he was "long a resident," and stated an erroneous belief that he had been "born here."

The early life of Duncanson has been a mystery to art historians. Indeed, the years between his birth in 1821 and his arrival in Cincinnati in the early 1840s have been largely a blank. Duncanson is generally recognized as one of the earliest American black artists of importance. He is usually identified with the Hudson River School of painting. See Appendix, Figure 1; *Monroe Gazette,* 17 Apr. 1838 to 9 Apr. 1839; Charles Cist, *Sketches and Statistics of Cincinnati in 1851* (Cincinnati: Wm. H. Moore, 1850), p. 126; *Monroe Commercial,* 14 Sept. 1871, p. 3, 26 Dec. 1872, p. 3; James A. Porter, "Robert S. Duncanson, Midwestern Romantic-Realist," *Art in America* (Oct. 1951), pp. 99–103; Edward H. Dwight, "Robert S. Duncanson," *Museum Echoes* 27 (June 1954): 43–45; Guy McElroy, "Robert S. Duncanson (1821–1872): A Study of the Artist's Life and Work," in illustrated brochure *Robert S. Duncanson: A Centennial Exhibition* (Cincinnati: Cincinnati Art Museum, 1972), pp. 5–16; James Dallas Parks, *Robert S. Duncanson: 19th Century Black Romantic Painter* (Washington, D.C.: Associated Publishers, 1980).

17. *Compendium of the Enumeration of the Inhabitants and Statistics of the United States, 1840* (Washington, D.C.: Thomas Allen, 1841), p. 94; *Statistical Report of the Secretary of State of Michigan*

for the Years 1849–1850 (Lansing, Mich.: R. W. Ingals, 1850), p. 65; *Seventh Census of the United States, 1850* (Washington D.C.: Robert Armstrong, 1853), p. 893; *Census and Statistics of the State of Michigan, May, 1854* (Lansing, Mich.: George W. Peek, 1854), pp. 246–47; *Statistics of the State of Michigan Compiled from the Census of 1860* (Lansing, Mich.: John A. Kerr, 1861), p. 189; *Census and Statistics of the State of Michigan, 1864* (Lansing, Mich.: John A. Kerr, 1864), pp. 382–83; *Statistics of the Population of the United States at the Ninth Census, 1870* (Washington, D.C.: U.S. Government Printing Office, 1872) 1: 173; *Census of the State of Michigan, 1874* (Lansing, Mich.: W. S. George, 1875), pp. 32, 103; Mach 102 *Population Schedules of the Tenth Census of the United States, 1880* Roll #596 *Michigan* vol. 18 *Monroe (part) and Montcalm (part) Counties*, p. 540; *Census of the State of Michigan, 1884*, 2 vols. (Lansing, Mich.: Thorp and Godfrey, 1886) 1: 230; *Report of the Population of the United States at the Eleventh Census, 1890* (Washington, D.C.: U.S. Government Printing Office, 1895), pt. 1: 190; *Census of the State of Michigan, 1894* 2 vols. (Lansing, Mich.: Robert Smith, 1896) 1: 84; *Census Reports of the Twelfth Census: 1900 Population* (Washington, D.C.: U.S. Government Printing Office, 1901) 1, pt. 1: 210; *Census of the State of Michigan, 1904, Population*, 2 vols. (Lansing, Mich.: Wynkoop Crawford, 1906) 1: 165–66; *City Directory of Monroe, Michigan, 1904* (Monroe: Goodrich, 1904), pp. 17, 27, 43, 47, 63, 87; *United States Thirteenth Census of Population, 1910* T624 Reel 664 *Michigan* vol. 62 *Monroe (part) and Menominee Counties*, Monroe City, First Ward, sheets 3A, 3B, and 20B, Second Ward, sheet 5B, Third Ward, sheet 21A; *State Compendium: Michigan, Fourteenth Census of the United States, 1920* (Washington, D.C.: U.S. Government Printing Office, 1924), p. 35; *Fifteenth Census of the United States, 1930* (Washington, D.C.: U.S. Government Printing Office, 1932), 3, pt. 1: 1133.

18. *Population Schedules of the Eighth Census of the United States, 1860* Roll #554 *Michigan* vol. 13 *Marquette, Schoolcraft, Mason, Osceola and Monroe Counties*, p. 546; *Population Schedules, 1880*, p. 540.

19. In 1880, the Foster family appeared as black in the decennial manuscript census. Twenty years later, they were recorded in neighboring Monroetown as white. *Population Schedules, 1880*, p. 550; *United States Twelfth Census of Population, 1900* T623 Reel 733 *Michigan* vol. 55 *Monroe (part) and Montcalm (part) Counties*, p. 277.

20. *Population Schedules, 1910*, Monroe Township, sheet 2B.

21. Compare *United States Twelfth Census of Population, 1900*

T623 Reel 733 *Michigan* vol. 55 *Monroe (part) and Montcalm (part) Counties,* pp. 221A, 224A, 232A, to *Population Schedules, 1910,* Monroe City, First Ward, sheets 3A and 3B, and Third Ward, sheet 21A. These families were the Duncansons, Hermanns (related to Duncansons), and Mays.

22. *Census, 1904,* 165–66 and *City Directory, 1904,* pp. 17, 27, 37, 43, 63, 87. In the directory, seven individuals were recorded as residing in the First Ward and four in the Second Ward. The state count places four Negroes in the Fourth Ward. A total of fifteen is thus certain. Even this number most likely underestimates the black population since the city directory did not list children. The whole question of errors and carelessness on the part of federal and state census marshals involves the issue of passing and is treated in the conclusion.

23. A detailed list of Negro surnames between 1830 and 1915 was compiled from these sources and then cross-referenced. The constant repetition of certain Negro names in the records made the outlines of several black kin networks in Monroe discernible.

24. Katzman, *Before the Ghetto,* pp. 25–32, 59–80, 112–15, 217–22; Kusmer, *A Ghetto Takes Shape,* pp. 19–24, 38–44, 66–90, 161–65, 281–88.

25. See *Population Schedules, 1850* to *1910.*

26. Herbert Gutman's caveat that kinship networks cannot be reconstructed from census data of course is true. Yet when augmented by other sources, as will be demonstrated, their existence becomes apparent. Herbert Gutman, *The Black Family in Slavery and Freedom, 1750–1925* (New York: Pantheon, 1976), p. 433.

27. The Fosters left the city in 1894 for adjacent Monroe Township, where they were enumerated in the 1900 and 1910 decennial schedules. See *Population Schedules, 1900,* p. 277; *Population Schedules, 1910,* Monroe Township, sheet 3B. Their farm was "just outside" the city boundaries and they always maintained a strong identification with Monroe activities. Their names appear frequently in the city newspapers, in local business records and account books, and elsewhere.

28. One of the difficulties encountered was the different spelling of Negro names. In the manuscript censuses between 1860 and 1880, for example, the same individual appears as Fanny Dunkinson, Fanny Duncan, and Fannie Duncanson respectively. Aaron Bromley appears as Aaron Bramble on his Civil War enlistment record, as Aaron Brumley in the 1874–75 city directory, and as Aarn Brumle on a deed record. In the 1870 census, Alexander Wickliffe has the surname Wickley and his daughter, Rebecca, is listed

with the last name of Wickoff. The too-frequently illegible pen of the federal enumerator was also troublesome. On the county level, vital records were often kept in haphazard fashion. On more than one occasion, a birth or death in the community was noted in the newspaper but was not recorded at the courthouse as required by law. The use of the appellation "col'd" following the names of some individuals in early city and state directories was inconsistent and capricious. In fact, the majority of Monroe's Afro-Americans were not designated as such.

29. See Niara Sudarkasa, "African and Afro-American Family Structure: A Comparison," *The Black Scholar* 11 (Nov.-Dec. 1980): 37–60. In this important essay, Ms. Sudarkasa takes to task American historians for conceptualizing black family relationships within the context of the nuclear household. She points out that it is just as reasonable and more accurate to view these matters from a lineage-consanguineal perspective.

30. "Fictive kinship is a binding relationship between individuals similar to that of close kin but not based on the bond of birth, marriage, or descent." Oriol Pi-Sunyer and Zdenek Salzmann, *Humanity and Culture: An Introduction to Anthropology* (Boston: Houghton Mifflin, 1978), p. 250.

31. If naming practices are taken into consideration, the tentative connection with Lasselle's slave seems reasonable. An Anthony Smith, son of Stephen, appears in the 1850 and 1860 schedules for Monroe and Raisinville townships respectively.

32. Wing, *History of Monroe County,* pp. 500–501; John Bulkley, *History of Monroe County Michigan,* 2 vols. (Chicago: Lewis, 1913) 1: 422–23; Boyd's Young Ladies Seminary and Collegiate Institute Collection, Monroe County Archives, Monroe County Historical Museum. From 1850 to 1879 Erasmus J. Boyd served as principal of this institution. A major Monroe showpiece, it afforded "the girls of Monroe and the State and of the country generally all the advantages of a school of the highest grade, where they might be fitted and qualified to hold positions in the scientific, musical, literary or social sphere in the world." Bulkley, *History,* p. 422. For most of this period, there were over one hundred young females in attendance, about half of whom were out-of-city boarders. The school closed its doors in 1883.

33. Monroe County Probate Court, Commitment Proceedings of Mrs. Phoebe Duncanson, 16 May 1890, number 4104. Three other children, Robert M., Louise, and Barney, are in the 1860 enumerations. It is unclear who their parents were.

34. Monroe County Probate Court, Estate of John Deane Dun-

canson, 16 Oct. 1871, number 1994; Estate of Charles Hermann, 30 Jan. 1923, number 10698.

35. Monroe County Probate Court, Guardianship of Wickliffe Fox, 16 May 1892, number 4386, 7 June 1892, number 4431; Estate of Mary Dickinson, 9 Apr. 1914, number 8273.

36. See Glen V. Mills, *Ann Arbor City Directory, 1903* (Ann Arbor: Glen V. Mills, 1903), p. 150, *1904*, p. 143; R. L. Polk, *Toledo City Directory, 1905* (Toledo, Ohio: Toledo Directory Co., 1905), p. 556, *1906*, p. 552.

37. Monroe County Probate Court, Estate of Ellen Francis Johnson, 14 Feb. 1923, number 10687.

38. The best discussion on the Monroe ward structure is in Mrs. Edmund Childs's interview with Doris Soleau, city clerk, 24 June 1958, "Recollections," p. 306. From 1837 to 1845, the city had five wards. The first three wards were located south of the River Raisin. Monroe Street marked the eastern boundary of the First Ward and the western limit of the Second Ward. The western boundary of the Third Ward was set by Scott Street, which marked the eastern line of the Second Ward. The Fourth and Fifth wards were located north of the River Raisin with the boundary set by a line drawn north from the river to the Michigan Central depot. The Fourth Ward was west of that point and the Fifth was east. Beginning in 1850 and lasting until 1870, Monroe was divided into three wards. The First and Second wards were south of the river with Washington Street marking the eastern boundary of the First Ward and western extent of the Second Ward. The Third Ward included all the city north of the river. After the 1870 decennial census, which revealed a population of more than 5,000 for the city, Monroe was allowed to add another ward. The area north of the River Raisin was designated as the Fourth Ward. South of the river, Cass Street was the boundary line between the First and Second wards and Scott Street marked off the Second and Third wards. Technically speaking, the city of Monroe constituted a single ward when a new charter was adopted in 1913; however, the four voting precincts that were created had boundary lines that were coterminous with the old ward arrangements. The basic division of the city was the same between 1870 and 1920. See *Charter of the City of Monroe* adopted 8 Dec. 1913 (Lansing: State of Michigan, 1913), p. 2.

39. A number of maps and atlases depicting nineteenth- and early twentieth-century Monroe have survived. They are Map of Monroe, Monroe County, Mich., 1871, Willets, Waters, and Bird, Civil Engineers, *County Atlas of Monroe, Michigan* (New York: F. W. Beers, 1876), pp. 79–80; 1888 Monroe Insurance Maps, Monroe

County Archives, Monroe County Historical Museum, *Standard Atlas of Monroe County Michigan* (Chicago: George A. Ogle, 1896), pp. 14–15; 1899 Monroe Insurance Maps, Sanborn-Perris, Monroe County Archives, Monroe County Historical Museum; Map of Monroe County, Mich., 1901 (Carleton, Mich.: George E. Lang, 1901). Unfortunately, they are not always useful in pinpointing the precise site of businesses or dwellings since they did not place an individual's name over his or her store's location. An additional problem was the business changes in the same building over the years. The 1871 map was the first to indicate businesses and homes in any kind of detail, yet neither the Duncanson paint shop on Washington Street nor the Miller tailoring establishment on Front Street can be placed with any certainty. It should be noted that the cartographic sources designated property ownership and not residency. People who were renters or boarders do not appear on these depictions; however, a careful working back and forth between the maps and atlases, Monroe city directories, decennial manuscript census schedules, and information in newspapers makes it possible to establish where the majority of these people lived and worked.

40. Monroe County Liber 73, p. 623, 1 Mar. 1871.

41. *Population Schedules, 1880,* p. 507; *Monroe City Directory, 1874–75,* p. 20; *Monroe City Directory, 1892–93* (Monroe: Frank Wilder, 1892). The oral tradition of the 1950s indicates that the Bromleys were "brought to Monroe as slaves" by the Comptons. This is not true. Rather, this misunderstanding reflects a false inference made by individuals living at the time regarding the board and work arrangement between Bromley and Compton.

42. Monroe County, Marriage Record 4 1867–86, p. 18, 13 Jan. 1869.

43. Katzman, *Before the Ghetto,* pp. 25–32, 59–80, 112–15, 217–22; Kusmer, *A Ghetto Takes Shape,* pp. 19–24, 38–44, 66–90, 161–65, 281–88. See also Gerber, *Black Ohio,* pp. 60–92, 297–319.

44. One of the best essays on the proper utilization of city directories is Peter R. Knights, "Using City Directories in Ante-Bellum Urban Historical Research," Appendix A in *The Plain People of Boston 1830–1860: A Study in City Growth* (New York: Oxford University Press, 1971), pp. 127–39. Knights found sexual, racial, economic, and areal biases in all the Boston antebellum directories. For twentieth century directories, between 1910 and 1951, Sidney Goldstein, "City Directories as Sources of Migration Data," *American Journal of Sociology* 60 (Sept. 1954): 169–76, and *Patterns of Mobility 1910–1950: The Norristown Study* (Philadelphia: University of Pennsylvania Press, 1958), pp. 58–123, offer some useful in-

sights. Among Goldstein's important conclusions were that there was virtually 100 percent coverage of adult males and that "satisfactory information on occupations was supplied, with the possible exception of the laboring groups for whom, as measured by the federal census, the directory over enumerates the unskilled laborers at the expense of the skilled and semi-skilled," pp. 122–23.

45. The 1850 U.S. population schedules do not list the occupations of females. Beginning in 1860, the U.S. census would begin this task. It is clear from evidence in local newspapers and from "oral history" that many women in Monroe worked during the entire period under consideration but were not reported as such in either the decennial censuses or city directories.

46. *Population Schedules, 1870,* p. 408.

47. *City Directory, Monroe, Michigan, 1901,* See also *Monroe Democrat,* 19 Oct. 1899, p. 5; *Monroe Record,* 27 Nov. 1902, p. 5.

48. Reference is made to Foster's teaching efforts in Bulkley, *History of Monroe County Michigan,* 2: 942, and Hermann is listed as a teacher in the Monroe city directories from 1905 to 1914.

49. Steiner Hardware Store collection account book 1865–71, and G. F. Grant Jewelry Store account book 1855–65, Monroe County Archives, Monroe County Historical Museum; Lauer note in possession of Charles Verhoeven, Jr.

50. Munch's Cigar Store, Tavern, Bus Stop and Hotel account book 1884–97; Dr. Amos Long dental register; Record Publishing Company 1900–1906 records in Monroe County Archives.

51. John A. Kirschner Collection, Monroe County Archives.

52. *Monroe Gazette,* 17 Apr. 1838 to 9 Apr. 1839; *Monroe Democrat,* 4 Mar. 1886, p. 1, 13 Oct. 1892, p. 1, 1 June 1899, p. 5.

53. Minutes and Records of the Monroe Baptist Church 1874–1914, *passim.*

54. Record of Monroe First Methodist Episcopal Church 1867–99.

55. *Monroe Democrat,* 23 Sept. 1880, p. 1, 21 Apr. 1881, p. 1; *Monroe Commercial,* 22 Apr. 1881, p. 1.

56. Record of Monroe First M. E. Church, p. 16; Minutes and Records of Baptist church, p. 190; *Monroe Democrat,* 25 Nov. 1904, p. 8.

57. See David Gerber, "A Politics of Limited Options: Northern Black Politics and the Problem of Change and Continuity in Race Relations Historiography," *Journal of Social History* 14 (Winter 1980): 235–55, for an excellent discussion of this issue.

58. Michigan Historical Collections, Bentley Historical Library, Monroe County Papers 1819–1903, vote on equal suffrage to col-

ored persons, 1850, *Monroe Commercial,* 16 Apr. 1868, p. 3, 24 Nov. 1870, p. 2. Unfortunately, a breakdown of the vote in the city is not available for 1870. The 1850 tally showed particularly lopsided majorities, in both city and county, against granting male Negroes the right to vote. Only 19 out of 265 votes in the city favored the amendment and in the county the count was 170 for and 1,370 against. Eighteen years later, when the people voted on a new state constitution with equal suffrage, the city and county again turned a large majority against the proposition. This time, however, the figures of 204 for and 578 against in the city and 1,365 for and 3,080 against in the county revealed that at least some white Monroe males were moving in the direction of political equality. The statistics for the county in 1870, when the state again submitted the amendment for ratification, showed that two years later Monroe's voters had not moved further in that direction. This time the county turned down equal suffrage by a vote of 1,938 to 1,034.

59. City of Monroe Register of Electors 1859–1912.

60. Bulkley, *History of Monroe County Michigan,* 2: 941; City of Monroe party enrollment, First Ward 1906–10.

61. *Monroe Democrat,* 5 Feb. 1904, p. 8, 14 Aug. 1884, p. 1, 21 Aug. 1884, p. 1, and 18 Mar. 1886, p. 1.

62. Herbert Gutman, *The Black Family in Slavery and Freedom 1750–1925* (New York: Pantheon, 1976), pp. 185–201.

63. The major exceptions to this generalization are the Billmires (under various spellings) and Louis Young. While there is some indication that the Billmires had a lengthy family connection with the Monroe environs, the existing evidence is inadequate for establishing definite or approximate genealogical ties. See *Population Schedules, 1830, 1850, 1870, and 1880,* and various newspaper references: *Monroe Commercial,* 6 June 1872, p. 3; *Toledo Morning Commercial,* 4 June 1872, p. 4; *Monroe Democrat,* 27 June 1889, p. 1. Louis Young, who appears in the Monroe population schedules for the first time in 1910, can be documented as residing in the city as early as 1903. His name is in numerous sources after that time and he continued to live in Monroe until his death in 1967. Louis Young did not marry and does not appear to have been "linked" to any black kin network in the community. The family of Oscar May appears in the 1900 and 1910 decennial censuses and city directories between 1901 and 1920. It would seem that they had some measure of family identity in the community. Apparently, they were light-skinned because their racial designation in the population schedules changed from black to white between 1900 and 1910. Unfortunately, not much is known about these people.

64. Martha and Thomas Tims, Beverly, Betsy, Thomas, Nathaniel, Blanche, and Elizabeth Harris, Elizabeth Billmire, Joseph, Caroline, and A. J. Williams, Betsy and Mary Jacobs, William Stanton, George and Mary Williams, Sarah Brewster, William, Elvira, and Alexander Wilks, Philip Jackson, Jane Mistu, Harriet Night, and George Gaitor in Microcopy 432 *Population Schedules of the Seventh Census of the United States, 1850* Roll #359 *Michigan: Monroe and Montcalm Counties,* pp. 691–760; Henry, Matilda, and Sarah Nims, Alma Dusaro, John, Priscilla, Matilda, and Andrew Jackson in *Population Schedules 1860,* pp. 521–618; Woodie, Rona, Hattie, and Loiza Woodfolk, Dennis, Tolinda, Cornelia, Julia, and John Grew, Abram Paudo, and Martha Johnson in *Population Schedules 1870,* pp. 394–459; Alexander Billsmire, Stephen, Mary E., Enanias, and Sarah Stuart, Nancy Booth, and Jake Cummings in *Population Schedules, 1880,* pp. 503–51; and Edward, Gertrude, Eugene, and Gertrude (daughter) Pool in *Population Schedules, 1900,* p. 251A. For the nineteenth century see Joseph and Montgomery Simmons, *Monroe Democrat,* 25 July 1889, p. 1; Fred Newberg, *Monroe Democrat,* 30 Aug. 1888, p. 1, 11 Feb. 1892, p. 1; Sidney Edmire, *Monroe Democrat,* 6 Feb. 1896, p. 1; Thomas Irving and John Cole, *Monroe Democrat,* 14 July 1898, p. 1; colored woman named "Brooke," *Monroe Democrat,* 2 Apr. 1891, p. 1.

65. A fire destroyed the Monroe County Courthouse on 28 Feb. 1879 and some governmental records were lost. Fortunately, the early marriage records survived. See Monroe County Marriage Record 3, 1852–70, Elizabeth Brown to Noel Cox, 10 Feb. 1868, p. 200; Ms. Brown may have been a member of a family which dated its Monroe origins to the territorial period. See *Population Schedules, 1820;* Charles Lanman, *Adventures in the Wilds of the United States and British American Provinces,* 2 vols. (Philadelphia: John W. Moore, 1856) 1:147; Marriage Record 4, 1867–86, Alexander Belmore to Mary S. Hill, 13 Jan. 1869, p. 18 (Belmore has already been noted); John A. Fields (race not included) to Annie E. Cooper, 11 Nov. 1873, p. 91; Marriage Record 6, 1887–1903, Thomas Hayes to Florence George (white), 31 Oct. 1889, p. 41. For the Civil War enlistments see Frances Warren, comp., *Michigan Manual of Freedmen's Progress* (Detroit: Freedman's Progress Commission, 1915), George Griffin, p. 232, James Pike, p. 243, Frank Taylor, p. 249, and Zachariah Wallace, p. 251. The race of some individuals listed in the early city and state directories is indicated with "(col'd)" following their names. Daniel Lowrie (col'd) appears as a barber in George W. Hawes, *Michigan State Gazetteer and Business Directory 1860* (Detroit: F. Raymond, 1859), p. 248, and in Charles F. Clark,

Michigan State Gazetteer and Business Directory 1863–64 (Detroit: Charles F. Clark, 1863), p. 408. A. Dunken and Henry Mims are listed as colored in George W. Hawes, *Loomis and Talbott's Monroe, Hillsdale and Coldwater Directory, 1860–61* (Detroit: Hawes, 1860), pp. 19, 26, 33. After the publication of the *Monroe City Directory, 1874–75* (Detroit: Burch, Montgomery, 1874), no local directory designated the race of any person. Charles Madison is in the Monroe City party enrollment register 1906–10 (race included) for the Fourth Ward between 1904 and 1906. It is certainly not accidental that Monroe citizens, who recalled their pasts at mid-twentieth century, could generally not remember any "coloreds" who could not be connected to an obvious extended kinship network. See Childs, "Recollections," *passim*.

66. It would seem that the newspapers "bared" the entire community to itself in their local columns. Items covered ranged from the size of watermelons to prodigious swine litters to family squabbles. The most intimate kind of information was sometimes disclosed. Although inconsistent, Monroe editors at times designated individuals who appeared in their columns as "colored." Those Afro-Americans who were members of established family networks were rarely addressed under that appellation, but those who were temporary residents or passing through usually were.

2

The Problem of The South and the Child-Negro Stereotype in Monroe, 1900–1915

> The Rev. Dr. Weaver (colored), under the auspices of the Presbyterian Board of Freedmen, will give a stereoptican lecture on the Freedman of the South at the Presbyterian church Friday evening of this week at 7:30. . . . All interested in the problem of the South are invited to attend.
>
> *Monroe Democrat,* 6 Oct. 1898

> Sambo goes out with the bell
> Swings it brisk and hearty
> Shouting "Come ye Darkies all
> to the Niggers' Party"
>
> *The Funny Little Darkies*
> (New York: McLaughlin, n.d.)[1]

For a brief period after the Civil War, blacks living in the North and Midwest seem to have enjoyed a status that was "almost equal" to that of whites. Upward income, property, and occupational mobility was not an atypical circumstance for Negroes who chose to carve out their lives in mid-American communities. Afro-Americans in Detroit, Cleveland, Monroe, and elsewhere experienced measurable improvement in their socioeconomic positions in the 1870s and 1880s. Both races appear to have cooperated and worked together in many areas. Schools and churches were often integrated. Most of the Negro-owned business serviced the white community, and it was not unusual for Afro-Americans of the "better sort" to socialize with Caucasians. In the larger cities, blacks played an important role in the political process, and discrimination in public accommodations had not become a general practice. The times seemed to lean in the direction of the total integration of society.[2]

By the 1890s, however, this trend was reversing. The promise of full equality disintegrated as scientific racism and the Jim Crow system in the South gained acceptability. While the rigid rules of southern racial etiquette were not reproduced in the North, a "color line" was drawn and the black population suffered greatly. A virtual caste system for Afro-Americans evolved in the large urban areas. Opportunities of all kinds contracted severely. European immigrants gradually pushed blacks out of their traditional positions as barbers and waiters, and the number of Negro proprietors declined. The new and more specialized trades, such as electrician, plumber, and paper hanger, that emerged during this time period were reserved for "whites only"; Afro-Americans were rarely hired into factories or as uniformed municipal employees. On the whole, blacks were excluded from labor union membership, and there was conscious racial discrimination in hiring for most jobs.

The intensification of racism also played a role in the area of housing in the larger midwestern cities. Where ethnic enclaves and a mixed pattern of residency had existed earlier, black ghettos began to take root. The political influence of the old Negro elite began to erode away. Racial discrimination by hotels, theaters, restaurants, and in public recreation facilities, despite its frequent illegality, became a standard practice in many northern communities. In addition, blacks were often set apart and received unequal treatment in public schools and hospitals.

The years surrounding the turn of the twentieth century witnessed a deterioration of race relations in all sections of the country, and this era is generally regarded as representing a low point in the history of Afro-Americans.[3] Monroe, of course, participated in this process but in ways that differed from Cleveland, Detroit, or Chicago. As a case study, Monroe provides another lens through which to view the consequences of race hatred and discrimination. Most important, blacks in Monroe lacked the demographic base to pose a serious challenge to the white community. Today, it seems that the nearly total closure of opportunity for Negroes in Monroe in this time period made little sense. After all, the city had allowed "token" Afro-Americans to hold various positions in the past, and the appointment of a black policeman or the hiring of a Negro operative in the town's burgeoning paper mills could not have threatened the prevailing social structure. Why then did Monroe become a closed society against new Negro residency in the Progressive Era?

The answer to that query is extremely complex and involves such matters as European and southern white immigration, the introduction of more advanced technology, and the appearance in Monroe of new industry and new occupations. For the most part, however, it involves the proliferation and maintenance of a nationwide white racist ideology that functioned to mold and limit the life chances of blacks in the community.

While the Negro obviously occupied a different "place" in northern as opposed to southern society, it is clear that white citizens in both sections shared certain perceptions about blacks. By the early 1900s, at least two competing general stereotypes—neither of them favorable—regarding the Afro-American's inherent characteristics were being put before the public. Important in the creation of this awareness was the existence of several nation-encompassing communication networks. Best selling books, articles in magazines with national circulations, silent films and "boiler plate" insides of national news, and items of general interest in local newspapers, ensured that few hamlets could mature without outside influence. Monroe was not isolated from the mainstream of national consciousness. Indeed, the phenomenon which has been termed "small town in mass society" was already a reality at the beginning of the twentieth century.[4] Monroe shared the same ideas and stereotypes regarding the social identity of Negroes as did much of the rest of the nation.[5]

It was mostly southern authors, speakers, and publishers who set the national tone on race relations in this era. To be sure, the North did not have the same pressing preoccupation with the "Negro problem" as the South. Southerners were vitally interested in creating the national climate of opinion on race because they were continuously confronted with the difficulty of dominating large numbers of Negroes whereas the northerners were not. Lacking an articulate or vocal white public to argue for his race after the abolitionist crusade had run its course, the Afro-American was abandoned to such racist southern publicists as Thomas Dixon, Jr., "Pitchfork" Ben Tillman, and Thomas Nelson Page. No contemporary northern writer had a comparable impact in affecting the quality of definition of American race relations. Rather, the ideas and attitudes of southern orators and essayists found fertile soil in the minds of white northerners, and by the turn of the twentieth century their perspectives were preeminent throughout the nation. As Ray Stannard Baker pointed out, "When we get right down to it, the controlling white men in the North do not believe in an inclusive democracy much more than the South. I have talked with many Northerners who go South, and it is astonishing to see how quickly most of them adopt the Southern point of view. For it is a doctrine which many of them, down in their hearts, really believe."[6] In a single statement, Baker had grasped the reality of the normative structure of race relations in the United States. The race question was not a sectional dilemma but a national one. An extremely small black population, an abolitionist crusade, an early end to slavery, and a continuity in political structure throughout the nineteenth century in the North had not resulted in an essentially different system of thought regarding the Negro.

If the South predominated in getting nationwide acceptance of its views, it would be an error, George Fredrickson has suggested, to see it as monolithic in its creation of the social identity of the American Negro. Rather, there were two southern racist traditions, often confused but nonetheless separate, which competed for national prominence. The first convention, which Fredrickson has termed the black degeneracy myth, was a competitive racism which viewed the Negro as a beast, ranking below whites on the evolutionary scale.[7] Most popular among negrophobes, the primary spokesmen for this hypothesis were such southerners as James K. Vardaman, Ben Tillman, and Thomas Dixon, Jr. The other view, one which gained much wider acceptance, both in the North and the South, was "accommodationist" racism.[8] In this neopaternalistic view, the moderates or accommodationists emphasized the childlike nature of the black race, its helplessness, and its submissiveness. Fredrickson contended that the "views of the southern accommodationists are significant . . . because they helped establish a new national consensus of 'enlightened' and 'liberal' opinion on the race question" during the Progressive Era.[9]

These white perspectives had a decided impact on the quality of race relations in Monroe. The racist stereotypes of the child-Negro and beast-Negro constrained and deeply affected the life of every black person residing in Monroe. In this chapter, the primary concern will be with developing an understanding of the role played by "accommodationist" racism, the child-Negro, in defining and shaping racial interaction in special settings in the community. The ways in which Monroe citizens utilized these racist understandings in actual interactions with blacks will be analyzed. Vastly different situations will be investigated in the following chapter, which uses the black degeneracy myth as a unifying theme.

Chapter 4 employs biography and the direct experience of selected local blacks in order to look at the city's Afro-American past.

In assessing the development of racial thought in Monroe, it is apparent that the community did have access to all the writings of southerners. The reading public of Monroe was certainly familiar with such best sellers as Thomas Dixon, Jr.'s, *The Clansman* (1905), Thomas Nelson Page's *Red Rock* (1909), and Walter Hines Page's *The Southerner* (1909). During the Progressive Era, Monroe citizens also had available to them many of the articles on blacks in magazines having a national circulation. Even Monroe's youngsters shared in this process. Children's books, such as *Ten Little Niggers,* the underlying theme of which was racial genocide, and *The Funny Little Darkies,* in which a caricatured and brightly hued "Sambo" appears, were part of the formative socialization experience of at least a few of Monroe's white progeny.[10] Of major significance here is the fact that no competing views of the Negro enjoyed a large national audience. Even the moderate Ray Stannard Baker, in his series of articles and his book about the Negro, was taken in by some of the negative stereotypes.[11]

A nationwide visual communication network which Monroe citizens participated in, from as early as 1902, was the silent movies.[12] Typically, moving pictures arrived in Monroe after showing for several weeks in Detroit. The nascent film industry found an avid nickelodeon clientele in Monroe. Most of the city's people apparently indulged in the medium. In November 1909, for example, the Family Theatre, after a particularly brisk showing of a single film, reported an attendance of 3,500 patrons (more than 50 percent of Monroe's population!) at ten performances, while turning away hundreds.[13]

Although a complete listing of early twentieth-century film offerings in Monroe is unavailable, it is clear that the community's movie patrons had access to the "bigger" celluloid productions of the times in local theaters. The Monroe Armory Opera House offered the "Great Train Robbery" in November 1904; the 1911 "Indianapolis Auto Races" played at the Family Theatre in July 1911; and films of the "Chicago Fire" were shown at the Little Gem in November 1911.[14] Apparently, Monroe was as much in the mainstream of film offerings as the large urban centers. As such, it would seem likely that the city's movie patrons had access to such racist productions as "Ten Pickaninnies" (1904), "Wooing and Wedding a Coon" (1905), and "How Rastus Got His Turkey" (c. 1910). In each of these motion pictures the child-Negro image manifested itself in full regalia.[15] It is likely that Monroe audiences increased their familiarity with the "Sambo" image by viewing films of this genre.

A major print network which Monroe shared with the remainder of the country was the large urban press. The southern viewpoint also worked its way into the major newspapers. The urban press of the early 1900s was filled with accounts of lynchings of blacks, jokes making light of Negroes, and with the appearances and speeches of such notables as "Pitchfork" Ben Tillman and Booker T. Washington on the "Race Question." If political reformers paid scant attention to the Negro question in the years following the turn of the century, the newspaper chains found that the public had a genuine interest in negative stereotypes about blacks. Tales of rape and revenge, of stupidity and docility regarding the Negro titillated the imagination of the public and sold papers.[16]

Monroe citizens often bought subscriptions to the larger urban midwestern newspapers. Not only were the Detroit and Toledo dailies available for purchase, but local agents sold to Monroe subscribers such papers as the *Chicago American,* the *Cincinnati Enquirer,* and the *Chicago Chronicle*.[17] For years local gadfly and writer John McMillan operated a news agency for the *Detroit Free Press* in Monroe, and another native, Ed Mauer, ran a metropolitan newspaper route in the city.[18] Sunday editions of the urban presses were especially popular with Monroe's populace since the local newspapers were printed only once weekly, on a Thursday or Friday.[19] It is clear that the racist offerings in the national newspapers were available to the reading public in Monroe during the early twentieth century. What is also apparent, according to Kenneth Kusmer, is that "shifts in public opinion on the race question during this period were actually national rather than sectional in nature."[20]

Undoubtedly, the most important print communication network in Monroe was the local press. The city was never without at least two competing weekly local papers between 1900 and 1915. The *Monroe Democrat* (1880–1915) represented the Democratic interests in the city and county, and the *Monroe Commercial* (1856–1904), the *Monroe Record* (1900–1904), and then the *Record-Commercial* (1904–21) were Monroe's Republican organs. The newspapers claiming no political affiliation were the *Monroe Independent* (1898–1901), the *Monroe Bulletin* (1908–15), the *Monroe Daily Graphic* (1896), and the *Black Iconoclast* (1900).[21]

The more important papers, the *Bulletin, Commercial, Record, Record-Commercial,* and *Democrat* were typically eight to twelve pages in length, and the usual yearly subscription price was $1.00

to $1.50. Each paper, according to the annual newspaper directories, enjoyed a countywide circulation of more than one thousand during their heydays.[22] Most of the pages of the newspapers were devoted to local news columns, but all but the *Bulletin* contained a "boiler plate" inside which offered international and national news and items of general interest.[23] Important to note here is the fact that Monroe's reading public had available to them, through the "boiler plate," material in the large urban presses which, at times, reinforced and reestablished the negative social identity of Negroes.

Most important in considering the local newspapers is the fact that the "'spontaneous' nature of the material reflects the values of both the ongoing society and the publishers."[24] If the local press relates nothing else, it mirrors something of the normative system and collective consensus of the community in general and by definition shows something about what people think important. The basic premise here is that the normative structure of race relations in Monroe can be inferred from the multitude of local newspaper items dealing with blacks. The content of Monroe's version of "Sambo" is clearly discernible from items in its own press.

The "old-time darkey" image of the Negro was a well-established and familiar stereotype for blacks during the Progressive Era. Adjectives such as indolent, cowardly, lazy, good-natured, careless, cheerful, childlike, faithful, imitative, helpless, harmless, shiftless, loyal, stupid, immoral, submissive, docile, credulous, kindhearted, and tractable were used to describe what Fredrickson has called the "child half of the perennial racist dichotomy between the Negro as child and the Negro as beast."[25] Blacks, as depicted by this stereotype, were the complete antithesis of all those qualities of character valued as important and worthwhile by Americans.

The basic problem here is to demonstrate the manner in which the "Sambo" image was passed down from the national level to Monroe's citizens. While there were, as indicated, several mediums through which that caricature was proliferated, material in Monroe's newspapers regularly reaffirmed and reconstructed the "old-time darkey" stereotype to the city's people.[26] This function of the press was particularly crucial in an environment where interactive possibilities between whites and blacks were limited.

One vehicle for conveying the Negro's place in Monroe was humor. Humor, of course, is actually a very serious business, and what is being suggested here is that jokes in the "nigger genre" functioned to reconfirm the normative structure of race relations and the Negro's social identity to whites. The meaning of jokes involving blacks rested with the societal position implied for Negroes. Afro-Americans were commonly the subject of jokes and racist jibes in the Monroe press, and the traditional childlike image emerged in its quintessence when blacks were the butt of Anglo-Saxon wit.[27]

The occasion for a joke about blacks in Monroe newspapers often had nothing to do with Afro-Americans themselves. In speaking about a since-forgotten local issue, the *Monroe Record* likened it to the supposed gastronomic prowess of Negroes. In a little pearl of local wisdom the *Record* declared that "a possum [i.e. a social or political issue] is never dead until it is safely away in the darkey's digesting apparatus; Watch dat possum."[28]

In another instance, when a local debate was taking place over the relative merits of a new duck shooting law before the state legislature, several caricatured Negroes appeared in a *Monroe Democrat* cartoon on the subject. M. A. Duquette, proprietor of the Monroe Art Store, was the artist for the page-one illustration. A white officer was depicted standing over the group of blacks: Officer: "What are you'se fellers doin'?" Darkey: "Shootin' craps boss. Nothing mo' to shoot since de new law."[29] The issue of the social position of blacks is implied in this scenario. Apparently, the proposed law, if passed, would turn everyone into dice-tossers, a Negro and lower-class diversion, or worse yet, into Negroes themselves.

In 1909 a position of mail carrier opened up for the Monroe post office. The *Democrat,* at that time, could not resist relating the manner in which a fictional black boy appeared before the civil service commission. "'How far is it from this earth to the moon?' was the first question asked of him. 'How fah am it from de earf to de moon?' he repeated. 'Say boss, if you's gwine to put me on dat route, I doesn't want de job.'"[30] The underlying message in that little script was that Negroes need not apply because the position was beyond that which blacks could be expected to fill.

The *Monroe Record* felt that a story in the *Youth's Companion* about Negroes was worth repeating to its readers. The tale involved a black regiment in the Civil War. The colored men had just finished fighting and marching all night and thus were in the state of complete exhaustion. One of the troops was carrying a dog. When the white captain asked why, the reply was, "The dog's tired." The lesson from the story, according to the paper, was that the "negro is famous for his irrepressible good humor, even under the most trying conditions. His ability to see the 'silver lining' to a cloud, however obscure might well be emulated by many a morose white man."[31] The real message, as far as Afro-Americans were concerned, was again one involving status. If Negroes had inferior positions in society, they were to accept them with equanimity and even joy, and if Caucasians were so unfortunate as to face similar conditions, a like response was expected. Such stories served to verify white opinions regarding the irrepressible, childlike nature of blacks. Accordingly, Negroes were thought to be happy regardless of what inferior roles they were allowed to play. Important to note is the fact that no one suggested that the adverse conditions the Afro-Americans faced be changed. Instead, they were complimented on the good-natured way they adjusted to adversity.

In addition to jokes and humor, the Monroe newspapers recorded, from time to time, the Olympian observations of commentators on blacks and the Negro problem, which served to make clear and reintensify the structural boundaries of the child-Negro role. In a 1901 editorial, for example, the *Monroe Record* heartily agreed with Booker T. Washington that Negroes should be furnished work only where fine results could be shown. Outside of his "proper sphere," the *Record* insisted, the Negro was "crowded to the wall by his white brother." Accordingly, farming was an appropriate activity. Though the black man had little land, the proposition that he be given forty acres and a mule, the *Record* reported, was "worthy of notice."[32] Again, the key to interpreting this statement is the concept of status. The pure and simple meaning to this script was that Negroes would not be considered eligible for the better jobs.

The contention that "the better established the norms are, the less likely it is that people will be aware of them" certainly holds true relative to what Monroe's white population in the Progressive Era regarded as the Negro's place.[33] Despite much evidence to the contrary, the Monroe press continued to talk about the "golden opportunities offered the colored race." The failure of black achievement rested not with the rigid and noncompromising normative structure but with the lack of responsibility on the part of blacks in taking advantage of opportunities. Unfortunately, the *Record* contended, so few Negroes "appreciat[ed] the glorious freedom so dearly purchased for the black slaves of the South by whites."[34]

The childlike image of the Negro gained its highest and most complete expression in the Monroe press in a 1902 editorial in the *Record* that is worthy of quoting in its entirety:

> In a sermon preached recently at Macon, Georgia, the Rev. W. W. Lucas, a Negro minister said: "I have decided that the only way to get rid of the 'Jim Crow' car is to get rid of the 'Jim Crow' Negro. If I could use 200,000 bars of soap on the unwashed Negroes that travel on trains and hang around depots I would solve the Negro problem

> about twenty per cent. Lazy, ragged, barefeet fellows, longing for silver slippers and long white robes and counting themselves worthy, neglecting to provide a home for their families on earth, and yet claiming a home not made with their hands in God's heaven. The white man is trying to make this earth blossom as a rose, and the Negro is getting ready to die. The white [*sic*] man is organizing societies to turn out at their funerals. Now I object to a $100 funeral for a fifty cent Negro. The Negro eats up and dresses away all he makes. One square meal on Sunday sweeps away all the wages of the week. He reminds me of the mule who ate the shipping tag from his leg. An old Negro exclaimed: 'Gee, dat mule dun eat up his whar-he's-gwine.' That's what the Negro does; he eats up his living."[35]

The concern here is not with the fact that a Negro delivered the homily but with the fact that a Monroe paper elected to print it. The statement shows that at least the *Monroe Record* refused to assume any form of responsibility for the Negro's status in America and by inference in Monroe. In the final analysis, the *Record* judged that the black man's failure to progress rested with his own dilatory, childish attributes.

While racial pronouncements, jokes, and humor in the local presses conveyed to Monroe's people the childlike social identity of the Negro, the idiom which had the greatest impact on codifying this stereotype was the minstrel show. A genuine American genre, minstrelsy originated in the late 1820s when it was introduced by black-faced white entertainers.[36] After the Civil War, Negro minstrels began to appear, and by the 1870s "genuine darkies" were very much in public demand. It is generally recognized that as an entertainment form, minstrelsy far outdistanced any of its rivals until the 1890s.[37] So important was this "folk and popular form" in the nineteenth century that one authority on the subject has viewed it as a key to understanding the thought and social realities of America's common people in this era.[38] A truly national medium, it reached virtually every town and hamlet in America in the late nineteenth and early twentieth centuries. In fact, it could be accurately stated that most northerners of that time period learned about "Negroes" from the minstrel shows.

By the beginning of Reconstruction, minstrelsy had attained a fixed form which would continue to endure into the twentieth century.[39] The "onstage" performance was usually preceded by a street parade with band playing to whet the appetites of prospective ticket buyers. Playing before local crowds in "opera houses" in the winter and under canvas in summer, the actual show consisted of three parts.[40] The first portion included a semicircular seating arrangement with a middleman, known as the interlocutor, and two end men, Tambo and Bones, engaging in a banter which reinforced the child-Negro stereotype. The interlocutor was usually in white face, and the remainder of the troupe wore burnt cork. This part of the presentation ended with everyone joining in a Walk-Around.

Excitement usually increased among the audience as the second part, or olio, commenced. Consisting of both individual and group specialties, the olio was characterized by wild dancing, clapping, and song. The finale to this part was a genuine southern hoedown with all the troupe engaging in music, dance, and song. The third and last part, a farce, playlet, or comic opera, ended the evening's entertainment. The forerunner of burlesque, this portion "often as not consisted of a burlesque of Uncle Tom's Cabin—the most frequently performed work in America."[41]

A crucial element in this medium was the fact that none of it, despite an almost universal popular opinion to the contrary, had anything to do with Negro life. Reputed to be an accurate mirror of plantation life in the Old South and supposedly giving a genuine rendition of the "old-time darkey," minstrelsy was, above all, a white-generated medium.[42] According to leading historians of the subject, a "close analysis of the minstrel shows reveal very little Afro-American influence in the music, dance or inspiration."[43] Indeed, its images of Negroes were "shaped by white expectation and desires and not by black realities."[44] Actually, a high percentage of minstrel men were foreign or northern-born white men who had no knowledge whatsoever of black subculture. Although blacks did enter minstrelsy as it opened up, their actions were mostly a reflection of limited economic opportunities and did not, in any way, indicate an acceptance of the idiom at face value. "Nothing seemed more absurd," black minstel George Walker wrote, "than to see a colored man making himself ridiculous in order to portray himself."[45]

Demonstrating Monroe's connection with this national ceremony is not difficult.[46] Indeed, all the Monroe newspapers of the era proliferate with advertisements announcing the arrival of minstrel troupes in town. Among the more prominent shows which played to Monroe audiences during the Progressive Era were John Vogel's Afro-American Mastodon Minstrels, Scott's Refined Negro Minstrels, Harrison Brothers Minstrels, Rockwell's Sunny South Company, Guy Brothers Famous Minstrels, and the all-white Hi Henry's Minstrels.[47] Closely related to minstrelsy were "Tom" shows. Monroe citizens looked forward to the "Tom" shows which performed regularly at the Armory Opera House. These productions remained standard entertainment for Americans throughout the early years of the twentieth century, and a town without its annual "Tom" presentation was hardly a town at all. As with minstrelsy, there were street parades, buck-and-wing dancers, and "African mandolin" (banjo) players.[48]

Typically, all these productions sent advance notices to the local news media to ensure a good attendance. What is most striking and offensive to the sensibilities of those not familiar with the jargon of the era is the alacrity with which these newspaper advertisements referred to Negroes as "coons." So patently racist are some of the advertisements that a reasonably accurate picture of the childlike Negro can be inferred from them without ever viewing or knowing much about the minstrel show itself.

For example, the *Monroe Democrat,* in reporting the arrival of "John Vogel's Afro-American Mastodon Minstrels combined with Darkest America," in June 1899, revealed that ticket holders would be able to see "Voodoo Dancers and thirty cake-walking 'coons.'"[49] The last show of the Monroe Armory Opera House session in 1901 was "Rusco and Holland's Big Double Minstrel Company." The advertisement for the group promised "50 dusky hired performers who were fairly bubbling over with effervescent mirth."[50] A notice in the *Democrat* indicated that, in addition to the company's two bands, there would be a "Pickaninny Drum Corps."[51] The Harrison Brothers Minstrels, which appeared under tent in the summer of 1900, boasted "the largest company, the sweetest singers, dancers, musicians, comedians and cakewalkers of the colored race."[52] "The Big Minstrel Show of November 14, 1907, featured the 'Belles of Fashion and the Browne Coon Brigade,' introducing some of the clever character singing, buck and wing dancing, and all the tricks and trials of the typical Southern Negro."[53]

The *Record-Commercial* gave page-one treatment to the Sunny South minstrel company in 1907. The paper assured its readers that "those . . . who patronize the opera house, and others who want to see a good coon show will be glad to see by the ad in this issue that Rockwell's Sunny South Company will be with us on Monday evening, February 25th." The advertisement promised Monroe citizens "An Army of Real Colored People," and "The Kings of Coon Town Comedy."[54] The end result of the rather extensive media attention was that Rockwell's retinue played to a packed house, and according to the *Record-Commercial,* the people got their "money's worth."[55]

This ceremony of racism penetrated the Monroe community on an even deeper level than simple observation of traveling shows. It cut to the very marrow of the town's normative structure. As the larger professional companies began to lose out to other entertainment forms, such as vaudeville and moving pictures in the first decade of the twentieth century, whites who were members of small communities often found themselves participants in minstrel shows. For the most part, these affairs were money-raising endeavors by local social clubs and various other groups.

As early as 1905 in Monroe, the program for the yacht club's third annual muskrat carnival included one Frank Shannon as "Black Face Comedian."[56] By 1912 the Monroe Yacht Club had moved to a complete "Mammoth Minstrel Show" to generate funds. The thirty club members who were to take part in the gala affair had practiced for over a month under the directorship of Caucasian William Blodgett of Detroit, a former professional minstrel. Running for two nights at the local opera house, the show included an old-time minstrel parade, six end men, a chorus of thirty men, and an orchestra of eight pieces.[57] The *Record-Commercial* and the *Monroe Democrat* declared the presentation a great success. To the joy of seeing minstrelsy there was the added bonus for the Monroe crowd in trying to guess which local "heroes" were hiding behind the burnt-cork faces. In summing up the event, the *Record-Commercial* stated that "the show bore more resemblance to a professional production rendered by veteran footlight artists than it did to a strictly amateur production."[58] How well the black-faced locals adapted to their training and darkey roles was reflected in the $400 gain to the club's treasury and the decision by the organization's officers to make the event an annual one. For the next five years, the Monroe Yacht Club would continue to "pack the house" and enrich its coffers with minstrel productions.[59]

As Monroe was always a good minstrel town, other groups began to profit from the community's interest. In 1913 the female employees of the Weis Manufacturing Company, a local concern, broke the all-male minstrel tradition by offering a black-faced production. While they were greeted by a full house, apparently the show was not a theatrical success, for the *Record-Commercial* noted that they suffered from onstage fright.[60] The next year, however, the Weis employees took no chances and trained for two months under the professional direction of Leon E. Shafer.[61] Playing two nights before the Monroe crowd, the seventy-five "girls" were praised for their bright and witty dialogue.[62]

Such activities illustrated the fact that the childlike social identity of the Negro lived in the minds of Monroe citizens during the Progressive Era. In reading best-selling books, articles in popular journals, and urban and local newspapers, and in viewing those participating in minstrel shows, Monroe's people could not avoid internalizing that conception. Indeed, it was through these kinds of processes that the "ole-time darkey" stereotype was forged in the minds of Monroe's inhabitants. The most insidious part of this cultural role was that it was white-created and white-maintained and had little to do with actual Negro life. Yet most of Monroe, and most of the rest of America, believed the role to be accurate. What this implied for black America was most tragic: Negroes encountered in everyday life were expected to play the clown—the submissive fool.[63] Indeed, that role was demanded of them. During the Progressive Era in Monroe, this framework was brought to most interactions and dealings between whites and blacks.

In their daily interactions with Negroes, the racist perceptions of Monroe's citizens were brought into play. The framework of the childlike Negro was raised to consciousness whenever blacks who were not personally known appeared on city streets. Indeed, Negroes who arrived in Monroe in the early twentieth century found that their presence was carefully noted. Several of these occasions can be rescued from historical oblivion by making inferences from testimony in the local newspapers.

Known as a "Gretna Green" for Ohioans during this era because of its nearness to Ohio's border and Michigan's lax marriage license requirements, Monroe was commonly the site of marriage ceremonies for out-of-towners.[64] The city's booming wedding industry, on occasion, witnessed in the county courthouse the union of black couples from Ohio towns. The local press usually managed to make special note of such occasions. The *Monroe Democrat* of 10 February 1898 announced that "Thursday noon a colored couple from Toledo called on County Clerk Leonard and asked for a marriage license which was duly granted. . . . So far as the *Democrat* is able to learn this is the first colored couple married in Monroe since the law requiring the procuring of a marriage license went into effect." Three years later, the *Record* reported the "first marriage license to be issued to a colored party since county clerk Mauer has been in office was issued. . . ." In 1904 the *Democrat* informed the public that county clerk Betz had issued a marriage license to a colored couple for the first time.[65] Monroe racism took a more explicit form in an interracial marriage at the county courthouse in 1908. The occasion merited a page-one treatment in the *Record-Commercial;* the byline, appearing in capital script, read "Mixed Marriage." Harvey Williams, colored, and Mrs. Rosa Cahill, white, both of Toledo, had taken the interurban to Monroe in hopes of having a private and quiet ceremony. Their hopes were ill-founded: "excitement galore" greeted the news of the promised union and as "soon as it was noised about that a mixed marriage was about to come off, everybody got busy and flocked to the clerk's office." The board of supervisors, which was in session, "took recess to witness the ceremony and the county clerk's room adjoining was jammed to full capacity. The ceremony over, the bride, who has been married four times previously and has passed the bashful stage, imprinted an echoing smack on the justice's lips, caught chairman Francisco after a sprint and treated him likewise, but came out a poor second when she took after County Clerk Ready." Almost as an afterthought, the *Record-Commercial* noted in the last sentence of the article that "they rather kicked on the amount of attention they excited and vowed as far as they were concerned Monroe would be henceforth wiped off the map."[66]

That the child-Negro social identity was trundled out by the paper's editors is patently clear in the above scenario. While interracial weddings violated Monroe's understandings of the proper relationship between the races and were potentially explosive affairs, this situation retained its comic flavor when the white partner in the union was shown to be of questionable character. Demeaning the oft-married Mrs. Cahill to the status of Negro had made the entire event an enjoyable one for the community. In the final analysis, the couple were viewed as subhuman, comic, and laughable. Even their objection to their treatment at the hands of Monroe was regarded as comic behavior. After all, minstrel-like folk could not be taken seriously in their rejection of such a fine place as Monroe. In any event, it really did not matter.

This condescending attitude toward blacks was also manifested in the field of sports in Monroe. In the two decades surrounding the turn of the century, local sports heroes and local teams played a large part in the life of small-town America, and Monroe was no exception. To be sure, Monroe citizens were always anxious and ready to observe and evaluate the performance of blacks by white athletic standards—particularly in the ring and on the ball diamond. Whenever her white citizens had a chance to watch Negro athletes perform, a great deal of excitement was generated.

Indeed, the mere appearance of a renowned black athlete in Monroe and the thought of a match often energized the community. In 1893, when the "celebrated colored pugilist, Peter Johnson," was traveling through the city by train, his presence was noticed at the Lake Shore depot on a short stop-over. The result was that the "big fellow was the center of attention for a little while."

But "none of the Monroe Athletic Club ventured to challenge him."[67]

Monroeites, however, had an opportunity to attend a boxing match in 1896 in which the issue was white versus black. On 10 February of that year the committee of the Monroe Athletic Club flooded the town with handbills announcing their latest fight card. The main attraction the following evening was to be Oliver Freeman of Saginaw, known as the "colored cyclone," against George Campbell of Detroit, ex-trainer of the current lightweight champion, Kid Lavigne. The ten-round glove contest was to take place at the Monroe Athletic Club gymnasium at the corner of Monroe and Front streets. The committee assured the readers of its broadsides that "both men are professionals who are desirous of becoming top notchers and will not let a chance to win pass by and the contest will be [a] decidedly warm one and will be won on its merits."[68] A sizable crowd turned out for the event only to discover that the vaunted "cyclone" had exhibited his "yellow" by failing to appear. A white opponent, Obed Silverwood, was substituted in his place, but he proved to be no match for the talented Campbell. Despite their initial disappointment when the black-white contest failed to materialize, all was not lost for those in attendance. The illusion of white superiority in this instance had been successfully maintained because to Monroe whites, Freeman's absence was evidence of cowardice.[69] Freeman appeared in "a glove match" in Monroe the following month. He fought Obed Silverwood to a draw and knocked out another challenger, Charles Albright of Monroe, in the first round. This time, the press praised "Mr." Freeman who "acted like a perfect gentleman and left town paying all his bills without any hitch."[70]

On the national fight scene during the Progressive Era the illusion of white superiority was being sorely tested. In the heavyweight ranks, champion Jack Johnson was pummelling all comers, and in the lightweight division, another Negro, Joe Gans, one of the greatest prizefighters of all time, was trouncing most of his opponents. So out of frame were their victories, so unlike the "coon" stereotype, that their bouts instantly galvanized the interests and the passions of the entire prizefighting public. Constance McLaughlin Green, in her study of the nation's capital, has noted that whenever Joe Gans stepped into the ring to defend his title, "a boy of either race who ventured alone into Washington's streets beyond his own immediate neighborhood risked a beating from a gang of the enemy intent upon upholding the honor of Gans or his white rival."[71]

Monroe's fight fans, of course, were keen observers of boxing on the national sports scene, and their reactions to the 1906 Gans-Nelson bout are of interest here. In September 1906 when lightweight champion Joe Gans defended his title against "Battling" Nelson, "a large crowd of fight followers hung with eagerness about the Western Union telegraph office . . . to get the returns."[72] The *Monroe Democrat* reported that "after the fifteenth round had been reached the sentiment [of those gathered] seemed to be that Nelson would tire out his colored opponent and it came like a bombshell to many to learn that the negro had won in the 42nd round."[73] It was inconceivable to Monroe's white boxing public that a child-Negro, the image of which they mistook for reality, could dominate and defeat a good white challenger. Gans's continuing victories provided a serious challenge to the myths of white superiority and Negro subhumanity, but a measure of comfort regarding those delusions would be regained in 1908, when the "white hope," Nelson, avenged his earlier loss by knocking Gans out in the seventeenth round for the title.[74]

Racism also played its part in the national sport, baseball. While there were thirty or more Negroes in the various white leagues during the post-Civil War years, there were none from 1898 to 1947.[75] The extension of Jim Crow in the South, the disenfranchisement of the Negro there, and a general lessening of economic opportunities for blacks throughout the nation were the main characteristics of the system of race relations which evolved in the decades surrounding the turn of the twentieth century. This period was certainly the nadir of Negro life in America. Many of the gains made by Afro-Americans during Reconstruction were wiped away between 1880 and 1910, and integrated baseball was one of these casualities. Desired on white teams immediately following the Civil War, blacks by the 1890s were no longer invited to play with established professional teams.

Barred from white professional baseball, several all-black teams acquiring the best talent of the Negro race were soon formed. Often backed by white men, these teams were seen by their owners as business investments. The simple fact was that while white America did not desire to see integrated teams play baseball, it would pay good money to see local nines test the best of the black race.[76]

Monroe was no exception to that generality. Playing colored teams was a common event in Monroe. On 6 August 1903, the *Record* reported that the local nine would play the Page Fence Giants at Monroe's Johnson Island Park the next week.[77] The Page team, the *Record* contended, was "the best aggregation of colored players in the world."[78] The more than 500 fans who attended the game saw the local heroes humiliate the Giants 24 to 1.[79] Although the Page Fence Giants were not staffed with the original black team members as first announced, Monroe citizens still took great pleasure in their victory. The *Democrat* was especially waggish in remarking that there "were no 'fast blacks,'" and that "the Coons darkened the plate but once, so it was easily brightened up." The paper went on to relate how Big Connally, a Monroe player, "ran clean over the base-man Brown, and for a while it was hard to tell what was Brown and what was white. . . ." The *Record* relished the idea that "the coons were under the impression that Enz was Sam Thompson [a former National League batting champion], and they watched him carefully."[80]

If there was a loss to a black team by the local Monroe players, a mitigating explanation was needed. When the Monroe nine played the Colored Giants of Detroit, "one of the strongest semi-professional ball clubs in the state," in July 1911, the *Democrat* made light of the latter's triumph. Even the fact that the game was played at Monroe's own Driving Park before hometown fans seemed to matter little. "The smokes got one in the third on a walk and two errors" and went on to win the ball game 3 to 2. The *Democrat* reasoned that the Giants "must have [their] pockets filled with lucky bones or rabbits' feet."[81] In other words, to Monroe citizens, a victory for whites was a measure of Caucasian superiority and Negro ineptitude, while a black success was simply the result of their good fortune. It is easy to see the ever-present child-Negro social identity peering out from the pages of the *Democrat, Record,* and *Record-Commercial* in each of these scenarios. "Athletic prowess," Constance Green has written, "which in post-World-War-II years would begin to bridge racial cleavages, merely widened the gulf" during the first decade of the twentieth century.[82] Negro athletic prowess, with its bottom-line equality, she might have added, was the last thing wanted by the American public. What was wanted were clown Negroes who played at being athletes.[83]

Another form of black activity in which the Monroe community evinced more than a moderate interest was "ragtime." Indeed, Monroe citizens maintained an intimate acquaintance with Negro tunes and songs throughout the Progressive Era. Black singers and musicians often performed in Monroe. The Monroe Piers, a recreation area on Lake Erie, frequently "imported" Afro-Americans from Detroit or Toledo to amuse the crowds during the summer months. For instance, colored waiters from Toledo, hired to work at the Piers' Lotus Hotel, organized a Lime Kiln Club in 1901 to entertain guests. The *Democrat* reported that "for simon pure, unadulterated fun, this quintet takes the bun."[84]

Monroe whites also appreciated the "novelty and antics" of Lee's six-piece colored orchestra, which appeared at the Piers for two consecutive seasons, 1913 and 1914.[85] A Detroit group, Lee's orchestra was so well liked that in the summer of 1913 "there were encores till the six big black funny musicians were nearly exhausted."[86] Playing at the casino's dancing pavilion, Lee's orchestra drew on that engagement one of the largest crowds in the Piers' history. The next year, when Charles E. Greening, manager of the Piers, asked the colored musicians to play again at the casino for the Monroe Yacht Club's Fourth of July Regatta, the big event of the season, the Monroe Cornet Band threatened to dissolve. Its members were angry because "citizens who require a band go outside the city to hire musical talent."[87] Since it was a Monroe organization, the band felt that a choice of local playing dates was rightfully theirs and, in this instance, they had not even been asked. The Monroe group, whose fortunes were declining, needed the money but pride was central to their complaint. Apparently, the band had suffered a setback which could not be tolerated: it had lost its public to the Lee musicians. Despite the protests, Monroe citizens listened and danced to the beat of the Negro artists at the regatta in 1914. The Monroe Cornet Band managed to survive this challenge but in weakened form. When it came to musical entertainment, black, at least in this instance, was preferred to white.

The winter season saw black groups playing the opera house. Finney's orchestra, a Detroit organization of colored men, held a concert in the fall of 1901. Two years later the "Colored Canadian Concert Company of Hamilton" scheduled a performance at the armory. Private organizations and clubs in Monroe also hired Negroes for entertainment purposes. In 1913, when W. C. Sterling, Sr., one of the city's leading citizens, celebrated his fiftieth year as a hunter by hosting a banquet for his friends, "six colored men from the famous Shook Orchestra of Detroit furnished music." The next year, the "Watermelon Jubilees" gave a "high class entertainment under the auspices of the local Knights of Pythias." That the Negro singers were well received is attested by the comment that "it was the general opinion that there wasn't a troupe on the road that could hold a candle to this organization."[88]

Despite the eagerness with which the Monroe public apparently embraced the product of black musicians, the writer of a local "Musical Review" column found the trend disheartening. The issue, it was explained, was one of musical standards which the "coon songs," "little trivial affairs of the most ephemeral nature," were lowering. Negro ragtime, which was listened to "ad nauseum," did not, in the columnist's view, even have the merit of the "original darky songs of the South." The southern tunes were, at least, "embodied with life and characteristics of a people." Ragtime, on the other hand, was "something borrowed from vaudeville" and "certainly could not please a cultivated fastidious taste for very long." Real musicians, the critic contended, "prefer something better" but were often forced at social events to listen in "silent protest" to the "frothy music." The writer concluded by calling upon "our girls" to "use their voices and talents to better advantage" and to regard music "as a sacred art never to be lowered by such trivial things."[89]

Undoubtedly the Monroe critic was following the current national habit of demeaning ragtime music. While popular demand for black music was generally acknowledged, ragtime was viewed as "symbolic of primitive morality and the perceptible moral limitations of the negro type." "There is a certain sway and swing," *Forum* writer Walter Kenilworth commented in 1911, "a certain indescribable sensuous something appealing and suggestive about the ring and melody, the rhythm and versification of this music. Scrutinizingly criticised, all of the songs are insidiously perverting; they are indicative of relaxative morality, of disparagement of the marital tie, of triviality in relationship of sex, etc., and the entire moral code might be included. There is not even an attempt made at concealment of the thought conveyed in the song. It is out-and-out vulgarity."[90] Kenilworth concluded that the increase in America's divorce rate and the general relaxation of moral standards was due primarily to the deleterious influence of Negro ragtime.

Symbolically, this theme of ragtime sensuality represented the perceived threat that a Negro musical contribution would weaken white group dominance. The attraction of ragtime promised to steal away the American people from "good" music, but more important, it foreboded a movement in the direction of equality. It represented a chink in the armor of white superiority. In the end, this challenge to the white group position was perceived, as it almost always is, in terms of sexual threat.

Despite the critics' concerns with standards, taste, and morality, Monroe and most of the rest of the country continued to enjoy black music. It is doubtful that most whites really took seriously all the folderol regarding the sensuality of ragtime and the threat to moral standards. The Monroe critic and Mr. Kenilworth were definitely in the minority. Instead, most white Americans and Monroe citizens viewed ragtime as a frivolous but thoroughly enjoyable activity. "Real music" and concerts remained the province of those devoted to the classics, and "coon songs" were relegated to light, informal occasions, where people danced, ate, and drank. Inevitably, ragtime, as with most other Negro activities, implied the child-Negro stereotype to most whites. Even though the activities which lent themselves to Negro music were important to Monroe's community life, there was no respectful recognition of this Afro-American achievement. While enjoyed, the popular Negro bands and songs were not appreciated as the genuine contribution to American folk art which they were. The childlike social identity of Afro-Americans precluded that possibility.

"Coon" music, minstrelsy, and religious sentiment were combined in what whites certainly regarded as another form of entertainment, the Negro camp meeting. Apparently, these gatherings provided not a few Afro-Americans with a livelihood in the early years of the twentieth century. Much like the minstrel troupes, groups of blacks toured the Midwest in the summer and fall, performing outdoors for whites. It is clear that Negro camp meeting exercises did take place in the Monroe environs during this time period.[91] One such gathering in nearby Dundee in 1900, the *Monroe Record* noted, was "attended by whites" and "owing to strong exhortations, fine choir singing and big collections, was a success."[92] In that same year, Jenny Sawyer, one of the most respected white citizens of the community, indicated her disappointment at not being able to "go out" to a different "nigger camp meeting" because of inclement weather.[93]

A far more serious form of entertainment were the Fisk Jubilee Singers. The Tennessee group warmed the hearts and opened the pocketbooks of Monroe citizens on at least two occasions. In 1886 and 1891, the world-famous group played to packed audiences in the local armory.[94] Their spirituals and religiosity projected a rather different view of black existence. In a word, they were "Christians," subject to the same kind of human experiences and dilemmas as their white counterparts.

It would seem that their performances tapped into a sense of mission on the part of more than a few of Monroe's white populace. Actually, certain northern churches continued to show an interest in the freedmen long after the Civil War. At the turn of the century, several Monroe congregations were still contributing to Negro missions in the South and showing a concern for the freedmen.

Monroe's First Presbyterian Church was particularly active in this sphere. In its annual budgetary report for 1898, this institution showed that $136.22 of its total budget of $2,198.99 was set aside for the freedmen. In addition, the Women's Missionary Society of the Presbyterian church was supplying funds and clothing for freedmen missions. This society allotted $18.15 of its budget of $104.37 for freedmen in 1899 and also sent boxes of clothing valued at $160 "to the Freedmen and Park College." Twelve years later, the Women's Missionary Society was still appropriating money and sending packages to the freedmen. The 1911 contribution was a "freedman special," consisting of a barrel of clothing "for Miss Anna Dunston, a sewing teacher in Albion Academy, North Carolina." For the year 1912, the society gave $16 to the freedmen. In addition to providing financial support to Presbyterian freedmen missions located in the South, the Monroe church opened its doors to black and white lecturers who had worked with the missions. The Rev. Dr. Weaver, an Afro-American, gave a stereoptican lecture on the freedmen in 1898, and in 1913 Mrs. H. L. O'Brien and Mrs. J. K. Mitchell, both of Ohio, "spoke interestingly on the freedman and on work in the home field." Typically, there were no admission charges for these lectures, but a "free will" offering was taken up after the presentation for the benefit of the missions.[95]

Monroe's Trinity Lutheran Church, Missouri Synod, also gave support to Negro missions in the early years of the twentieth century. The Trinity congregation gave $14.60 in 1898, $6.60 in 1900, and $60 in 1902 to Negro missions. Like the Presbyterian church, Trinity Lutheran on occasion offered its pulpit to guest lecturers who spoke on the southern missions. On 30 July 1903, Trinity Lutheran Church announced that at half past seven "Rev. A. Lankenau of New Orleans, La., will deliver a lecture on the Progress of the Lutheran Mission among the Negroes in the south." The presentation was to take place before both Lutheran congregations in the city, and it was also opened to the general public. A collection was taken up after the lecture "for the benefit of the Negro mission." The 1913 report on Negro missions made at the annual meeting of the Missouri Synod, held in Monroe, revealed that the Lutheran church continued to support forty-six missions in eight southern states. These missions were cared for by thirty-six missionaries who served a membership numbering 2,297 souls, which included 1,674 school children. Significantly, the report indicated that Negroes had contributed $5,692.17 to the support of these endeavors.[96]

A third Protestant congregation that continued to exhibit an interest in the freedman was St. Paul's Methodist Episcopal Church. St. Paul's Freedman's Aid Society received $4 in contributions in 1900 and monies again in 1901. St. Paul's doors were also open to presentations from outsiders, and in 1910 "The Southland Nightingales, a company of colored people representing educational work in the South," gave a musical entertainment.[97] As a fund-raising venture, no admission was charged, but a silver offering was taken.

In searching for a reason why Monroe's white citizens continued to show an interest in southern Negroes, the subject of a speech given in 1898 by Rev. W. H. Rees, D.D., of Cincinnati, gives a partial answer. Delivered before the Epworth League of Monroe's M. E. church, the presentation was entitled "The Black Man, What Shall We Do with Him?" Though the speech itself has not survived, its subject revealed a great deal. The statement assumed an essential lack of power and effectiveness on the Negro's part, while implying quite the opposite for the white race. This attitude was again reflected in a speech, given six year later, at the graduation ceremonies of Monroe High School. Francis P. Ready, the orator for the evening, talked on "Our Duty to the Negro." "In treating of America's black past," the *Democrat* reported, "he took forth the usual stand of Northerners, claiming that we are largely to blame for the negro's present condition and must, by educating, encouraging and protecting him, help him to a higher plane of development."[98] In effect, both presentations evinced the most subtle form of racism: Negro helplessness mollified through white beneficence. A collective form of paternalism and guilt played some part in Monroe's continuing concern with the South.

The contributions from the three congregations, while not monetarily outstanding, do indicate a willingness on the part of some Monroe citizens to assume a continuing measure of responsibility for destitute southern Negroes in need of an education and a place to worship. Yet the child-Negro myth kept poking its head throughout all this activity. In the end, the southern Negro was viewed not only as a victim of war and poverty but as helpless.

This church activity, however, told something else, something as important as the child-Negro myth. To whites in Monroe, America's Negro problem was remote; it was confined to the South. Indeed, as Ray Stannard Baker observed, "Northern white people would seem to be more interested in the distant Southern Negro than in the Negro at their doors."[99]

On no occasion during the Progressive Era did Monroe citizens evince a concern for Negroes who lived outside the South. Instead, they assumed that conditions in the North were basically equal and democratic. In their eyes, the American Dream was a reality in the North; Negroes who failed in that section did so because of deficient desire, aptitude, or character—again the infantile social identity—not because of inequities. Little did Monroe's white inhabitants realize that they were an integral part of the whole "problem." Monroe, as it has been demonstrated in this chapter, was not isolated from the rest of the country; it participated intimately in the nation's racist consciousness during the Progressive years.

The potency in Monroe of the child-Negro myth came through nowhere more clearly than in the events surrounding Booker T. Washington's visit to Monroe in 1899. The managers of the high school lecture series, which provided Monroe with indoor winter entertainment at the Armory Opera House, had booked Booker T. Washington as one of their speakers for the season. The *Democrat* proudly reported that on "Monday, January 30th, the citizens of Monroe and surrounding county will be greatly favored by having an opportunity to hear the foremost Negro in America, Booker T. Washington of the Tuskegee Normal and Industrial Institute." This page-one feature article went on to credit the Tuskegee founder with many accomplishments, quoting encomiums from such contemporary notables as Joseph Choate and President McKinley. Never before had an Afro-American received such praise in the Monroe press. The essay had the desired effect and "there was a grand rush for the reserve seats" to the "star number of the course." A paying and interested public turned out with great expectations to hear and judge the "Moses of the Negro Race." The *Democrat* in reviewing the occasion reported that

> the lecture by Booker T. Washington Monday evening was largely attended and proved to be the star number of the course. While the speaker did not come up to the expectations of the audience in some respects he nevertheless proved himself to be an orator of great ability. He gave a fine description of the work in which he is engaged in, and spoke entirely from the negro point of view. He left unsaid many things upon which the people would like to have heard him express his opinion. Mr. Washington is a mulatto, and upon the whole makes an awkward appearance upon the stage, but through his zeal, and intelligent handling of the negro question he has gained the respect of the whole country both north and south.[100]

Between the lines of the *Democrat*'s reporting, the child-Negro was bursting forth. To Monroe citizens, the simple fact was that Mr. Washington, or any other Negro, did not belong on the stage in an oratory capacity. The crowd had come wondering if they would find a minstrel man and, to the audience, beneath his articulate veneer, Washington was just that: an out-of-place, awkward mulatto with not a great deal to offer (except his "intelligent handling of the negro question"). While the attack was muted because Washington was a well-respected national figure, it was still there. In Monroe's eyes, "a nigger was a nigger was a nigger . . ." even if he also happened to be one of the greatest men of his era.

Looking at the child-Negro stereotype in terms of normative structure, it can be appropriately regarded as a role prescription. In essence, it reflected the unchangeable social position which whites discerned blacks as occupying. It is not insignificant that whites played continually at being the child-Negro. Indeed, Monroe citizens, as has been demonstrated, were taught deliberately and step by step the "Sambo" role in their rehearsals for their minstrel shows. These activities served to reify "ole darkey" in the minds of the participants and meant that the production was taken as mirroring Negro activity in everyday life. To use the language of the symbolic interactionists, they took the role of the other, but the other was not real. The impact of this tragic and incorrect inference had devastating effects on black people. The end result was that the larger society demanded from Negroes clownish, servile, and foolish behavior on most occasions. Indeed, even when blacks attempted to play serious roles, they were taken for parody. James Weldon Johnson has commented on this point. In discussing the social life of a black club in Harlem, Johnson recalled that

> there was one man, a minstrel, who whenever he responded to a request to "do something," never essayed anything below a reading of Shakespeare. How well read I do not know, but he greatly impressed me; and I can say that at least he had a voice which strangely stirred those who heard it. Here was a man who made people laugh at the size of his mouth, while he carried in his heart a burning ambition to be a tragedian; and so after all he did play a part in a tragedy.
>
> No matter how well he may portray the deeper passions, the public is loath to give him up in his old character; they even conspire to make him a failure in serious work, in order to force him back into comedy.[101]

To be sure, for Negroes, the "Sambo" role prescription was inescapable. Reflecting the comparative group positions of whites and blacks, the child-Negro social identity flourished in fertile ground during the Progressive Era. Monroe and the dominant white society loved their nation of child-men and eternal "pickaninnies."

A less favorable note was present in the thoughts of the city's inhabitants regarding another dimension of the so-called Negro personality, the beast-Negro. If the Afro-American was servile, fawning, attentive, and comical, he was also capable of behavior that was insolent, savage, defiant, and "uppity." "When his bad nature erupted, it was like a volcano; the Negro would do anything—commit arson, murder, outrage a child."[102] This beast-Negro image, as will be seen, came into play in Monroe at various times during the Progressive Era.

NOTES

1. Children's books, Monroe County Historical Museum. This book belonged to a local citizen, Alfred Sawyer, and dates from the 1880s or 1890s.

2. See David M. Katzman, *Before the Ghetto: Black Detroit in the Nineteenth Century* (Urbana: University of Illinois Press, 1973), *passim*, Kenneth L. Kusmer, *A Ghetto Takes Shape: Black Cleveland, 1870–1930* (Urbana: University of Illinois Press, 1976), *passim*, and David A. Gerber, *Black Ohio and the Color Line 1860–1915* (Urbana: University of Illinois Press, 1976), *passim*, for excellent discussions of the black experience in the late nineteenth century.

3. See especially Rayford W. Logan, *The Betrayal of the Negro from Rutherford B. Hayes to Woodrow Wilson* (New York: Collier-Macmillan, 1965).

4. Arthur Vidich and Joseph Bensman in their classic sociological study, *Small Town in Mass Society*, rev. ed. (Princeton: Princeton University Press, 1968), demonstrated how the major institutions of society worked into the fabric of community in Springdale, New York, in the 1950s. In the case of Monroe, this process had occurred by the end of the first decade of the twentieth century. The nearness to Detroit and Toledo, three major railroad trunks traversing the city, a completed interurban system by 1904, and a myriad of other factors ensured that Monroe was subject to the same influences affecting the rest of the nation.

5. A social identity is an identity imposed by the larger culture on individuals who have stigma. As such it is regarded in this book as the rough equivalent of stereotype, and the terms are used interchangeably. See Erving Goffman, *Stigma: Notes on the Management of Spoiled Identity* (Englewood Cliffs, N.J.: Prentice-Hall, 1965), pp. 2, 4, 57, 105, 138. Goffman has suggested that Afro-Americans in the United States possess a tribal stigma. Stigma is the social disgrace attached to the condition of having unusual or spoiled physi-

cal attributes or a blemished character. The major thrust of Goffman's volume is toward understanding how people who possess stigma manage social situations. Accordingly, stigmatized people have three identities: social, personal, and ego. A social identity means the normative dimension of role expectations held for those with stigma in general. Personal identities reflect the unique and highly individualized qualities of those with stigma that are generally recognized by people who "know" them. It should be noted that both social and personal identities deal with the perspectives of persons who do not possess stigma. An ego or "felt" identity deals with the stigmatized individual's subjective sense of his or her own situation.

6. Ray Stannard Baker, *Following the Color Line* (New York: Doubleday, 1908), p. 268.

7. Fredrickson, *The Black Image in the White Mind: The Debate on Afro-American Character and Destiny, 1817–1914* (New York: Harper Torchbooks, 1971), pp. 256–82. Fredrickson's primary interest in his book is to delineate and discuss the predominant racist ideologies during various periods of American history between 1817 and 1914. As a writer of intellectual history, his main concern is to perceive and describe the doctrines and ideas of the leading thinkers on race during various eras. Between Reconstruction and the end of the nineteenth century, the beast-Negro image dominated southern thought on race. Once white supremacy became a reality, a less harsh, accommodationist view celebrating the child-Negro prevailed.

As previously indicated, both stereotypes had existed in American minds since colonial days, and the preeminence of one over the other reflected, in addition to the evolutionary historical experience, the realities of the life situations. In other words, the beast-Negro reigned when the relationship between the races was fraught with conflict and the child-Negro gained ascendance when whites had established control. Fredrickson analyzes how each of these images changed through time and shows clearly and perceptively those developments in the minds of the foremost "experts" on race. Even though Fredrickson contends that these stereotypes entailed separate traditions, nowhere does he suggest that they were mutually exclusive. In fact, both images were held simultaneously in American minds. The problem is one of emphasis.

While Fredrickson's emphasis is intellectual history, the primary concern in this study is social history. As such, this author's major question is: how did the ideas of the major thinkers on race filter down into the thoughts and minds of the average Monroe citizen?

The findings of this study give no indication that the city's populace perceived the subtle distinctions that the opinion-makers made between the social identities of blacks as beasts and blacks as children. The typical Monroe resident held both images at the same time in his mind, and the precedence of one over the other was basically situational. If Negroes "behaved," the child-Negro was raised to consciousness; if not, the beast-Negro appeared. Both "pictures in the mind" were closely tied to role expectations.

Fredrickson's typology was crucial in providing a viable basis for organizing, interpreting, and discussing real events and experiences in Monroe's past. Fredrickson's and the present study do not disagree, but they do operate on different levels.

8. Ibid., pp. 283–319.

9. Ibid., p. 299. See also Rayford Logan, *The Betrayal of the Negro* chapter entitled "The Negro as Portrayed in Representative Northern Magazines and Newspapers," pp. 371–92.

10. Both these books belonged to Monroe citizens. *Ten Little Niggers* is the life-long possession of a native Monroe woman now in her eighties, and *The Funny Little Darkies,* which belonged to Alfred Sawyer, another local, is in the Monroe County Historical Museum.

11. For example: "Two classes of coloured people came North: the worthless ignorant, semi criminal sort who find in the intermittent high-paid day labour in the North, accompanied by the glittering excitements of city life, just the conditions they love best. . . ." Baker, *Following the Color Line,* p. 112. Baker also talks about half-ignorant bumptious Negroes who stir the animosity of whites. Ibid., p. 125.

12. *Monroe Democrat,* 1 Aug. 1902, p. 5.

13. *Monroe Democrat,* 5 Nov. 1909, p. 7. The fascination with the film medium was nearly limitless. In 1913, Monroe partook of a craze affecting the larger cities by having itself filmed by a professional cameraman. In 1,000 feet of celluloid, taken over a three-day period, an expert from Chicago, with "camera and crank" in hand, filmed Monroe street scenes, businesses, monuments, parks, public buildings, and citizens. Promoted as a booster project, the film footage of Monroe was intended to provide documentary evidence of the city's business potential to prospective investors and industries. While there is no evidence that the movie aided in this end, it is clear that the city's people gloried in seeing themselves on the silver screen. The Family Theatre played to packed houses at each of its showings. See *Record-Commercial,* 11 Sept. 1913, p. 7; *Mon-*

roe Democrat, 12 Sept. 1913, p. 7, 19 Sept. 1913, p. 1, 28 Sept. 1913, p. 7.

14. *Monroe Democrat,* 12 Nov. 1904, p. 5, 28 July 1911, p.1, 24 Nov. 1911, p. 1. In addition, "twenty-six actual views" of the Triangle Shirtwaist Company fire in New York City were shown in the Family Theatre in April 1911. *Record-Commercial,* 20 Apr. 1911, p. 7. Unfortunately, the Monroe movie entrepreneurs did not advertise in the weekly newspapers, and it was not until mid-1915, when the city had its first permanent daily, that their film offerings appeared with regularity in the pages of the local press. Previously, only the most "special attractions" were noted in the community's newspapers. This writer spent a great deal of time and effort trying to document a showing of D. W. Griffith's "Birth of a Nation" in Monroe in 1915 but was unsuccessful. It would have played to Monroe audiences during the first quarter of 1915. The *Record-Commercial,* the only Monroe newspaper extant for that time period, listed no film offerings in local theaters. Nonetheless, given the evidence that does exist regarding Monroe's picture show industry, it is almost certain that "Birth of a Nation" was viewed by Monroe's movie clientele.

15. The most exhaustive study on blacks in films is Thomas Cripps, *Slow Fade to Black: The Negro in American Film 1900–1942* (New York: Oxford University Press, 1977). In his first chapter, "The Unformed Image: The Afro-American in Early American Movies," pp. 8–40, Cripps points out that for at least its first decade of existence the cinema provided more than stereotyped roles for Negroes. All films portraying blacks in this formative period were not racist. After the perfection of the techniques of editing, cutting, and rhythm, the screen image of Afro-Americans assumed a more rigid and negative form. By the time of Wilson's presidency, the movie medium had locked Negroes into an inflexible racist configuration. See also Peter Noble, *The Negro in Films* (Port Washington, N.Y.: Kennikat Press, 1948), pp. 27–31; Donald Bogle, *Toms, Coons, Mulattoes, Mamies, and Bucks* (New York: Bantam Books, 1973), pp. 3–10; Dwight Hoover, *The Red and the Black* (Chicago: Rand McNally, 1976), pp. 263–64.

16. Kusmer points out that while the white press generally paid scant attention to affairs in Cleveland's black community, it "inflamed racial hatreds with lurid stories of lynchings and black criminal activity." See Kusmer, *A Ghetto Takes Shape,* pp. 56–57.

17. *Monroe Democrat,* 9 May 1901, p. 5; *Monroe Record,* 3 July 1902, p. 5.

18. *City Directory, Monroe, Michigan, 1901* (Monroe: Record, 1901), back outside cover; *Record-Commercial,* 17 Nov. 1910, p. 7.

19. The development of the Sunday edition, according to the leading historian of American journalism, Frank Luther Mott, was one of the chief publishing phenomena of the period after the Spanish-American War. "Sunday papers of fifty pages or more soon became common." Frank Luther Mott, *American Journalism: A History of Newspapers in the United States through 260 years: 1690 to 1950,* rev. ed. (New York: Macmillan, 1950), p. 584.

20. Kusmer, *A Ghetto Takes Shape,* p. 54.

21. The *Black Iconoclast* published by local Afro-American James Bromley will be treated in the final chapter on blacks. George W. Graves, editor of the *Graphic,* published forty newspapers in different locations over a twenty-six-year period. *Monroe Democrat,* 29 Oct. 1896, p. 1, 15 Mar. 1900, p. 5.

22. N. W. Ayer & Sons *American Newspaper Annual,* 1899 (Philadelphia: N. W. Ayer & Sons, 1899), p. 389; *1901,* p. 406; *1905,* p. 407; *1906,* p. 412; *1907,* p. 417; *1908,* p. 406; N. W. Ayer & Sons *American Newspaper Annual and Directory, 1910,* p. 410; *1911,* p. 429; *1912,* p. 427; *1914,* p. 437; *1915,* p. 442; *1916,* p. 448; Pettengill *National Newspaper Directory and Gazetteer, 1899* (New York: Pettengill, 1899), p. 282; Edward P. Remington *Annual Newspaper Directory, 1906* (Pittsburgh: Edward P. Remington, 1906), p. 128; *1907,* p. 130; George P. Rowell & Co. *American Newspaper Directory, 1900* (New York: George P. Rowell, 1900), p. 478; Charles P. Fuller *Advertisers Directory, 1908–9* (Chicago: Charles P. Fuller, 1908), p. 152.

23. Mott, *American Journalism,* p. 479.

24. Sidney Goldstein, *The Northern Study: An Experiment in Interdisciplinary Research Training* (Philadelphia: University of Pennsylvania Press, 1961), p. 40.

25. Fredrickson, *The Black Image in the White Mind,* p. 285.

26. A normative system is a changing, mercurial entity and is in constant need of attention, reconfirming, and redefining. When the systems of interactive frameworks draw the boundaries of norms where few opportunities exist for interaction between two racial groups, as in this case, the printed medium takes on a special significance. In the South, where daily life experiences reconfirmed a racial etiquette, the function of the press in establishing a normative context was less important than in the North.

27. The Cleveland press of the 1850s and '60s indulged in the same practice. See Kusmer, *A Ghetto Takes Shape,* p. 9. Humor was

not used, at least in public print, to convey the beast-like image of Negroes, but then a public lynching offered little to laugh about.

28. *Monroe Record,* 13 Dec. 1900, p. 1.
29. *Monroe Democrat,* 7 Mar. 1901, p. 1.
30. *Monroe Democrat,* 15 Mar. 1909, p. 1.
31. *Monroe Record,* 9 Aug. 1900, p. 5.
32. *Monroe Record,* 25 Apr. 1901, p. 4.
33. Tamotsu Shibutani, *Society and Personality* (Englewood Cliffs, N.J.: Prentice-Hall, 1961), p. 44.
34. *Monroe Record,* 20 Nov. 1902, p. 4.
35. *Monroe Record,* 7 Aug. 1902, p. 4.
36. The best overall historical treatment of minstrels remains Carl Wittke's *Tambo and Bones* (Westport, Conn.: Greenwood Press, 1971; reprint ed. Winston, N.C.: Duke University Press, 1930). Hans Nathan, *Dan Emmett and the Rise of Early Negro Minstrelsy* (Norman, Okla.: University of Oklahoma Press, 1962) is excellent for the antebellum period and contains much of the dialogue and many of the songs from the era. Constance Rourke's *American Humor: A Study of the American National Character* (New York: Doubleday Anchor Books, 1953), pp. 74–90, interprets minstrelsy as a viable segment of the American folklore tradition. Marshall W. Stearns, *The Story of Jazz* (New York: Oxford University Press, 1958), pp. 109–22, sees the minstrel shows as significant vehicles for presenting Negro jazz to the American public. Albert F. McLean, Jr.'s, *American Vaudeville as Ritual* (Lexington: University of Kentucky Press, 1965), pp. 21–28, has some insightful conclusions on the relationship of vaudeville to the black-face shows. Joseph Boskin's "Sambo: The National Jester in the Popular Culture," in *The Great Fear: Race in the Mind of America,* eds. Gary B. Nash and Richard Weiss (New York: Holt Rinehart Winston, 1970), pp. 168–73, points out that while the minstrel shows' heydays were gone by the 1890s, the tradition continued in the form of neighborhood productions well into the 1940s. Also valuable is Robert C. Toll, *Blacking Up: The Minstrel Show in Nineteenth-Century America* (New York: Oxford University Press, 1974). Although it deals with a time period before the era under consideration, Toll's book provides the most detailed analysis of the origins and growth of this national institution. While many other books make at least some mention of minstrelsy, the best interpretation of the idiom in terms of societal roles is Nathan Irvin Huggins, *Harlem Renaissance* (New York: Oxford University Press, 1971), pp. 244–86. Huggins attributes the absence of an indigenous black ethnic theatre in the twentieth cen-

tury to the negative and determining effects of the minstrel shows. A movie rendition of minstrelsy from the Negro perspective was recently presented on television. The Columbia Broadcasting System's "Minstrel Man," aired for the first time on 2 March 1977, was superb, and this writer would recommend viewing it to any student of black history or American culture.

37. Stearns, *The Story of Jazz,* p. 109.

38. Toll, *Blacking Up,* pp. 281–82.

39. Huggins, *Harlem Renaissance,* p. 247.

40. See Stearns, *The Story of Jazz,* pp. 116–17; Huggins, *Harlem Renaissance,* pp. 249–50; Wittke, *Tambo and Bones,* pp. 135–209.

41. Stearns, *The Story of Jazz,* p. 117.

42. As developed in the 1820s and 1830s, the medium attempted to portray two different Negro figures, the plantation darkey and the city dude. See Boskin, "Sambo," p. 168. Zip Coon was the urban counterpart of Jim Crow. The superficial differences between the types are of no great concern in this essay. Even before the Civil War, the stereotypes had been merged and could not be separated.

43. Huggins, *Harlem Renaissance,* p. 248.

44. Toll, *Blacking Up,* pp. v-vi.

45. As quoted in Huggins, *Harlem Renaissance,* p. 282.

46. While there is some disagreement among sociologists and anthropologists regarding the definition and proper use of the concept, "ceremony," as defined and explained by Julius Gould and William L. Kolb, eds., *A Dictionary of the Social Sciences* (New York: Free Press, 1965), pp. 82–83, matches quite well with several aspects of minstrelsy. One of the foremost difficulties in using the term is distinguishing it from "ritual." See Edmund R. Leach, "Ritual," in *International Encyclopedia of the Social Sciences,* ed. David L. Sills (New York: Macmillan and Free Press, 1968) 13: 520–26; Gould and Kolb, *A Dictionary of the Social Sciences,* pp. 607–8.

47. See *Monroe Democrat,* 1 June 1899, pp. 1, 8, 31 Jan. 1901, p. 1, 15 Apr. 1904, p. 5, 10 Dec. 1909, p. 16; *Monroe Record,* 31 Jan. 1901, p. 5, 19 July 1901, p. 8, 30 May 1901, p. 5, 27 Feb. 1902, p. 5; *Record-Commercial,* 14 Nov. 1907, p. 1, 21 Feb. 1907, p. 5, 27 Aug. 1908, p. 7. In their 1901 Monroe performance, the innovative Hi Henry troupe used automobiles in their grand entrance parade. *Monroe Record,* 31 Jan. 1901, p. 1.

48. See *Monroe Record,* 13 Dec. 1900, p. 5. Of the many traveling "Tom" companies, Stetson's "Uncle Tom's Cabin" was the perennial favorite of the Monroe crowd. Appearing in the city in 1900, 1902, 1903, 1905, 1907, and 1908, the Stetson troupe consisted of

"white and colored musicians, and colored people from the colored belt." Ibid., 20 Aug. 1903, p. 1.

49. *Monroe Democrat,* 1 June 1899, p. 1.

50. *Monroe Record,* 30 May 1901, p. 5.

51. *Monroe Democrat,* 30 May 1901, p. 5.

52. *Monroe Record,* 19 July 1900, p. 8.

53. "The Big Minstrel Show," *Record-Commercial,* 14 Nov. 1907, p. 1.

54. "The Sunny South," *Record-Commercial,* 21 Feb. 1907, pp. 1, 4.

55. *Record-Commercial,* 28 Feb. 1907, p. 5.

56. "Program 3rd Annual Muskrat Carnival of the M.Y.C." in W. C. Sterling, Jr., Collection, Monroe County Historical Museum, Monroe, Mich.

57. *Monroe Democrat,* 2 Feb. 1912, p. 7; *Record-Commercial,* 1 Feb. 1912, p. 6.

58. *Record-Commercial,* 15 Feb., 1912, p. 1.

59. See *Monroe Democrat,* 24 Jan. 1913, p. 1, 20 Feb. 1914, p. 1; *Monroe Bulletin,* 12 Feb. 1915, p. 11; W. C. Sterling, Jr., Collection, box #9, scrapbook #15, Monroe County Historical Museum, 1915 and 1916 programs. During the 1913 affair an "aged woman succumbed to heart failure as the curtain rose on the minstrel troupe" (*Monroe Democrat,* 7 Feb. 1913, p. 1), but according to the *Democrat* that untoward event did not dull the appetites of the crowd.

60. *Record-Commercial,* 10 Apr. 1913, p. 7.

61. Ibid., 26 Mar. 1914, p. 6.

62. Ibid., 9 Apr. 1914, p. 7. In December 1914 the Monroe Owls put forward a minstrel show in Monroe. As with the M.Y.C. and the Weiss employees, they called in a professional, William Bayers of Steubenville, Ohio, to teach them how to do it right. See ibid., 3 Dec. 1914, p. 1, 10 Dec. 1914, p. 1, 16 Dec. 1914, p. 1; *Monroe Bulletin,* 10 Dec. 1914, p. 4.

63. The serious dilemma that this conception presented to blacks, in terms of their self-concepts, will be discussed in the final chapter.

64. "Monroe the Gretna Green," *Record-Commercial,* 17 Feb. 1910, p. 1; "St. Joe, Michigan's Flourishing Gretna Green Caught in Idea from Historic Monroe," *Detroit News-Tribune,* 7 July 1901.

65. *Monroe Democrat,* 10 Feb. 1898, p. 1; *Monroe Record,* 10 Oct. 1901, p. 4; *Monroe Democrat,* 29 July 1904, p. 5.

66. "Mixed Marriage," *Record-Commercial,* 17 Dec. 1908, p. 1; *Monroe Democrat,* 31 Aug. 1893, p. 1.

67. *Monroe Democrat,* 31 Aug. 1893, p. 1.

68. Monroe Athletic Club Papers, Monroe County Archives, Monroe County Historical Museum.

69. *Monroe Democrat,* 13 Feb. 1896, p. 4.

70. Ibid., 26 Mar. 1896, p. 1.

71. Constance McLaughlin Green, *The Secret City: A History of Race Relations in the Nation's Capital* (Princeton: Princeton University Press, 1967), p. 161.

72. *Monroe Democrat,* 7 Sept. 1906, p. 7.

73. Ibid.

74. Frank Menke, *The Encyclopedia of Sports,* 5th rev. ed., revisions by Suzanne Treat (New York: A. S. Barnes, 1975), p. 276. Interestingly, Monroe fans gathered again at the Western Union office to receive the results of the Jeffries-Johnson fight in 1910, but nothing beyond this fact was stated in the Monroe press. See *Record-Commercial,* 7 July 1910, p. 7.

75. Robert Peterson, *Only the Ball Was White* (Englewood Cliffs, N.J.: Prentice-Hall, 1970), p. 3. Mr. Peterson's work, obviously the product of careful historical research, contains much valuable information but few interpretive themes.

76. See *Monroe Democrat,* 30 Oct. 1903, p. 5, 17 Feb. 1905, p. 5, 4 Mar. 1910, p. 7, 11 Mar. 1910, p. 7, 5 Aug. 1910, p. 7; *Monroe Record,* 13 Aug. 1903, p. 4.

Recapturing the significance of small-town baseball during the Progressive Era is not an easy task. Suffice it to say that of all the entertainment activities open to people of this era, baseball was the favorite. A truly national sport, towns took the greatest pride in producing winning teams. Struggles with teams from nearby towns were not simple athletic contests but battles of mythic quality. Indeed, the honor of each community depended on the outcome. Some of the most impassioned items in the local newspapers involve losses that resulted from an umpire's error in judgment or an unethical action by an opposing player. For Monroe, the game with nearby Carleton was the highlight of the season, and an otherwise dismal record would be forgiven for a victory in that contest. "Ringers," who were not native to the community, were often hired to play ball by local teams. In the years before the development of the major league farm system, small town teams often functioned as feeders for the major leagues. Monroe sent "Ki Ki" Kissinger and "Chick" Lathers to the Detroit Tigers, "Rip" Egan won a contract with the Cincinnati National League team, and Bert Lerchen signed a contract with the Boston American League team during the first years of the twentieth century.

77. *Monroe Record,* 6 Aug. 1903, p. 5. The Page team appeared in Monroe on at least two earlier occasions; see *Monroe Democrat,* 13 June 1895, p. 1, 13 Aug. 1896, p. 1. In 1895, the Page Fence Giants were owned and operated by three white men from nearby Adrian, Michigan. Peterson indicates that the Giants paraded in the streets before the game to create community interest. Peterson, *Only the Ball Was White,* p. 49. See also Thomas E. Powers, "The Page Fence Giants Play Ball," *Chronicle* 19 (Spring 1983): 14–18. Powers's research shows that the original Page team, managed by John W. "Bud" Fowler, disbanded between 1898 and 1899. The 1903 edition of the Adrian Giants had an inferior and entirely different roster. There is some evidence that Fowler, a Negro, was "imported" to play for a Monroe baseball team on occasion. *Monroe Democrat,* 3 Aug. 1899, p. 5. For instances not cited below, see *Monroe Democrat,* 11 July 1901, p. 5; *Monroe Record,* 20 Mar. 1902, p. 5; *Monroe Democrat,* 1 July 1910, p. 7; *Record-Commercial,* 16 June 1914, pp. 6, 9 July 1914, p. 7.

78. Ibid. See also *Monroe Democrat,* 14 Aug. 1903, p. 1.

79. "Only Got One Score," *Monroe Record,* 20 Aug. 1903, p. 1; *Monroe Democrat,* 21 Aug. 1903, p. 5.

80. *Monroe Democrat,* 21 Aug. 1903, p. 5; "Only Got One Score," *Monroe Record,* 20 Aug. 1903, p. 1. As their careers folded, it was not uncommon for former major leaguers to continue playing baseball with the small-town team that would pay the most. "Big" Sam Thompson played for Monroe in 1903. See *Monroe Democrat,* 19 June 1903, p. 4.

81. *Record-Commercial,* 22 June 1911, p. 7; *Monroe Democrat,* 14 July 1911, p. 11.

82. Green, *The Secret City,* p. 161.

83. It is not surprising that Negro ball teams soon found themselves resorting to "minstrel" baseball, with acrobatics, ball tricks, and an imaginary ball routine. Peterson, *Only the Ball Was White,* p. 70.

84. *Monroe Democrat,* 11 July 1901, p. 5.

85. *Monroe Bulletin,* 17 July 1913, p. 1.

86. *Monroe Democrat,* 18 July 1913, p. 1; *Record-Commercial,* 11 Sept. 1913, p. 7.

87. *Record-Commercial,* 2 July 1914, p. 7, 9 July 1914, p. 6.

88. *Monroe Democrat,* 19 Oct. 1901, p. 5; *Monroe Record,* 3 Dec. 1903, p. 5; *Monroe Democrat,* 19 Dec. 1913, p. 12; *Record-Commercial,* 26 Nov. 1914, p. 7.

89. "Musical Review," *Monroe Democrat,* 24 July 1903, p. 2.

90. Walter Winston Kenilworth, "Negro Influence in American Life," *Forum* 46 (Aug. 1911): 177–78.

91. How common these performances were in Monroe is not apparent. The local news media rarely made reference to such occasions, and news of these events must have been passed by handbill or word-of-mouth. Because Monroe had so few indigenous Negroes, these gatherings of necessity were played by outsiders.

92. *Monroe Record,* 14 Oct. 1900, p. 5.

93. Jenny Toll Sawyer, diaries, Sunday, 12 August 1900, Michigan Historical Collections, Bentley Historical Library, University of Michigan.

94. *Monroe Democrat,* 11 Feb. 1886, p. 1, 5 Nov. 1891, p. 1, 12 Nov. 1891, p. 1.

95. *Monroe Democrat,* 14 Apr. 1898, p. 1, 9 Mar. 1899, p. 5; *Record-Commercial,* 9 Feb. 1911, p. 7; *Monroe Democrat,* 16 Feb. 1912, p. 1, 6 Oct. 1898, p. 1, 7 Nov. 1913, p. 7.

96. *Monroe Democrat,* 13 Jan. 1898, p. 1, 11 Jan. 1900, p. 1; *Monroe Record,* 16 Jan. 1902, p. 1, 30 July 1903, p. 5; "Successful Meeting Closed," *Monroe Democrat,* 4 July 1913, p. 1.

97. *Monroe Democrat,* 11 Jan. 1900, p. 1, 10 Jan. 1901, p. 1, 26 Aug. 1910, p. 7.

98. *Monroe Democrat,* 6 Jan. 1898, p. 1, 1 July 1904, p. 1.

99. Baker, *Following the Color Line,* p. 118.

100. "Booker T. Washington," *Monroe Democrat,* 19 Jan. 1899, p. 1, 26 Jan. 1899, p. 5, 2 Feb. 1899, p. 5.

101. James Weldon Johnson, *The Autobiography of an Ex-Colored Man* in *Three Negro Classics* (New York: Avon Discus, 1969), pp. 451, 486.

102. Nolen, *The Negro's Image in the South,* p. 16.

3

The Beast-Negro Stereotype in Monroe, 1900–1915

> The last words spoken by the sheriff before he went on the operating table was to his dear and personal friend Perry F. Knapp, chief of police of Toledo. He said, "Perry, get the nigger."
>
> "ALL MONROE COUNTY MOURNS Bravest, Cleanest Official in Michigan Shot Down by a Negro while in the Discharge of his Duty,"
>
> *Record-Commercial*, 4 Aug. 1910

> Five Little Niggers going
> in for law;
> One got in prison, and then
> there were Four.
>
> *Ten Little Niggers*,
> Bo-Peep Series, (c. 1890)

If white America found a warm spot in its heart for the child-Negro, the "ole-time darkey," the reverse was true for the opposite side of this social identity. Indeed, it is hard to imagine the animosity of the white-dominated society being more stimulated than it was by the image of the brute-Negro. The stereotypes of the childlike and beast-Negro were, if not invented by, at least developed and articulated by southern Negrophobes who perceived a threat to the white group's position in the land south of the Mason-Dixon Line. When Negroes behaved, i.e. accepted their social positions, the lovable and endearing "darkey" stereotype was brought to consciousness, but when a Negro chose to protest or challenge white dominance, the beast-Negro image burst forth in all its fury.

In the end, both social identities reflected the same social reality: the relegation of Afro-Americans to an inferior place in American society.

If the North had not participated in the invention or articulation of the beast-Negro, it was not without responsibility for its proliferation. Citizens outside the South were clearly remiss in not constructing counter images. If accommodationist racism won out in the North, it was because the Negro was potentially less threatening to white dominance there. Admittedly, "Sambos and clowns" presented little menace to the established order of things, and white citizens throughout the nation could feel rather free to indulge in their fantasies about child-Negroes. In the end, they might rationalize that "no one had been hurt." To a point, sentiments about the beast-Negro played through the minds of Caucasians—particularly when they felt menaced. To be sure, citizens North and South were very much aware of the ritual attached to this image—lynching. Illegal hangings were not uncommon and people all over the country learned the grisly details of many of these incidents by reading the newspapers. Through the "boiler plate" in their local press, Monroe's inhabitants read detailed and lurid news accounts of violent racial confrontations. Almost every month a stirring story about a lynching was related in the Monroe papers. Typical by-lines were "Downing a Colored Brute," "Fierce Race Fight," "Shot and Strung Up," and "Foil Plan to Lynch Negro."[1]

Monroe's white citizens had more than just a passing interest in lynchings. In 1906 the *Democrat* announced the arrival in town of Maurice Turner, a former Monroe native. Turner, the paper related, was in Springfield, Missouri, when a mob of 5,000 whites hanged three Negroes and so could give a first-hand account of the mob action. More than a few Monroe whites saw lynchings as a legitimate course of action. One Tuesday in February 1900, "Prof. Bauer's IX grade class in Civil Government spent their recitation hour . . . in debating the question 'Is lynching justifiable?' The class was evenly divided and the debate good. Although hard to decide the decision was given the negative side." In an incident in 1902 involving an unlawful entry of a Negro into a Monroe residence, the only occupant of which was a little girl, the specter of lynching was brought forward. While the man escaped, the *Record* commented that "it's lucky for this same colored gentleman that he lives north of the Mason and Dixon Line." A Monroe mob did kill a white man accused of rape in 1902, and so closely were mob action and Negroes connected in the minds of Monroeites that almost fifty years after the incident people incorrectly reminisced that the victim had been black.[2]

While there is no question that Monroe citizens had an acquaintance with the beast-Negro stereotype, the major problem in this chapter concerns how the town's inhabitants and legal structure adapted to the question of Negro deviance. How, in other words, did Monroe react to and deal with black lawbreakers and criminals? Did the social identity of the Negro as fiend have any bearing on outcomes? Only an analysis of criminal incidents, as reported in the local press and remembered by Monroe citizens, can begin to answer those questions.

During the Progressive Era, Monroe newspapers paid a great deal of attention to the issue of law and order. Local court proceedings, arrests, and criminal incidents were followed closely by the editors of the papers. Indeed, it is difficult to unearth an issue of any of the Monroe newspapers from this time period which makes no reference to illicit activities. The city's newspaper establishment printed and scrutinized closely the county prosecutor's semiannual report, which revealed the nature of the crimes and the success of the legal process.[3] In a town where crime was everyone's business, a conviction rate of over 95 percent of those arrested was not uncommon. So concerned were the inhabitants with their normative structure that the following class of incident was not atypical. In 1902 the *Record* reported that "a couple of young men came into the Piers the latter part of the week with a yacht and were brought to the city until they could satisfy the officers that they were entitled to possession the yacht."[4] For the most part, the race of offenders was carefully noted in the Monroe press. In only one incident, which will be discussed later, was a Negro offender not identified as "colored." Consequently, the Monroe press provided an excellent bird's-eye view of what punishments and treatment awaited the black criminal in Monroe.

Suspicion usually greeted unknown Negroes who arrived in Monroe during the first years of the twentieth century.[5] A Negro playing an unaccustomed role or possessing property blacks did not normally have was in for a hard time. In July 1905, William Green, colored, came into Monroe and tried to sell a Reliance bicycle at Kopf's repair shop. Needing money, the "coon" offered the wheel "for $10.00 claiming that a man had given it to him on Fourth street and told him to sell it for that price and keep $3.00 as his commission." Officer Navarre, who had been called by Kopf, "couldn't swallow such a story and an investigation was started."

As Green passed his time in the local jail, "Sheriff Dull sought to locate where the wheel was stolen but without success."[6] Word from Toledo and the surrounding area had failed to turn up evidence of a missing Reliance.

Mr. Green, however, was not released but instead was charged "with being in a strange land without visible means of support." Pleading guilty before Justice Mathews, he "was given twenty minutes in which to find the city limits. He warmly congratulated the learned judge on the leniency shown and said he would endeavor to make the limits in five minutes. He bounded out of the court room like a rubber ball and never stopped to ask for the bicycle, which he claimed had been given him to sell."[7]

The tension between the images of the beast-Negro and the child-Negro in the white mind is apparent in the foregoing script. The incident began on a very serious note, a potential badman had been collared, but it ended, at least as far as the white community was concerned, on a note of mirth. Green emerged as a clown, a child-Negro, and the press justified the denouement of the controversy by implying, despite the lack of proof, that the item had been stolen. It seemed that if Green had been telling the truth, he would have demanded the wheel. It never occurred to the white observers that the terrified Green might have been most concerned with simply getting out of town in one piece rather than with scoring fine legal points in the matter.

Acquaintance with the criminal social identity meant that the countenances of strange blacks were closely inspected and scrutinized by Monroe citizens. Negroes with scars or pockmarks which matched those on wanted posters were detained in the local jail. Blacks suspected of being fugitives from the law were often taken into custody by Monroe officers. In 1903 two local papers reported that Arthur Good, a colored man who was employed in Monroe as a pavement worker, had been arrested by city officials. "With a record as black as his countenance," he was wanted for attempted murder in Toledo.[8] In another instance, a certain Mike Allen, wanted for obtaining money under false pretenses in Flint, was spotted working as a horse trainer at the Monroe Driving Park in July 1913 by Undersheriff Cronenwett. Like Good, Allen was also taken into custody and was later returned to the offended city.[9]

In another instance, in 1901, a Negro male accompanied by a white female drew a violent response from Monroe police. A colored man, observed walking with two little girls, one of whom was white, on the railroad tracks near Monroe's Warner switching yards, was chased and shot at by officer Boudrie. Fortunately, the bullets ranged wide of their target. The man eluded Boudrie but was later captured and jailed by other officers. Convinced that he was wanted in Toledo, Monroe officials sent several inquiries there and discovered that the black girl was his daughter and the other youngster was a member of a white family with whom he shared the same Toledo address. The white girl's parents decided to press charges and the Negro was taken to Toledo to await trial.[10]

Misfortune awaited some Negroes who appeared on Monroe streets during this time, although the city's watchful eye erred on more than one occasion. When he selected Monroe as a likely spot in which to solicit funds for a building for colored people in Washington, D.C., little did Brother Reverend E. W. Thomas realize that he was in for one of the most difficult times of his life. Thomas had been canvassing the streets for only a short time when he was arrested by Chief of Police Duclo. On the way to jail, Duclo noticed that his prisoner answered the description of a Charles Savage, alias Charles Stevens, who was wanted in Kansas City for the theft of a registered mail pouch containing upwards of $50,000. The reward for information leading to the culprit's capture amounted to $3,000. News of Thomas's detention was immediately sent via Western Union to Kansas City, and a man who could make positive identification was soon on his way. This official, Inspector Birdseye, after a good look at Thomas concluded that he was not the man wanted. Notwithstanding, the Monroe prisoner did "resemble Savage in nearly every particular, being of the same age, practically the same height and weight, the same shade of color, exactly the same features and scars, there being of the latter one on the bridge of his nose, one in the outer edge of each eyebrow and right side of the forehead. . . . General Stuart, inspector in charge at Chicago, said that is was the most remarkable resemblance he had known in his thirty odd years experience."[11] Birdseye complimented Duclo on his "shrewd discernment in picking up a person resembling so closely the man wanted." Monroe admitted the mistake, and after almost a week of intensive questioning, "Brother" Thomas was sent on his way. No apologies were necessary because even the "two post office secret service men were in doubt for a time whether to release or hold him."[12]

More embarrassing was the arrest in the same year of another Negro by the ever-diligent Dulco. "On a tip furnished from a party in Erie, a colored man, said to have been Henry Durand, wanted in Toledo for a cutting scrape, was arrested on the 10 o'clock car . . . and placed in police headquarters on suspicion." "After a searching inquiry," the *Record-Commercial* reported, "he was let go, having proven he was a resident of Erie," a community only ten miles south of Monroe![13]

More serious incidents pointed in an unsuspected direction. If the beast-Negro always came into play, once a case entered the courts a concern for justice was present and there was a relatively evenhanded administration of the law. While ruder passions ruled some of the populace in Monroe, the city and county officials and leaders allowed concerns about fairness and equity to determine outcomes on more than one occasion. Perhaps the major difference in racism between the North and the South was the manner in which this shared stereotype was reified. It is difficult to imagine similar situations occurring in the South without the unwarranted loss of life.

During 1901, groups of colored men ran afoul of the law in Monroe several times. During the first decade of the twentieth century, blacks were often brought into northern towns to work on streets, railroad grades, and other construction projects. The work was physically exhausting, but Negro laborers were always available for the arduous tasks at a low rate of pay. Smart contractors took advantage of the large national Negro labor pool. Southern blacks, in search of employment and other opportunities, often traveled far from their original homes, moving from one town to another as jobs started and ended.

John J. Strong, a Monroe County contractor, imported a number of blacks into the city in May 1901 to work on a grading and building project for the Detroit and Toledo Shore Line Railroad, with which he had secured a contract.[14] Before a month was up, racial tensions surfaced in a "row between the 'coons' and white men at the Shore Line Camp." Local law officers called to the scene had to draw their revolvers to rescue three white teamsters who were being held by the group. Later, when the "dark bunch" was arraigned before Judge Noble, John Madden, "Moxey" Reed, and Charles White, all colored, were each fined two dollars for assault and battery on the teamsters. The three were not imprisoned but released to the custody of their employer, John Strong, after he had paid the assessments.[15]

The incident, however, had not run its course. Two weeks later, when the workers were paid, the three who had been fined discovered that they had been docked for the sum. John Madden, the toughest of the lot, became enraged when he discovered that he had no money coming to him for the previous pay period. "He started on the warpath singing, 'I ain't got no money, but I will have some.'" Within a short time, "the bad 'nigger' and a worse gun caused lots of excitement." Madden had pulled his forty-five revolver on Strong and demanded payment of the two dollars. After taking the money, the "dangerous man" escaped but was later captured a few miles from Monroe in Rockwood on a northbound freight. The *Democrat* reported that "when Madden was searched he had a monster revolver and a belt of cartridges about his person and had he suspected that the Rockwood men intended to arrest him, someone would have been shot. He seems a desperate character."[16]

Here, then, seen emerging from this scenario, is the desperate, wicked, criminal Negro type *par excellence.* John Madden matched the characteristics usually present in the beast-Negro social identity. The local press had cast him in that mold, and undoubtedly more of Monroe's citizens accepted the description. Given these facts, what is most surprising is the legal denouement of the affair.

Two months later, when Madden was taken before Justice Kinne, he was charged with the serious crimes of assault and attempt to commit highway robbery. Convinced that he did not have a chance, Madden pled guilty to both counts but was taken aside by the judge for private consultation. "Upon returning to the court room Judge Kinne announced that he was not satisfied with the plea of the prisoner, stating he believed the prisoner at bar should be furnished with counsel since he had pleaded guilty to the charge fearing that if he did not and he was given a trial that his color would count against him and he would not receive justice. . . ." Intent on showing Madden that justice was color-blind in his court, Kinne appointed John O. Zable counsel. The incident ended with Madden pleading guilty to the lesser charge of assault, for which he was sentenced to sixty days in the county jail.[17] A concern for justice, at least in this instance, resulted in a relatively light sentence for an armed Negro. A fair-minded evaluation of the circumstances surrounding the crime and Madden's character had revealed that the beast-Negro was pretty much human after all, and the stereotype had been rejected in the name of judicial equity.

Another incident involving the same colored camp again caused excitement in Monroe in August 1911. Thirty-six of the eighty-five men employed by the Shore Line were engaged in a work stoppage. The strikers had been shipped from South Carolina with the understanding that their fares would be paid from their first two weeks' wages. Apparently, they misunderstood the agreement or had been misled. The thirty-six lined up for pay after their initial fourteen days but were told they had no money coming. Bitter arguments ensued, and the southern blacks refused to return to their jobs. As the situation reached a crescendo, Monroe police were summoned to the camp. On arrival, the officers drew their revolvers, forced the Negroes into waiting boxcars, and summarily sent them away. The *Democrat* explained that they "had been doing nothing and making trouble" and were "an ignorant, troublesome lot of southern negroes."[18]

The camp continued to be troublesome as "war was waged" there in September. In the mix-up, John W. Hart, colored, was cut severely on the right arm by another Negro, Sarah Marts, for which he required treatment by a Monroe physician. After four months of nothing but problems, Monroe citizens must have rejoiced when work in the vicinity was completed. In October, the colored camp was moved north to Newport.[19]

Blacks were involved in even more serious and potentially explosive situations during the Progressive years in Monroe. A "stabbing affray," which occurred during Decoration Day celebrations in 1901, threatened to result in a public lynching. "While the memorial exercises were being conducted at the Armory in celebration of the freeing of the negro," the *Democrat* harangued in its coverage of the event, William Stokes, "one of the freedmen, nearly ended the career of one of the race of his liberators."[20]

The culprit, Stokes, the story went, had arrived in the city several months earlier from Columbus, Ohio, and set up a "fake healing" store, where he practiced the laying-on of hands and dispensed herbal remedies. At first calling himself "Dr.," Stokes was soon forced by local authorities to change his title. After that the "Professor's" business declined, and he began to "work" for a living by painting.[21]

On the fateful day, Stokes was in Jacob Herman's saloon with his plastering tools and whitewash brush enjoying a few cold beers. At the same time, William Rudert, a local butcher who enjoyed baiting the "Dr." about his decline in status, entered the establishment. Rudert, as was his custom, had been drinking heavily, and he immediately began to shower abuse on the colored painter. Three times, the *Record* reported, Rudert left and then returned to continue the verbal assault on the Negro. Stokes, an eyewitness later recalled, begged Rudert to go away and leave him alone, but the mean drunk would not relent. "The last time Rudert re-entered the saloon Stokes stepped over toward the door and the butcher picked up a chair and jammed it into the colored man's face, cutting his forehead."[22] Stokes in retaliation buried his putty knife in Rudert's chest. "The knife entered between the lower two ribs on the left

Robert S. Duncanson, the noted American landscape artist (courtesy Allen Van Deusen)

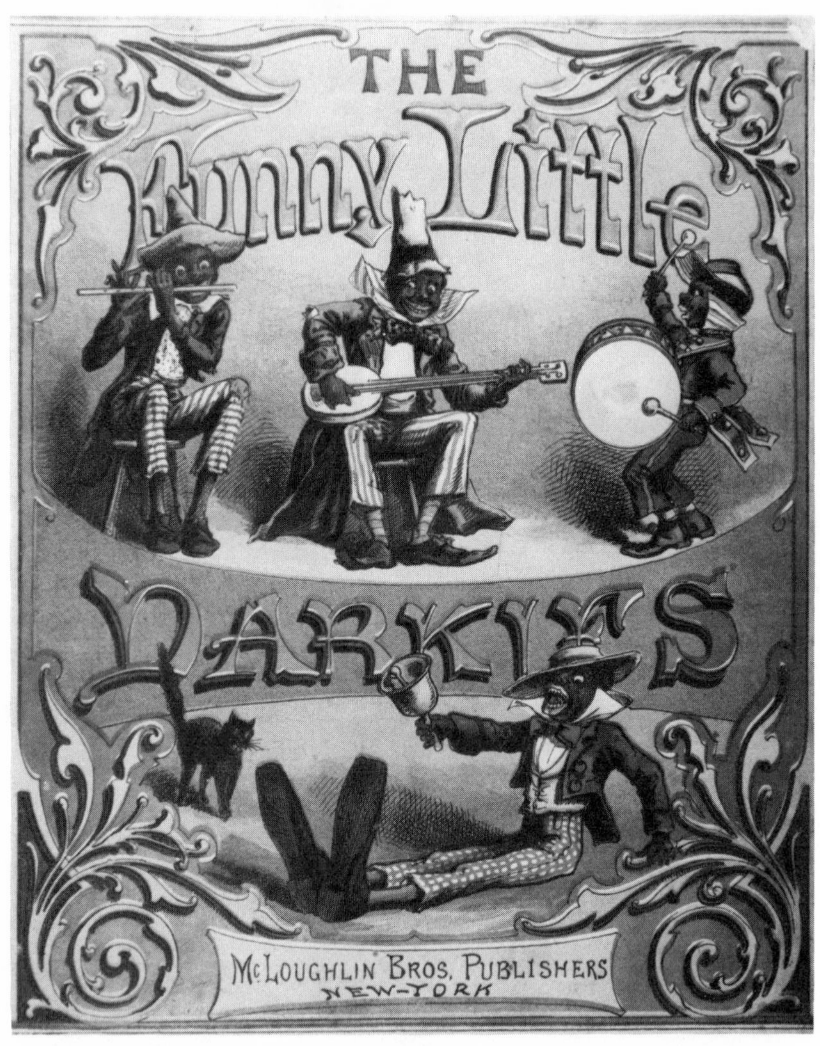

This booklet, belonging to a white Monroe family, was typical of the racist literature written for children (courtesy Monroe County Historical Society)

MONROE, MICH., THURSDA

Two Dead Prisoners!

They Attack the Turnkey and are Surprised at the Warm Reception Given Them.

His Pistol is Responsive to the Touch, and Two Coons are Converted into Cloud Pushers.

A Poor Jail but a Good Jailer.

A warning to Crooks to Keep from Monroe Co.

A NEW JAIL, YES!

The *Monroe Democrat* regaled in the killing of two Afro-American criminals (*Monroe Democrat,* 30 Apr. 1891, courtesy Monroe County Library System)

THE RECORD-COMMERCIAL

"MONROE FIRST, ALL WAYS."

COMMERCIAL VOL. 71, NO. 32. MONROE, MICHIGAN, THURSDAY, AUGUST 4, 1910. RECORD VOL. XI, NO. 13.

SHERIFF EDMOND DULL IS FATALLY SHOT.

ALL MONROE COUNTY MOURNS

Bravest, Cleanest Official in Michigan Shot Down by a Negro while in the Discharge of his Duty.

MAYOR ISSUES PROCLAMATION TO SUSPEND BUSINESS.

PROCLAMATION

The sudden and tragic death of the sheriff of the county, shot down in cold blood, while in the performance of his sworn duty, calls for suitable action on the part of the community of which he has been a resident, during his years of public service.

His remains will lie in state at the Sheriff's residence from noon on Thursday, August 4th, to noon of Friday August 5th. Services will be held there at one o'clock P. M., of Friday when the remains will be taken to St. Paul's M. E. Church, where public services will be held, at the conclusion of which the remains will be taken to Temperance, Michigan, for interment.

In honor to his services and the manner of his death, I most earnestly enjoin upon the citizens of this city that during the hours of the funeral services, from 12:30 to 2:30 P. M., of Friday, August 5th, that business be universally suspended, and all places of business, of whatever character, be absolutely closed during those hours and that our business men personally join in paying the last tribute to a brave and earnest officer.

Given at the Executive office of the City of Monroe, Michigan, this third day of August, A. D. 1910.

JACOB MARTIN,
Mayor.

The *Record-Commercial* captured the community's sentiment about their slain sheriff (*Record-Commercial*, 11 Aug. 1910, courtesy Monroe County Historical Museum)

THE RECORD-COMMERCIAL

"MONROE FIRST, ALL WAYS."

COMMERCIAL VOL. 71, NO. 34. MONROE, MICHIGAN, THURSDAY, AUGUST 18, 1910. RECORD VOL. XI, NO. 15.

ASPHALT BLOCK

PAVING MATERIAL SELECTED BY COUNCIL

ANOTHER STORY OF THE CAPTURE

TOLD BY ONE OF THE REYNOLDS BROTHERS.

MURDERER HARRIS SENTENCED

TO SOLITARY CONFINEMENT AT HARD LABOR FOR LIFE.

ANNUAL REUNION.

Members of the 11th Michigan Will Meet at Constantine Aug. 24, 25.

RENNER FAMILY RE-UNION.

CHRISTIAN SCIENCE SERVICE.

AT HOME WITH CUSTER

SOFTER SIDE OF INDIAN FIGHTER DESCRIBED BY MRS. YATES, A FRIEND OF FRONTIER DAYS IN THE WEST.

(Continued on Page Six)

William Harris, who confessed to shooting Sheriff Dull, sat silently as the verdict of guilty was delivered (*Record-Commercial*, 18 Aug. 1910, courtesy Monroe County Historical Museum)

Front Street, Monroe business district, about 1900 (courtesy Monroe County Historical Museum)

flesh wound on the left arm. "Then, without a word, the negro, with his pistol still clutched in his hand, jumped over the prostrate form of his victim and disappeared in the darkness, followed by five shots from the wounded man's revolver." This final courageous act, the *Record-Commercial* observed, was "characteristic of the fearless nature and the indomitable will of Edmund Dull."[36]

The farmer, Reau, weighing his options carefully, decided not to pursue the felon, and instead remained behind to comfort and aid the mortally wounded sheriff. Meanwhile, the sound of gunfire had created a great commotion among people in the nearby area, and a crowd quickly gathered at the scene. After the serious nature of the lawman's wounds was ascertained, he was carefully carried into Erie. Once there, a Lake Shore passenger train was flagged down, and Dull was soon on his way to Toledo's Robinwood Hospital.

After a few hours had elapsed, the anxiously awaited word came from the hospital: "Sheriff Dull desperately ill . . . as ill as he could possibly be." Dr. Gillette, of Toledo, had performed an emergency operation but the effort was useless. Despite the fact that he survived the operation and even regained consciousness, Dull was doomed. The wounds were too severe; one of the projectiles had perforated the intestine nine times. The sheriff's family was called to Toledo to witness his passing.

News of the event galvanized the entire county, and Dull's last words before the operation to Perry Knapp, Chief of Police of Toledo, signaled the call to action: "He said, 'Perry, get the nigger.' Seldom, if ever [had] the entire county of Monroe been so suddenly wrought up." Arthur Lesow, a prominent citizen in the community, who first arrived in Monroe on 1 August 1910, remembered that all the town's men were armed with guns.[37] "The brutal murder . . . stirred the city and county as no event since the massacre of the Little Big Horn, and there was serious danger that, if the murderer was caught, he would be lynched. When the news of the shooting reached Monroe, the mayor promptly sent some of the police out to Erie and swore in a large number of deputies. Scores of people also organized themselves into volunteer searching parties from this city, and all along the territory between Monroe and Toledo farmers did likewise."[38]

The *Toledo Blade* reported that as soon as "Toledo police were notified of the shooting Chief Knapp summoned every motor and mounted policeman and every detective in the department and sent them in squads by different roads to search" north and west of Toledo.[39] The *Monroe Democrat* informed its readers that "news of the shooting was telegraphed to all parts of Michigan and Ohio where the fugitive might get on one of the railroads passing through Monroe County, and within an hour every crossing was under guard and every car and train was searched at every station." Despite the intense efforts, the Negro was not found that evening. "The elements favored the negro, for the night was pitch dark and for much of the time a heavy rain fell, so that the men could not see their hands before their faces."[40]

The next day, the manhunt gathered momentum. About thirty-five members of Company D, Monroe's contribution to the First Michigan Volunteers, armed with Springfields from the armory, left early in the morning for Erie, where it was rumored that the culprit had been sighted. The *Record-Commercial* observed that Captain Harrington's group "worked faithful and well and each was determined if he saw the murderer that process of law would not be needed if he offered any resistance." That same morning, East Toledo police joined in the search along the Michigan-Ohio border.[41]

Back in Monroe, Mayor Martin was posting hourly bulletins of Dull's condition outside his shoe store. The lawman's declining life signs told the story although the citizens of Monroe reported to Mayor Martin's store hourly to see if Dull's condition had taken a turn for the better. All day, the *Record-Commercial* commented, "the city was in a quiver of excitement and the effect of the bulletins served to keep the anxious populace on edge. Hopes and fears prevailed alternately, although every succeeding message undoubtedly pointed to the fact that the struggle for life on the part of the sheriff would end in a victory for the grim destroyer."[42]

Information was received on that same day that a man matching "in every detail" the description of Dull's killer was wanted for murder in Chatham, Ontario. Monroe citizens were convinced that the fiend they were looking for was a multiple slayer. On Tuesday, 2 August, word reached Monroe that a Negro fitting the murderer's description had been captured and arrested in Flint. Deputy Sheriff Emery Mills, ex-Mayor Alex Deinzer, and the witness, Hayes, left for the city when the news was recieved. At Flint the colored suspect was positively identified by Hayes as the Negro who had thrown him from the freight car. On the strength of this identification, the man, Travis Wilkerson, was taken to Monroe for further questioning.

In the meantime, word had leaked out that the culprit would be returning with Mills, Deinzer, and Hayes from Flint, and a large crowd began to mill around the Père Marquette depot. When questioned, Monroe officials continued to deny any knowledge of the matter. The *Democrat* later explained that "this was done to head off any of the threatened attempts at lynching the negro."

After his arrest in Flint, the captive Wilkerson "evinced considerable nervousness when he learned he was going to Monroe, and repeatedly asked if there was any danger of a mob meeting him." Despite the continued assurance by Mills and Deinzer that elaborate precautions had been taken, his fears were well founded. All along the route of the Père Marquette, people were waiting to catch a glimpse of the alleged felon. "A crowd of several hundred gathered at Plymouth and pretty near all of Ash Township were at Carleton," and a large crowd was waiting at the depot in Monroe.[43]

Fearing some sort of demonstration, the officers and Mayor Martin had devised a plan to get the prisoner safely into jail.

> On the arrival of the train but one passenger C. J. Kirby debarked and he seemed to be in dense ignorance about any officer or negro. Mills and his party were hid in the baggage car in which the lights were put out and on leaving the city the electric headlight was turned off and the tail lights screened. According to prearranged program a party consisting of Turnkey Cronenwett, Chief Forner, Mayor Martin, A. B. Bragdon, Jr., in two automobiles driven by Ben Greening and Lee Rauch met the train at Dunbar Road a mile south of the city. The train was swung down and Mills and the prisoner, Hays and Mr. Deinzer hurried into the awaiting automobile and the run to the city began at a speed as great as possible by the machines. At the corner of Sixth the automobiles left Monroe street and zig zagged to the rear of the jail. Here Wilkerson and Hays were hustled in, the doors slammed and locked and the officers drew a long breath at the success of landing the suspect safe in jail.[44]

Not one in the crowd was aware of what was happening until the prisoner was taken through the door. A cry went up and the disappointed throng soon swarmed about the jail. "Men, women and children seemed to have sprung from the ground so dense did the crowd become, but passage to the jail was guarded by militiamen and no demonstration occurred." The *Toledo Blade* reported that the crowds were "angry in demeanor, but they spoke in low tones, and did not allow their passions to rule their judgment." Undoubtedly, memories of a mob-killing less than a decade earlier in Monroe, which resulted in much grief and soul-searching in the community, still remained in the minds of many of those present in the crowd.[45] That memory plus the determined resistance of the men guarding the jail caused this aggregation to hesitate, and there was no mob action in Monroe on this occasion.

The crowd's indecison was fortunate because Wilkerson was not the man who had killed Sheriff Dull. Mr. and Mrs. Reau, Conductor Grau, and the members of the train crew, after having a good look at Wilkerson and comparing him to another Negro captured in a separate incident, insisted that he was not the man with whom they had had exchanges. Faced with a contradiction in testimony, Monroe law enforcement officials resumed their questioning of the original witness, Hayes. After several hours of a third-degree grilling, Hayes relented and admitted that Wilkerson was not the man with whom he had fought and that the Negro who had tossed him from the moving train had not robbed him of twenty-five dollars. There never was that much money involved in the exchange but, in a vengeful mood, Hayes had manufactured that part of the incident to ensure that his assailant would be pursued by the arm of the law. Revelation of these "facts" turned Monroe against Hayes, and he was pilloried and held responsible for being the "first step in the tragedy." Because of his lies, Hayes was given the maximum penalty for "being a vagrant and disorderly character," sixty-five days in the Detroit House of Correction.[46]

The other Negro had been taken by farmers on Wednesday about three miles south of Monroe on the Père Marquette tracks.[47] Shot in the neck and wounded, the *Blade* related that the suspect was "almost on the verge of collapse from fright." Several of the witnesses positively identified the captive, William Henry Harris, as the guilty party, and Monroe was convinced that the "slayer of one of the bravest, cleanest, dearest, efficient, fearless, officers that Monroe county" had ever had was "securely confined within the steel cage of the county jail."[48]

On the same afternoon of Harris's capture, Dull, after "hanging on" for what seemed like endless hours, finally succumbed in Toledo's Robinwood Hospital. Immediately the city of Monroe began elaborate preparations for the funeral. The proclamation issued by Mayor Martin outlined the procedures for the observances:

PROCLAMATION

The sudden and tragic death of Edmund Dull, sheriff of this county, shot down in cold blood, while in the performance of his sworn duty, calls for suitable action on the part of the community of which he has been a resident during his years of public service.

His remains will lie in state at the Sheriff's residence from noon Thursday, August 4th, to noon of Friday, August 5th. Services will be held there at 1 o'clock P.M. of Friday, when the remains will be taken to St. Paul's M. E. Church, where public services will be held at the conclusion of which the remains will be taken to Temperance, Michigan, for interment.

In honor of his services and the manner of his death, I most earnestly enjoin upon the citizens of this city that during the hours of the funeral services, 12:30 to 2:30 P.M. of Friday, August 5th, business be universally suspended, and all places of business, of whatever character, be absolutely closed during those hours, and that our business men personally join in paying the last tribute to a brave and earnest officer.

Given at the Executive Office of the city of Monroe, Michigan, this third day of August, A.D. 1910.

JACOB MARTIN, Mayor[49]

As Monroe prepared to lay its beloved sheriff to rest, the city's law enforcement officials were subjecting Harris to a gruelling and unrelenting line of questioning. While Harris continued to protest his innocence, his inconsistent statements and the positive identification by the witnesses convinced Monroe officials that they "had their man." Having no success in wresting a confession from the culprit, the city's lawmen called in outside professionals schooled in those matters. It was during this second battery of questioning that the treacherous nature of the Negro-beast image became apparent. On Friday morning, the second day after the capture, Detective DeLisle of the Murphy Detective Agency of Detroit uncovered a razor hidden on Harris's person.[50] "When asked what he had intended to do with it, he said that if he had been cornered too close he would have cut his [DeLisle's] throat. When further questioned if he thought of cutting any one else's he cooly remarked, 'Well two fellows did get pretty fresh with me in here the other day.' He referred to Prosecuting Attorney Root and County Clerk Ready who, on Wednesday had put him through some stiff questioning and had trapped him into some damaging contradictions. They were unarmed at the time and their feelings can be imagined when they learned of the danger they had been in."[51]

Friday, the day of Dull's last rites, found a great portion of the county coming to the city to attend the services. Buggies and automobiles were lined up in single file from Erie to Monroe, and most people could not get near the church. The *Record-Commercial* observed that their numbers were so great that they "resembled the concourse of people which gathered on 'Custer Day'" to see President Taft dedicate the Custer statue earlier that spring. During the funeral, "the jail yard was filled and the streets in all directions for more than a half block." Although at least one thousand had failed to gain entry to the church, they "waited patiently and reverently about during the ceremony."[52]

Taking precautions, the police had stationed many plainclothesmen in the throng. As the church bells pealed the end to the services, tensions in the city again rose to a fever pitch. "There was a strong undercurrent of indignation manifest, particularly among people from the country. 'He ought to be lynched,' said somebody in a crowd that had gathered. The word was passed around. The town began warming up. More people collected on the streets. They moved toward the jail. Once there the feeling ran higher and higher."[53]

On the inside, Harris was "almost on the verge of collapse from fear that he would be lynched." Detective McLaughlin of the Pennsylvania Railroad of Toledo decided to question the Negro a final time. Talking in a low pleasant voice,

> he began asking him "do you hear the tolling of that church bell out there?" "Do you know what that means?" To this Harris said "Yes, boss, I guess I do."
>
> "Don't you see that crowd gathered out there in the street and in this jail yard?" . . . Harris looked out the window for a moment, a shudder shook his frame and McLaughlin quick to notice the physical change said: "Don't you want to tell me where the gun is? It [a confession] might save your life." At this Harris looked at him and said: "Under some stones by mile post seven on the Pere Marquette, get me out of here and I will tell you the whole story."[54]

As men began to crowd around the jail urging each other to action, the officers understood that the building would not stand a determined assault.[55] There was an urgent need of a plan to evacuate Harris. "A conference was held in the sheriff's residence with Perry F. Knapp, chief of police of Toledo, and he planned the campaign for the removal of Harris. His trained master mind worked out the details in a second. . . ." All that was needed was a good fast car, so Lee Rauch, a local citizen of even temper, volunteered his vehicle for the project. The arrangement called for parking the automobile on the east side of the jail barn in the alley, where it would be hidden from the view of the mob by both the barn and Central School. At the appropriate moment, Chief Knapp would signal acting Sheriff Renner, and the desperado would be hurried from the back entrance of the jail to the waiting automobile. "While the plan was hurriedly arranged there was no excitement and there was no hitch. The negro handcuffed to Detective McLaughlin ran as fast as possible to the automobile and when it started north out of the alley Sheriff Renner, Deputy Sheriff Mills and A. B. Bragdon Jr., were aboard. As soon as Macomb street was reached Mr. Rauch 'let her go' and his 'Packard 30' was in perfect shape and when the party was going past Vine street the speed indicator registered 47 miles an hour."[56]

The idea was to speed out of the city northward, stop a Detroit-bound streetcar, and thereby set up a procedure for delivering Harris safely to the Wayne County Jail. When the Stoney Creek crossing of the D. M. & T. interurban was reached, "Sheriff Renner, Deputy Sheriff Mills and A. B. Bragdon Jr., got off the automobile to stop the Detroit limited while the automobile made the run to Hurd's crossing a half mile north. By a secret signal which was recognized and honored by Mortorman Charles Law the limited stopped, the party got aboard and a record run [was] made for Detroit."[57]

According to the *Democrat,* Harris had shown the better side of his nature during the race to Hurd Road. Overhearing Sheriff Renner's expressed fear "that men bent on lynching the coon might follow the auto," Harris asked the officer to slip him his gun if the occasion merited it. Harris stated, "You men amount to something and I wouldn't want you to lose your lives on account of me. I ain't worth anything. If that mob shows up, give me the gun and I'll take a chance with it."[58]

Once safely within the confines of the Wayne County Jail, Harris calmly repeated his confession to the authorities. No, he had not committed the murder in Chatham, Ontario, but he had slain Sheriff Dull. The *Free Press* characterized Harris's confession as "unconcerned as could be." The beast-Negro emerged in its distinctive form in the description of a reporter from the *Detroit News* who interviewed Harris. "'Harris!' called a deputy sheriff standing before the bars of section 'A' at the county jail. Down in the pit of the section a great hulk of a black man uncoiled his legs, arose from the stakeless crap game which he had been playing and looked up: Maybe his face is brutal. Maybe this man-killer is horrid to look on sometimes, but when he climbed those short iron stairs this morning his face was wrinkled into a sort of abashed, winsome smile. He looked guileless in spite of his giant shoulders and the pock marks on his face." As the conversation continued, the reporter noted that he smiled broadly as he lazily recounted the battle with Dull. "'I didn't know I hit him,' he said. . . . 'I'd shot him twice, but didn't know either one got him. I wanted to make sure. So I put the muzzle against his stomach and fired. Then I knowed I'd got him.'"[59]

For Monroe, the incident was not quite finished. Harris had to be returned to Monroe for arraignment and sentencing. Although the date and hour of the hearings were well-guarded secrets, when the officers and Harris got off the interurban at Second Street early in the morning of 16 August, the prisoner was recognized. News of the "trial spread like wild fire and a crowd of fifty to sixty followed the officers to the court house. Once a guilty plea had been entered, the arraignment, held by Justice Berthelote in the Supervisor's room, took only eight minutes."[60]

Immediately, Harris was whisked across the hall to the circuit court. Once there, Judge Golden heard testimony to determine the degree of murder and pass sentence. Following the examination of the eyewitness, William Reau, Golden found the defendant guilty of murder in the first degree. When asked if he had anything to say before sentence was passed, Harris answered, "I'm sorry it's done, that's all." Harris's penalty was solitary confinement and hard labor for life at the Michigan state prison at Marquette.[61]

The entire trial, from start to finish, had taken less than one-half hour. "It was exactly 10:37 when the last word in this awful tragedy was uttered." At eleven o'clock Harris was taken back to Detroit, and that same evening he was aboard the Michigan Central on the way to Marquette. Law enforcement officials were determined that Monroe would not get another chance to lynch its prisoner.

A *Democrat* reporter, who witnessed the proceedings, commented on the change in appearance that had overtaken Harris since his capture on 3 August. On that day "he showed no end of nerve, jollied the officers and in general acted in a care-free manner. On Tuesday [August 16] he showed unmistakable signs of fear, trembling from head to foot, hanging his head in the manner characteristic of the negro culprit, his eyes shifting, uneasily and at times closed tightly, avoiding the glance of the officers and spectators." A writer for the *Record-Commercial* saw something different: "When he [Harris] was told to sit down he did so and looked around the crowded courtroom with a look of absolute indifference and defiance."[62]

While these accounts seem contradictory, both relayed the same message: Harris was the beast-Negro incarnate. The two descriptions told a great deal about the way in which Monroe handled the tragedy. For exactly two weeks, the community had lived at the edge of sanity. The emotional fires had been thoroughly stirred and remained unquenched. Even though the limits of the law had been doggedly pursued and Harris had received the maximum sentence, people remained dissatisfied.

The *Record-Commercial,* in an editorial written after the final act of the drama, commented that "in the truer and juster sense there can be no 'retribution' for such a crime." While some solace was to be gained by knowing that "the darkness of the solitary . . . scanty fare . . . and an iron bed" would be Harris's until death, only God could repay and that would be in the last days.[63] Until then, the citizens of Monroe were left to their own devices to douse their emotions. What many did, including the local reporters, was conjure up images of the archfiend, guilty of so enormous a crime. Any movement, any word uttered by the Negro was interpreted negatively as further evidence of his despicable character. Harris emerged as evil personified, not only in the Monroe press, but in the Detroit and Toledo papers as well.

It should be noted, however, that the white man, Hayes, whose lie had started the chain of events, was viewed as a partner in the crime. "No power, human or divine," the editor of the *Record-Commercial* wrote, "can make from Hays and Harris the instrument for good which the lie of one and the deed of the other swept from an honored career to the deep forgetfulness of the grave."[64]

"Stringing the culprit up" would have given a great measure of satisfaction to many Monroe citizens, and for a while the situation was hanging in the balance. City and county officials, however, acted decisively when circumstances warranted it, and in the end the rule of law prevailed. There was no summary vengeance, and the *Detroit Free Press* congratulated Monroe on progressing through the tragedy without the loss of the prisoner's life.[65] While both Harris and Hayes had received "fair play" at the hands of Monroe, the real heroes in the drama were the city officials. They had not resolved the dilemma through mob action but had concluded the affair by observing the judicial process.

This was the approach taken in the majority of the dealings with black suspects or criminals in Monroe during the first decade and a half of the twentieth century. Of course, the close scrutiny of nonnative Negroes' behavior undoubtedly made it difficult for the Afro-American criminal to ply his trade in the city, but the simple fact was that the protagonists were judged according to the merits of the case and on the basis of their individual characters. In a day when law and order was everyone's concern, criminals, black or white, suffered stern penalties. When it came to the law in Monroe, there were good folk and bad folk, not whites and blacks. Although the beast-Negro social identity perhaps lived in the minds of some of the townspeople, it had relatively little to do with the legal resolution of criminal incidents. In the final analysis, the beast-Negro image was primarily a product of negative passions generated at the time of the incident and had only fleeting reality. Once a case entered the courts, equity and legality prevailed in Monroe. Nothing demonstrated this fact better than the drama involving the death of Sheriff Dull.

Although Monroe adopted some southern attitudes and perceptions about Negroes, it refused to appropriate lynching as part of its racial etiquette. Monroe, in the early years of the twentieth century, had some rather tense moments with Negro criminals, but the ceremony of lynching was not observed, and the community emerged from those experiences with its civilized and "northern" status intact.

The beast-Negro in terms of normative structure can be appropriately regarded as a role prescription for blacks, the opposite side of the child-Negro prescription. Of the two, the child-Negro was by far the stronger stereotype. If the brute lurked behind the child, he only appeared on a few occasions, and then his existence was temporary and evanescent. Even in the Dull drama, where the quintessential fiend appeared and the community lived dangerously, normal patterns of interaction resumed after a period of two weeks. The clown was ever present and was brought to every interracial interaction; the beast, on the other hand, sprang forth only under unusual circumstances. In the end, the Negro-criminal had great notoriety but in fact was rare, and the Negro-as-beast social identity had been created, perhaps unconsciously, like that of the child-Negro, to keep Afro-Americans in their place. In Monroe, as has been demonstrated, the beast had little to do with the administration of justice and as such must be regarded as a mental construct which functioned primarily to illustrate to the majority white populace the Negro's place or, rather, lack of place in the community. As with the child-Negro, the brute, beast, fiend social identity was unreal and reflected a tragic misperception on the part of white Monroe and white America.

NOTES

1. *Monroe Democrat,* 12 July 1900, p. 3, 28 Dec. 1901, p. 2; *Monroe Record,* 10 Mar. 1904, p. 6; *Record-Commercial,* 20 Jan. 1911, p. 1.

2. *Monroe Democrat,* 27 Apr. 1906, p. 7, "School Notes," ibid., 1 Mar. 1900, p. 4; *Monroe Record,* 24 July 1902, p. 5; Mrs. Edmund Childs, interviews with Mrs. George Navarre, n.d., and McMillan sisters, 30 Oct. 1958, in "Recollections of Life in Monroe County, Michigan, 1956–62" (Monroe County Library Board, unpublished),

p. 117, 389. For the incident see "Awful Tragedy," *Monroe Democrat,* 5 Sept. 1902, p. 1; "Unlucky Friday," *Monroe Record,* 4 Sept. 1902, p. 1.

3. The county prosecutor's semiannual reports are in the local press, in January and July, 1900–1915, *passim.*

4. *Monroe Record,* 31 July 1902, p. 4.

5. Afro-Americans were not alone in being carefully scrutinized by Monroe citizens for possible breaches of the law during this time period. Because of their reputations as consummate thieves, gypsies were usually hurried out of the country soon after being sighted. See *Monroe Democrat,* 2 Jan. 1903, p. 5, 10 June 1904, p. 4, 17 June 1904, p. 5; *Record-Commercial,* 9 June 1904, p. 5, 20 Apr. 1905, p. 5; Mrs. Edmund Childs, interview with Mrs. Delia Rowe, 14 Mar. 1958, in "Recollections," p. 237. Chinese were always fair game for apprehension as illegal immigrants. More than a few, who were spotted riding through the city on the interurbans, were removed from the cars and detained in the local jail to await investigation. See *Monroe Record,* 21 Jan. 1904, p. 1, 3 Mar. 1904, pp. 5, 8; *Monroe Democrat,* 22 Jan. 1904, p. 5, 29 Jan. 1904, p. 1, 11 Mar. 1904, p. 5, 23 Feb. 1912, p. 1, 7 Feb. 1913, p. 1, 30 May 1913, p. 7; *Record-Commercial,* 22 Feb. 1912, p. 1, 8 Aug. 1912, p. 7, 15 May 1913, p. 6, 29 May 1913, p. 7, 13 Nov. 1913, p. 7, 21 May 1914, p. 1. Finally, tramps, who posed an ubiquitous problem for most American communities, were closely watched as they made their trips through Monroe.

6. *Monroe Democrat,* 28 July 1905, p. 7, 4 Aug. 1905, p. 7; *Record-Commercial,* 3 Aug. 1905, pp. 4–5.

7. *Record-Commercial,* 3 Aug. 1905, pp. 4–5; *Monroe Democrat,* 4 Aug. 1905, p. 7.

8. *Monroe Record,* 24 Sept. 1903, p. 5; *Monroe Democrat,* 25 Sept. 1903, p. 5.

9. *Monroe Democrat,* 1 Aug. 1913, p. 7.

10. *Monroe Democrat,* 29 Aug. 1901, p. 5; *Monroe Record,* 29 Aug. 1901, p. 1.

11. *Record-Commercial,* 2 July 1908, p. 7, 9 July 1908, p. 7.

12. *Monroe Democrat,* 31 July 1908, p. 7.

13. *Record-Commercial,* 26 Nov. 1908, p. 12.

14. *Monroe Record,* 30 May 1901, p. 5.

15. *Monroe Record,* 13 June 1901, p. 4; *Monroe Democrat,* 20 June 1901, p. 5.

16. "Shore Line Hold-up," *Monroe Record,* 27 June 1901, p. 1; "A Dangerous Man," *Monroe Democrat,* 27 June 1901, p. 1.

17. *Monroe Record,* 29 Aug. 1901, p. 4.

18. "Strike!" *Monroe Record,* 15 Aug. 1901, p. 1; *Monroe Democrat,* 15 Aug. 1901, p. 8. Black women, who accepted "free transportation" to the North in return for jobs, often found themselves victims of similar schemes. See Kenneth L. Kusmer, *A Ghetto Takes Shape: Black Cleveland, 1870–1930* (Urbana: University of Illinois Press, 1976), p. 258.

19. *Monroe Record,* 12 Sept. 1901, p. 5; *Monroe Democrat,* 3 Oct. 1901, p. 5.

20. "Stabbing Affray," *Monroe Democrat,* 6 June 1901, p. 1.

21. "Was Stokes Justified?" *Monroe Record,* 6 June 1901, p. 1.

22. Ibid., and "Stabbing Affray," *Monroe Democrat,* 6 June 1901, p. 1.

23. "Stabbing Affray in Monroe," *Detroit Advocate,* 8 June 1901, p. 1.

24. *Monroe Record,* 13 June 1901, p. 4.

25. *Record-Commercial,* 26 May 1910, p. 6; *Monroe Record,* 30 Jan. 1902, p. 5, 6 Feb. 1902, p. 1.

26. *Monroe Democrat,* 11 Aug. 1898, p. 1, 25 July 1902, p. 5; *Record-Commercial,* 2 June 1904, p. 5.

27. *Monroe Record,* 29 Jan. 1903, p. 1.

28. *Monroe Democrat,* 14 June 1907, p. 7.

29. *Record-Commercial,* 5 Dec. 1912, p. 7.

30. *Monroe Democrat,* 14 July 1898, p. 1, 28 July 1898, p. 1, 23 July 1903, p. 5, 23 Aug. 1912, p. 7, 30 Aug. 1912, p. 7, 15 Nov. 1912, p. 7, 12 Sept. 1913, p. 7; *Monroe Record,* 23 July 1903, p. 5, 10 Dec. 1903, p. 5; *Record-Commercial,* 22 Aug. 1912, pp. 1, 7, 24 Oct. 1912, p. 7, 31 Oct. 1912, p. 5, 14 Nov. 1912, p. 7, 15 May 1913, p. 7, 11 Sept. 1913, p. 6, 19 Nov. 1914, pp. 1, 7; *Monroe Bulletin,* 19 Nov. 1914, p. 1.

31. *Record-Commercial,* 7 Sept. 1905, p. 5; "John Robbins or 'Black John' Confesses to Stealing in Monroe and Lenawee Counties," *Record-Commercial,* 18 July 1912, p. 1; *Monroe Democrat,* 19 July 1912, p. 7.

32. In an 1891 affair involving a felony and the subsequent shooting deaths of two Negro prisoners in the local jail, *Democrat* headlines related not only the news but revealed something about Monroe's racist attitude. They read: "Two Dead Prisoners: They Attack the Turnkey and Are Surprised at the Warm Reception Given Them. His Pistol is Responsive to the Touch, and Two Coons Are Converted into Cloud Pushers." See *Monroe Democrat,* 30 Apr. 1891, p. 1, and Mrs. Childs's interview with Mr. Albert A. Heck, 18 Dec. 1956, in "Recollections of Life in Monroe County, Michigan," 1956–62, p. 226. Although circumstances surrounding the event

suggested that the jailer, Albert Tedder, was not without blame, he was hailed as a hero. The *Democrat* reported that he had received "stacks of letters from various papers asking for his picture." The two victims, on the other hand, were cast as beast-Negroes. One Afro-American had purportedly considered killing one of the town's finest policemen, and the other was a known wife-deserter, bigamist, and procurer.

33. *Record-Commercial,* 4 Aug. 1910, p. 1.

34. "Sheriff Dull Slain," *Monroe Democrat,* 5 Aug. 1910, p. 1; "All Monroe County Mourns . . . ," *Record-Commercial,* 4 Aug. 1910, pp. 1, 6; "Posses Seek Negro Who Shot Dull," *Toledo Blade,* 2 Aug. 1910, pp. 1, 3.

35. *Monroe Democrat,* 5 Aug. 1910, p. 1.

36. Ibid.

37. Interview with Arthur Lesow in his home at 605 Humphrey Street, 30 Dec. 1976. Until he discovered the reason for the weapons, Mr. Lesow stated he was quite bewildered regarding "what kind of town" he had arrived in.

38. "Sheriff Dull Slain," *Monroe Democrat,* 5 Aug. 1910, p. 1.

39. "Posses Seek Negro Who Shot Dull," *Toledo Blade,* 2 Aug. 1910, p. 1.

40. "Sheriff Dull Slain," *Monroe Democrat,* 5 Aug. 1910, p. 1.

41. "All County Mourns," *Record-Commercial,* 4 Aug. 1910, p. 6; "Posses Seek Negro Who Shot Dull," *Toledo Blade,* 2 Aug. 1910, p. 1.

42. "All County Mourns," *Record-Commercial,* 4 Aug. 1910, p. 6.

43. "Sheriff Dies, Posse Shoots Second Negro," *Toledo Blade,* 3 Aug. 1910, p. 3; "All County Mourns," *Record-Commercial,* 4 Aug. 1910, p. 6.

44. *Record-Commercial,* 4 Aug. 1910, p. 6.

45. "Sheriff Dies, Posse Shoots Second Negro," *Toledo Blade,* 3 Aug. 1910, p. 6; "Unlucky Friday," *Monroe Record,* 4 Sept. 1902, p. 1.

46. "Harris Admits Murder," *Monroe Democrat,* 12 Aug. 1910, p. 1. This drama says a great deal about the American value system. Obviously, had it not been for the reputed theft, the criminal law machinery would not have been set in motion and the train of events that followed, including Dull's death, would not have occurred. Significantly, no one questioned the wisdom of a legal code which contained this property dimension.

47. "The Capture," *Record-Commercial,* 11 Aug. 1910, p. 1.

48. "Sheriff Dies," *Toledo Blade,* 3 Aug. 1910, p. 1; "All Monroe County Mourns," *Record-Commercial,* 4 Aug. 1910, p. 6.

49. "Sheriff Dull Slain," *Monroe Democrat,* 5 Aug. 1910, p. 1.

50. "The Capture," *Record-Commercial,* 11 Aug. 1910, p. 1.

51. "Harris Admits Murder," *Monroe Democrat,* 12 Aug. 1910, p. 1.

52. "The Ceremonies," *Record-Commercial,* 11 Aug. 1910, p. 11. In the spring, President Taft arrived in Monroe to take part in the dedication proceedings for a Custer equestrian statue. Monroe attracted national attention at the time, and it was the city's "biggest day."

53. "Harris Admits Murder," *Monroe Democrat,* 12 Aug. 1910, p. 1; "Negro Calmly Tells How He Shot the Sheriff," *Detroit News,* 6 Aug. 1910, p. 2.

54. "Negro Tells of Killing Sheriff," *Toledo Blade,* 6 Aug. 1910, p. 1; "The Confession," *Record-Commercial,* 11 Aug. 1910, p. 1. Jenny Toll Sawyer, a leading citizen in Monroe at the time, noted the "lynching" mood of the crowd in her diary entry of 5 Aug. 1910. See Jenny Toll Sawyer diaries, Bentley Library, Michigan Historical Collections, Ann Arbor, Mich.

55. "Negro Admits Murder," *Detroit Free Press,* 6 Aug. 1910, p. 1.

56. "The Confession," *Record-Commercial,* 11 Aug. 1910, p. 1.

57. Ibid.

58. "Harris Admits Murder," *Monroe Democrat,* 12 Aug. 1910, p. 1.

59. "Negro Admits Murder," *Detroit Free Press,* 6 Aug. 1910, p. 1; "Negro Calmly Tells How He Shot Sheriff," *Detroit News,* 6 Aug. 1910, p. 1.

60. "Sent Up to Marquette," *Monroe Democrat,* 19 Aug. 1910, p. 1; "Murderer Harris Sentenced," *Record-Commercial,* 18 Aug. 1910, p. 1.

61. *Record-Commercial,* 18 Aug. 1910, p. 1.

62. "Sent Up to Marquette," *Monroe Democrat,* 19 Aug. 1910, p. 1; "Murderer Harris Sentenced," *Record-Commercial,* 18 Aug. 1910, p. 1.

63. "Retribution," *Record-Commercial,* 18 Aug. 1910, p. 6.

64. Ibid.

65. As quoted in "Lynching Never Pays," *Record-Commercial,* 11 Aug. 1910, p. 6.

4

Home Grown: The Personal and Ego Identities of Monroe Negroes, 1900–1915

> They say that a woman of this city left her husband just recently because he refused to treat her white; and as a result of her action her husband is so mad that he is black in the face.
>
> *Monroe Democrat,* 1 Mar. 1902

> One Little Nigger living all alone;
> He got married and then there was none.
> One Little Nigger, with his dear little wife,
> Lived many years a happy life.
>
> *Ten Little Niggers,*
> Bo-Peep Series, (c. 1890)

That the social identities of the child-Negro and the beast-Negro were present in the minds of Monroe's white inhabitants during the Progressive Era is apparent from the foregoing analysis. The overwhelming demands placed on Negroes to act as the clown, buffoon, and fool have often been noted. James Weldon Johnson, for example, grasped the central reality of the "happy-go-lucky, laughing, shuffling, banjo-picking" stereotype by pointing out that blacks in serious roles were seen by the white public as a "sort of absurd caricature of 'white civilization.'"[1] Not only were foolish roles demanded, but any other traditional American role which blacks elected to play was seen by most Americans as comic opera. The truth was that the Afro-American could not escape these role prescriptions in his interactions with whites. As such, Negroes were not allowed to regard themselves as bona fide Americans, indeed not even as weak imitations. That right was reserved for naturalized citizens. Instead, they were forced to lead a schizophrenic-like existence, holding the same values and abiding by the same norms as white America while being required to live with the knowledge that white America regarded them as essentially un-American. If Americans were hardworking, Negroes were lazy; if whites were inventive, blacks were stupid; if Caucasians were law-abiding, blacks were criminals; the list could go on. White America measured its virtues and successes against the failures of the black population. No matter how far one fell on the socioeconomic scale, there was a saving grace to being white: one could not sink lower than a "nigger."

The child-Negro sterotype, in particular, placed Afro-Americans in an impossible role conflict for which there was no solution. The very attributes of character which the white public demanded from blacks were antithetical to success. Negro Americans were prevented from succeeding by a social identity invented by white America and then told that success, in this land of opportunity, was guaranteed to all with the proper character. Reality was turned on its head: blacks were required to be failures and then held responsible for their lack of success.

The essential problem in ascertaining the personal ego identities for selected Monroe blacks is to determine how greatly the onerous role prescriptions inherent in the Negro's social identities affected their lives. Did the fact that Monroe's Negroes were personally known in the community mean that they were exempt from the child-Negro and beast-Negro social identities? If so, in which ways? Were Monroe's blacks permitted or encouraged to be successes, i.e. Americans? If so, in which ways? Finally, how did Monroe's hometown Afro-Americans regard their position and existence in the community?

These questions can be answered in part by compiling, evaluating, perusing, and making inferences from data on some of Monroe's black individuals which appeared in newspaper items, city directories, family bibles, autograph books, library holdings, probate court proceedings, high school publications, and the memories of Monroe citizens. Since biography is the vehicle of communication, both the personal and ego identities of selected Monroe Negroes will be discussed, when possible, at the same time.

In evaluating the existing material, one fact stands out: each Negro had his or her own unique personal identity. To some degree, that identity was dependent upon the mask which was chosen for public display. Enough information exists about several individuals in the kinship networks analyzed in Chapter 1 to make some substantive statements regarding "who they were" to the larger community.

Some blacks opted for an identity which matched the child-Negro, and "ole-time darkey" tag. The description of Stephen Smith in a "mortuary" in a 1904 issue of the *Monroe Democrat* fitted "Sambo" perfectly.

> Dad Smith was slow minded, easy going, good natured and accommodating, he was engaged at various times as handy man and errand boy in every house . . . being welcome visitor everywhere. The doors of every home being open to him. Yet he was never known to sleep in a bed; in winter he would wrap himself in a few quilts and curl up near a stove and in the milder season he spent his evenings in barns or in the open air. Unlike most of his race, he did not vote the Republican ticket and often referred to himself as a "Democrat nigger." His friends whom he had served to the best of his ability during his life time did not forget him when he died, for they made up a purse and gave him a Christian burial. . . .[2]

Services for Smith, who "always had a smile and a cheery word for everyone," were held at St. Mary's Church, and his pallbearers were white.[3] The seventy-eight-year-old "boy" had gained the acceptance of the white community by smiling his way through a life of adversity and accepting his lowly status. His rewards for playing the child-Negro were the fulsome praise in the local press at his demise and a decent Christian burial.

Monroe citizens also had good words for "Aunt" Fannie Johnson. Ellen Frances Johnson and her husband, Alexander, had both been born slaves in Virginia and had on their migration northward in the early 1880s decided to make Monroe their home. In their forties and fifties when they settled in the city, the couple had no children while Monroe citizens.[4] Known as "top-notch" cooks and caterers, there was hardly a respectable home in Monroe during the late nineteenth century which did not receive their services. Before he reached an age when he was too ill to work, Mr. Johnson had labored at odd jobs and served as head cook for the Monroe Light Guard during their encampments. Apparently, their joint efforts met with some financial success because the couple owned a home in the First Ward at 114 West Fifth Street. Unfortunately, this early good fortune did not provide financial security for Mrs. Johnson in her declining years. After Alex "passed on," the aged Fannie continued to eke out an existence by "taking in washings" and cooking for many of the Monroe families for almost another two decades.[5]

Mrs. Johnson's personal identity was the subject of a feature article in a 1913 issue of the *Detroit Saturday Night*, a popular Detroit newspaper. John M. Bulkley, author of the most recent Monroe County history, and a local citizen who had spent no small proportion of his life writing articles for magazines and newspapers, penned "The Ante-Bellum Auntie Who Is Monroe's Pride" for the Detroit paper. Traditional southern literary themes found an able spokesman in Bulkley. In this essay, Fannie exemplified all those virtues that white America and Monroe preferred in Negroes. She was, in Bulkley's words, "Monroe's genuine befo-de-wah auntie." He wrote that "Aunt Fannie is a type of the best of that colored race that lived in slavery days, feeling perhaps, the unseen fetters of bondage as lightly as might be, a favored house servant in a good family. . . ." It was while a slave that Fannie acquired the "subtle art of cookery in all its delicate shades of ingenious combination, as well as the clever skill of laundering." These skills, "which she took up with her love for her old 'missus,'" had remained with her through the years. "Notwithstanding her advanced age and the sometimes remorseless rheumatism the 'quality folks' of old Monroe in this as well as in past generations have come firmly into the faith that unless Aunt Fannie at least directs and oversees and waves the magic wand in her own dexterous hand, in the process of 'fixing' for a to-be-given function—it is all 'off.'"

In reflecting on her "Ole Virginny" days, Fannie was quoted by Bulkley as saying, "Yes, dey was might good to me . . . they was suttingly good Christian folk, and I stuck to 'em when the 'mancipation days come, and they paid me wages—mighty small wages dey was, too, along at fust; but dey was poor, and what could the poor white folks do? Hit was only the slaves what was gettin' their freedom."

According to Bulkley, the ex-slave regarded the Civil War as the "most uncivilest wah I ever see or heard of." As for the South, she loved it still, but Monroe had "been a mos' pleasant home" for over thirty years. The minstrel image reached its purest form in the article when Fannie, in comparing the relative merits of both regions, was quoted as saying: "Watermelons? . . . I actchally never see no watermelons any more."[6]

Memories of Walter Fragner, a lifetime resident of Monroe, reaffirmed Bulkley's evaluation of Mrs. Johnson's personal identity. Fragner recalled how the Armitages, one of Monroe's "400" families, would send their horse and carriage after Fannie when they were having a party. Universally acclaimed as a "wonderful cook," Mrs. Johnson was "especially famous for her mince pies." How deeply cultural stereotypes had fastened onto the minds of the Monroe citizenry is perhaps indicated by Mr. Fragner's revealing description of the town's culinary expert: "She was very very fat and wore a red bandana tied around her head, just like Aunt Jemima of pancake fame today."[7]

With Mrs. Johnson, the qualities most appreciated were an unquestioning subservience, a feeling of empathy for the white people's burdens, and a thankfulness for the small pittance thrown her way. Her personal identity, like that of Smith's, mirrored the child-Negro.

Mrs. Johnson's demise in 1923 at the advanced age of ninety illustrates the foremost difficulty with personal identities: they are by nature fleeting. When people who know someone leave or die, an individual's personal identity vanishes. By 1923 most of the old residents who valued Mrs. Johnson and her community function were gone. Fannie had out-stayed and out-lived her contemporaries. In her obituary, the press paid no encomiums but simply stated "Old Resident Dies."[8] Her comfort at the time of her death was another native Monroe Negro, James Bromley, in whose home she died. After forty years of life in Monroe, Fannie expired, leaving no immediate relatives and in obscurity.

Monroe's Negro population pursued different strategies in establishing personal identities. The Foster family members, for example, appear to have denied any Afro-American connection and lived their lives within the majority context. Oral tradition states that the family "went around with white people."[9] The Fosters had an ambiguous racial status in the community. As indicated in Chapter 1, the family had different racial designations in different censuses. In 1880 the Fosters were enumerated by federal census marshals as black, in 1900 as white, and in 1910 as mulatto. Grace Foster Schmitt, the youngest daughter, died "white" in 1954. The first Monroe Fosters, James and Elizabeth, migrated from Canada with their children in 1879. Apparently light-complexioned, they were born of mixed parentage in Ontario. For reasons not entirely clear, each of their fathers expatriated from the United States to Canada during the abolitionist years. The 1861 Canada West Census returns indicate they were mulattoes. Elizabeth's father, William H. Butler, was a native of South Carolina, and James Foster's father, Levi, was originally from Ohio. Ann Calvert Butler, the mother of Elizabeth, was English and white, and James's mother, Elizabeth Waring Foster, a native of Virginia, was at least three-quarters Caucasian.[10]

The reasons for their selection of Monroe as a permanent home are not known. It does seem that Levi Foster, a leading black figure in Amherstburg, was not totally pleased with life in Canada. Between 1866 and 1873 he petitioned to end the separate school department for coloreds in the community. Each time the trustees turned back his request. Life was filled with obstacles for Negroes in Ontario, and James and Elizabeth Foster must have had those limitations in mind when they opted to migrate to Michigan.[11]

For years, the Foster family counted itself among the affluent in Amherstburg. James's father, Levi, operated a successful stage line, hotel, and livery business from 1848 to 1873. In 1861 his property included livestock valued at $1,000, seven carriages worth $7,000, and forty-four acres of land. When they arrived in Monroe in 1879, James and Elizabeth had the cash and the "know-how" to thrive in their new home. Soon after reaching the city, the Fosters purchased a home and a livery stable business. The enterprise, located at 22 Washington Street, was operated at a profit until 1893, when James retired and sold the business to J. D. Campbell. The family then bought a homestead of twenty-three acres on the outskirts of the city and ran a successful fruit and dairy farm for several years.[12]

An affluent family by all standards of the age, they resided during their tenure in Monroe in the Third and Second wards, in two of the community's better homes. The first dwelling at Third and Scott streets was sold to the Trinity Lutheran Church as a parsonage in 1884 for $1,900. In the next year, the family moved into a large and newly constructed Italianate home on Sixth Street, where they lived until 1894, when they moved to their farm in Monroetown. For the next six years Foster owned and operated the "Willow Bend Dairy" at that location. The Fosters also owned large portions of real estate in the city and county. At the time of his death in 1900, James Foster's estate was valued at over $10,000. This included real estate assessed at $5,500 and bank savings and credits totaling $4,530.82.[13]

In a time when few young people were allowed to pursue an education beyond the sixth grade, Elizabeth and James Foster saw each of their five children who survived into maturity, four daughters and one son, attend Monroe High School. Ella finished a two-year course, and Myrtle and Grace completed four years. At least two of the Foster girls, Mae and Grace, studied piano at Gale's Monroe School of Music. In October 1899, the family financially backed Ella in a candy store enterprise in the city of Monroe. Soon joined by her younger sister Mae in the endeavor, Ella Foster's "Sugar Bowl" offered ice cream and candies and boasted the first hot soda fountain in Monroe. Apparently the business was not a great success because in November 1902 the sisters moved their stock and store to Ann Arbor.[14]

Not only were the Fosters full participants in Monroe's economic life, they were active in a great range of institutions within the city. While he never ran for nor held political office, James was known as a good Republican who could be counted on for support when needed. When leaders in the community solicited donations for victims of a forest fire in the Saginaw Bay region in 1881, J. W. Foster was counted for a five-dollar contribution. City school officials also found the Fosters competent. Both Myrtle and Ella Foster were voted as speakers for their high school graduation exercises in 1889 and 1893 respectively. Myrtle was a successful part-time teacher for several years in the city's school system.[15]

The Minutes and Records of the First Baptist Church of Monroe best depict the level of acceptance the Fosters enjoyed from the white community. Their names figure prominently in these manuscripts. A close perusal of the minutes reveals that the Fosters were pillars in this Caucasian institution. During the last two decades of the nineteenth century, James W. Foster served continuously in some leadership capacity. Several times he was elected to the positions of deacon, treasurer, and trustee. When the flock was without an ordained leader, it was Foster who chaired the annual meeting. The daughters took leading roles in the Baptist Young People's Union. Meetings of that group and the ladies' aid society were often held in the Foster home. Each of the Foster children was baptized in the Baptist church.[16]

On more than one occasion conflicts arose in the congregation involving the Fosters and someone white. Each time the Fosters prevailed. When a move was made to exclude Brother D. E. Boyce from fellowship in 1881, one of the charges proven against him was his "abusive language and profanity to bro-Foster." In the 1890s the Fosters were at odds with the pastor, Rev. J. A. Davies, who accused Foster's eldest daughter, Myrtle, of writing an anonymous and defamatory letter to him. A special meeting of the trustees was called to look into the difficulty. On 1 May 1890, Davies and his witness, Eunice Bentley, and Myrtle Foster were summoned to the classroom of the church to give testimony. After a warm discussion, it was determined that nothing could be proven, and Davies asked that the matter be dropped "on the condition that the Foster family would walk with the church, and subscribe then and there for the Pastor's salary as they ever did." Both parties accepted these conditions and agreed to never bring up the subject again. It would seem that a great amount of bitterness resulted from this situation and things did not end there. Rather, several months later, the congregation dismissed Reverend Davies, and Eunice Bentley ceased playing an active role in the church.[17]

James Foster was active and prominent in the institution until his death in 1900. On the day he died, A. W. Gale, the church's secretary, eulogized him in the minutes. He wrote that "a deep sorrow and gloom has fallen upon our little band caused by the death of her beloved brother and deacon, J. W. Foster, which occurred suddenly July 11th. He has been a faithful leader and burden bearer, a wise counsellor, and one who always had the interest of the master's course deep at heart." Six months later, a note in the *Democrat* indicated that the church still felt his loss "most keenly."[18] Foster's wife and children remained loyal to the Baptists for the first two decades of the new century. It would seem that the Fosters experienced no racial barriers in their quest for Christian involvement.

So well recognized were the personal identities of the Foster family that they were granted city library privileges after moving outside of Monroe. City law enforcement officers responded to a call from Foster in 1899 and arrested eight white men, even though the family no longer lived inside municipal boundaries. So closely were the Fosters identified with Monroe's community life that the obituaries for James Foster in July 1900 in both the *Record* and the *Democrat* neglected to follow the custom of mentioning that the deceased was "colored." Moreover, when the widow Foster appeared in John Bulkley's *History of Monroe County Michigan* as one of the area's prominent citizens, more than a decade later, no reference was made to color.[19]

The degree to which the family had integrated the normative and institutional structure of Monroe and gained the acceptance of the city's people was no more clearly illustrated than in the events surrounding the death of a local white man who had been fatally wounded by Jay Foster, the couple's only son. On 22 June 1901, only a few hours after being bailed out of prison, William "Red" Breckenfelder was shot and killed while attempting to burglarize the Foster home. The *Monroe Record* captured the city's mood regarding the affair when it declared that "the dead crook was considered a tough proposition by the local police and if anything they were glad to know that he is out of the way. That they were not alone in this was evinced when the news became generally known Sunday morning, the universal opinion being that while not intentional the shooting was a good thing for the community." On the other hand, the *Record* went on to state, the Fosters were "among the city's most highly respected people."

As was customary with any fatality, a coroner's inquest was held to determine if there was any culpability on anyone's part. Significantly, the only testimony heard at the inquest came from the Fosters, and their explanation of what had happened went completely unchallenged. In the end Jay was completely exonerated "both in the eyes of the public and the jury," and sympathies were entirely with the Fosters. Throughout the entire affair there was no race baiting, no cries for lynch law, and the beast-Negro image played no part whatsoever in the drama. In fact, accounts of the tragedy in the local press included no mention of the fact that the Fosters were a colored family. The Fosters' special status and relatively high social position in Monroe, combined with the early demise of a perennial troublemaker, meant that most citizens accepted the outcome of the incident.[20]

For all practical considerations, by acting as white the Foster family had moved toward erasing its Negro stigma in the Monroe community. Although citizens continued to view their less-than-white complexions with some anxiety, for the most part, the Fosters' economic successes counted for more. Their relatively high position would have important consequences for Grace, the youngest of the Fosters' daughters and the only one of the children to remain in the Monroe vicinity. Caring for her mother, Elizabeth, until her death in 1921, Grace married a German immigrant, Carl Schmitt, who had worked on the Foster farm.[21] The descendants of that union still live in Monroe County today and pass completely for white.

If Mrs. Johnson and "Dad" Smith seemed to embrace the child-Negro, and the Foster family members were able to reject not only the stereotype but their black identity, James Bromley adopted a different strategy. Of all the black families who lived in Monroe during the Progressive Era, the Bromleys, about whom the most is known, are by far the most interesting. Between 1862 and 1928, four generations of the Bromley family lived in Monroe. The first Bromley to settle in the city was a thirty-two-year-old escaped slave who had fled his master's plantation near Florence, Alabama, in 1862.[22] Heading northward, Aaron Bromley found his way to Monroe County and settled in the city soon afterwards. Aaron worked for the next two years as a day laborer in Monroe.

Not long after the North opened its ranks to colored troops for service in the Civil War, Bromley was in uniform. On 29 August

1864 he enlisted as a substitute for John L. C. Godfroy of Monroe's Second Ward. After signing up for a one-year term, he was mustered into the First Michigan Colored Infantry in Detoit. Assigned to Company C of the 102d U.S. Colored Troops, Bromley joined his unit at Beaufort, South Carolina, on 11 October 1864. While there he contracted erysipelas and suffered from chronic rheumatism and general debility. It would seem that he saw no action but spent most of the time in the camp hospital. He was discharged by a surgeon's certificate of disability on 17 May 1864, several months before his enlistment was to expire.[23]

Undoubtedly, a major reason why Bromley decided to return to Monroe after the war was to renew his acquaintance with Ellen Cox. Ellen, also of Afro-American descent, had moved during the Civil War to Monroe from Bardstown, Kentucky, with her mother, a sister, three brothers, an aunt, an uncle, and five cousins. After a courtship of more than one year, Aaron and Ellen were wed on 5 July 1866.[24] Following their marriage, some of Ellen's family continued to live for several years with the couple at the Cass Street address. Aaron worked as a day laborer and Ellen "kept house." Their joint efforts met with some success since data from the U.S. census *Population Schedules* for 1870 show the family with real estate holdings valued at $800 and a personal estate estimated at $250.[25]

Much of what has survived about Aaron Bromley involves his Civil War experience. His pension records show that the illness he suffered in the service continued to plague him in later life. The erysipelas led to complete blindness in his left eye, and the rheumatism resulted in an almost useless right foot. During the last decade and a half of his life he hobbled about with a cane and was unable to do any manual labor. Bromley applied at various times for an invalid pension. The general affidavits signed by five white Monroe citizens between 1889 and 1896 are important testimony to the strength of his personal identity in the community. In effect, they all testified that Bromley "was all right when he received his discharge" in their efforts to gain the old man some compensation. His experience with the local Joseph R. Smith GAR Post was less satisfying. In 1891, nine years after the organization's inception, he applied for membership. The committee examining Aaron Bromley reported favorably, but when the ballot was passed it was found not clear and he was rejected.[26]

Despite what must have been for them many disappointments, the couple did their best to ensure that their children would become part of the community. During their marriage, Aaron and

Ellen had seven children, five of whom died in infancy.[27] Two sons, James born in 1867 and Noel in 1871, survived into adulthood. Realizing the importance of education, the Bromleys strove to provide their sons with the best schooling that Monroe could offer. James, in partricular, was a more than adequate scholar and was often commended for his efforts. While James and Noel did not graduate from the city's secondary institution, it is certain that they did attend Monroe Union School. Apparently each was fully accepted into the school's activities. James's high school autograph book showed that he played the tuba in the band and was a standout on the ball diamond.[28] Contemporaries of James and Noel, Kathy Nims and W. C. Sterling, Jr., remembered that both boys "were pretty much accepted as everyone else." Both also recollected that James and Noel were especially close friends of Horace Conant, son of one of the more prominent couples in Monroe. Sterling reminisced that "Horace Conant once entertained them along with some other friends at a breakfast in his home."[29]

After spending their entire adult lives in Monroe, both Aaron and Ellen Bromley died in the first decade of the twentieth century. Ellen died of a stroke at the age of sixty-three on 8 August 1903. Her memorial services were held at St. Paul's Methodist Church. The *Democrat* observed that this was the first death in a colored family in years in Monroe.[30] Seventy-six-year-old Aaron, "the oldest of Monroe's few colored citizens," followed her to the grave almost exactly three years later. At the time of his death, the *Record-Commercial* noted that "Mr. Bromley was a familiar character in the city and was a honorable, faithful employee." A younger contemporary, Charles Verhoeven, Sr., remembered that Aaron "looked just like Uncle Tom and was a fine old man."[31]

Not much is known about Noel's life. Apparently only his formative years were spent in Monroe. In 1903, when Mrs. Bromley died, he was living in Winnipeg, Canada, and three years later when Aaron died, he was stationed at the U.S. Barracks in Columbus, Ohio. In 1913, word came from Chicago that Noel had died in the Marine hospital.[32]

On the other hand, James Bromley, the focal personality in this chapter, remained in Monroe his entire lifetime and raised his family in the city. The six-foot-four or more "big" Jim made an indelible impression on all those around him. Known and respected as an educated man, he was "always reciting a poem." Many years after he died, Monroe citizens still remembered him. Kathy Nims, a life-long Monroe resident, summed up Jim's personal identity in the city and Monroe's opinion of him when she recalled that he was big, very black-skinned, handsome, talented, athletic, and nice-mannered. Others remembered him as a friendly, talkative, and refined individual who was good with his hands.[33] The most salient characteristic of James's personality was that throughout his life he remained his own person. No racial stereotypes or conventions barred his way, and on more than one occasion he violated the racial mores held by Monroe's white citizens. James Bromley was not reluctant to test the viability of his personal identity against the social identities held for Negroes by the white community.

Jim's most significant transgression was his mate selection. On 17 December 1888, he and attractive, white, Catholic, and French Elizabeth Willetts were joined in matrimony in the Baptist church.[34] Local tradition has it that Jim first met Libbie while working as a stable boy for her father, Frank, who operated a livery business on Monroe Street. While the former is likely, it is certain that the two were well acquainted in high school. Each signed the other's autograph book in 1886, Libbie simply penning her name and Jim writing "to the bitter end" after his signature.[35]

Local oral tradition speculates that she either married him to spite her parents because they had frustrated earlier marriage plans with a white boy or she "had to." While nothing is known about an earlier involvement with someone else, it is certain that Libbie was pregnant when she married Jim. She gave birth to the couple's first child, Leo Noah, on 8 February 1889, less than two months after the wedding.[36]

A valuable collection of oral history, "Recollections of Life in Monroe County, Michigan, 1956–62," contains more than a few references to the union. "Up to that time, the Bromleys had been regarded as highly respectable citizens." The marriage created a great furor in the community. "No one knew why she married him." Charles Verhoeven, Sr., remembered that "after the wedding, Jim was almost afraid to go out on the streets for fear he'd be mobbed. But things quieted down and they became accepted by their fellow townspeople." Mrs. Ben Dunlap recalled that "for a long time her family disowned her, but eventually took her back." Despite the fact that the marriage lasted until James died in 1927, and Libbie never remarried, Monroe never approved of the wedlock and Mrs. Bromley's choice was viewed as a "big mistake."[37]

While the marriage lasted, it was apparently strife-ridden, and Mrs. Bromley suffered from periodic illnesses. From time to time the local press commented gleefully and insensitively on this aspect of the union. In a statement that could only have referred to Jim and Libbie, a 1902 issue of the *Democrat* announced that "they

Elizabeth Willetts's marriage to James Bromley in 1888 caused a furor. This picture of Mrs. Bromley was probably taken in the 1930s (courtesy Monroe County Historical Museum)

debtors.

EMANCIPATION DAY BEING OBSERVED

Colored people from Michigan, Ohio, Indiana and Canada, opened a three day celebration in honor of Emancipation day at Peltier's woods, one mile south of Monroe today.

It is expected that during the three days celebration that at least 8,000 persons will be present.

James Bromley, Monroe, who has charge of the affair, stated this morning that he received a telegram from Toronto, Ontario, that a carload of people were coming from that city and are expected to reach here this evening.

Johnson's band, of Detroit, will furnish the music. D. McKinney, attorney, Detroit; Charles Cottrell, Toledo, ex-counsel to Honolulu, and Dr. Robinson, of Detroit, were on the program today to deliver addresses.

One of the features for Wednesday evening will be the breakfast dance, which will start at 12 o'clock midnight Wednesday night and continue until six o'clock on Thursday morning.

On Thursday a baseball game will be played.

Many Monroe people are expected to attend the gathering.

VOTING HEAVY IN THREE STATES

James W. Bromley organized the Emancipation Day celebration in 1922 (*Monroe Evening News*, 3 Aug. 1922, courtesy *Monroe Evening News*)

The former Bromley home at 610 Cass Street was in a quiet, respected neighborhood (courtesy Dennis Au)

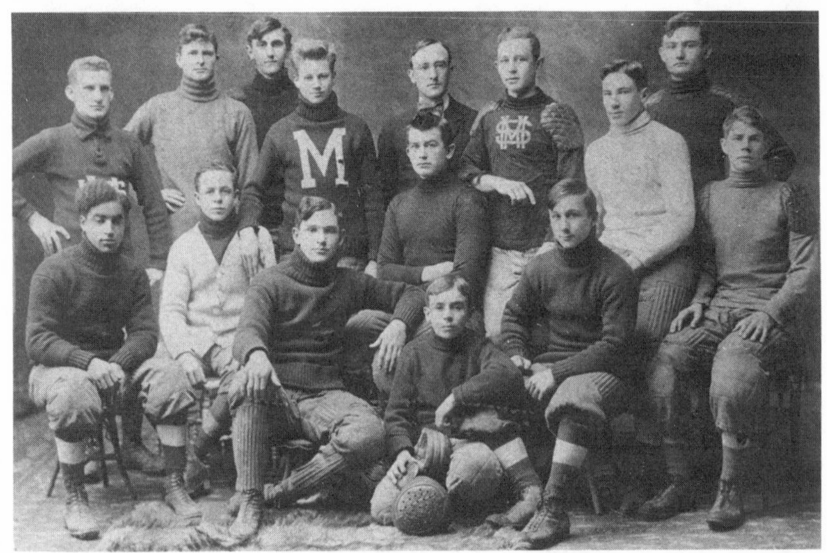

Alcayde Bromley was a star halfback on the 1909 Monroe High School football team (courtesy Mary Kay Kosa)

The 1907 Monroe Orioles were the pride of the community. Alcayde Bromley, although still in high school, was the starting pitcher (courtesy Monroe County Library System)

Monroe High School graduation, 1910. Alcayde Bromley, seated at the far left, did not participate fully in the ceremonies (courtesy Monroe County Historical Museum)

In 1921, Alcayde Bromley was hired by Monroe High School as a part-time orchestra director (courtesy Monroe County Historical Museum)

Alcayde Bromley and his first wife, Florence Woodson, in 1913 (*Brighten the Corner*, 1977, courtesy Monroe County Fine Arts Council)

say that a woman of this city left her husband recently because he refused to treat her white; and as a result of her action the husband is so mad that he is black in the face."[38] According to local tradition, Mrs. Bromley suffered beatings from her husband on more than one occasion. Mrs. Dunlap, who lived near the Bromleys as a child, remembered an incident when Libbie came running to her home "out of her mind," screaming, "Hide me from that big black nigger!" After a brief period of time, Libbie returned to Jim and on the whole, according to Mrs. Dunlap, they were a happy couple.[39]

Indications that Libbie was paying a physical price for the strife appeared in 1915 when she entered St. Vincent's hospital for a "very serious operation."[40] Two years later she had a breakdown. While the couple apparently cared a great deal for one another, an action initiated in 1917 by James and the couple's son, Alcayde, in the Monroe Probate Court proved that the marriage continued to be unhappy and difficult for most of its duration. Proceedings to declare Libbie legally insane had been started by James and Alcayde because Mrs. Bromley had been suffering from delusions of persecution and bodily harm and had threatened to take her life. The testimony given by James, Alcayde, Dr. Charles Southworth, and Dr. William Acker, together with a positive result on a Wasserman test, sealed the verdict. Both physicians agreed that Elizabeth was suffering from paresis, an advanced stage of syphilis. On 14 May 1917 Libbie was declared legally insane by the Monroe Probate Court. From Monroe, she was admitted to St. Joseph Retreat in Pontiac, Michigan, as a private patient.[41]

After a brief period of recuperation in Pontiac, Libbie returned to her Monroe home to stay. The basic burden which she faced after the marriage was ostracism by both relatives and the community. The refusal of Mrs. Olmsted, a neighbor, to exchange visits with Mrs. Bromley was probably not atypical.[42] Monroe did not let her forget that she had married a Negro. Deprived of the emotional supports that she had learned to depend upon in childhood, Libbie had recurrent "nervous breakdowns." Treated as a Negro, Elizabeth had never learned to survive as one. The marriage ended in 1927 with the death of James, and his widow would remain single and alone in their home until her death in 1955.[43] Distance, in terms of time, erased much of the bitterness, and Libbie's memories of Jim were always kind and positive. Local citizens recall her talking of "her" Jim, about his sensitivity and kindness.[44] Once James was gone, many of the old relationships were again open to her, and she spent her declining years in relative peace, enjoying occasional visits from her grandchildren.

All indications are that James provided his family with a comfortable state of existence. The couple had two children, but their first son, Leo Noel, died at the age of three of a "complication of diseases" while a second son, Aaron Alcayde, born 15 April 1890, survived into maturity.[45] As is usually the case, both were lighter in complexion than their father, but, as might be expected, this did little to alleviate Mrs. Bromley's "problem" regarding their pigmentation. Mrs. Dunlap recalled her mother saying that "Mrs. Bromley used to cover the faces of her babies when she took them out in the buggy."[46] Various references about community ostracism, town curiosity, or personal guilt could be drawn from this oral tradition. Yet it is probably most fair to judge that Elizabeth was not terribly anxious, for whatever reasons, to face "Monroe" with each public outing and solved this rather delicate dilemma by covering up.

Jim worked at many jobs during his lifetime. At the time of Alcayde's birth, Jim listed "cook" as his occupation, but for most of his life he was known as a whitewasher, painter, and decorator. The statement of a life-long resident of Monroe that "no job was too menial for Jim, because he was a good provider," while not accurate regarding his vocations, reflected a basic understanding: Jim Bromley "worked" for a living.[47]

Jim formed several partnerships in the paint business with local white citizens during his working years. In 1892, for example, he and Gus Renner opened a practical paint shop at Front and Cass streets. In 1899, James and Joseph I. Schnorberger formed a partnership and had fourteen painters on their payroll. In noting the appearance of their business, the *Democrat* declared that the two had "put in an up to date paint shop. They are young men and deserve a great deal of credit for their courage in starting a venture of this kind and deserve liberal patronage. Their shop is a novelty in the way of decorations." Conducting business under the name of Jim and Joe, the partners had letterheads and business cards printed up by the Record Publishing Company and advertised each week in the local press. Their store was located at 58 West Front Street and their motto was "We Want Come-Again Customers."[48] Items in the press noting the contracts which Jim and Joe had secured indicated that the enterprise was a success.

One of their first big jobs was redecorating the interior of the First Presbyterian Church. The *Democrat* declared after they had completed the task that "their work would do credit to any of the best firms in the large cities." While Jim and Joe had been assisted by William Shields, a decorator from Detroit, Monroe could "boast one of the best firms of painters and decorators in the state." In 1901 the business partners did tasteful work in their repapering and repainting of the office and display room of local photographer C. W. Hill. Apparently in some demand by the community, the two completed many projects during their three-year partnership. Their more successful contracts included putting "up a neat sign for Adolph Munch's saloon" and painting the exterior woodwork of St. Mary's Church.[49]

Jim and Joe found time to take off from their paying pursuits on occasion. In 1902, for example, they completed some work without charge for a local women's group. The Monroe Civic Improvement Society, whose primary goal was to beautify the city, publicly thanked and commended Jim "Brombly" for "decorating the fountain and painting the signboards" at Memorial Place, a cemetery which the group was rescuing from total destruction.[50] Bromley and Schnorberger were also active in establishing the wages and laboring conditions for painters and decorators in Monroe. In 1901, at a meeting of the "Master Painters of the City of Monroe," Jim and Joe and eight others increased the wages for painters from twenty to twenty-five cents per hour and fixed the price of hanging wallpaper at twelve-and-one-half cents per single roll.[51]

Despite their apparent financial success and involvement in community life, Bromley and Schnorberger dissolved their partnership for unknown reasons but by mutual consent in October 1902. After the partnership had ended, Bromley continued to pursue the painting and decorating occupation. He continued to receive contracts on his own. In August 1904, for instance, he and Donald Heath refurbished the old Loranger Hotel for Charles E. Greening. Five years later he was awarded a major contract for decorating the hall and several rooms of the Monroe County Courthouse.[52]

Through the years Jim had the opportunity to work in other capacities. In the winter of 1904–5, he served as deputy game and fish warden for Monroe County. Patrolling the marshes in search of hunters who were illegally destroying muskrat houses, as was the custom in the area, Bromley had cause on several occasions to arrest members of the white community. Significantly, all were found guilty by the judge and each was sentenced and fined accordingly.[53]

Perhaps the most serious entrepreneurial enterprise which Bromley attempted was a restaurant business which he operated from 1910–12 in Monroe. Apparently a life-long dream, the endeavor was financed with money from an estate that an aunt in

Washington, D.C., had left him. James's Elite Restaurant was located at 51 West Front Street; the menu included a wide range of items which promised to satisfy the taste of any palate.[54]

James's culinary calling ran awry in 1911 when he was caught selling liquor illegally. At the time, it was virtually impossible for new businessmen to obtain liquor licenses in Monroe. Prohibition and the local option craze were gaining momentum in the state and there were several "drys" in places of influence in Monroe who were interested in decreasing the number of saloons in the city. Operating a restaurant without the added attraction of alcoholic beverages, especially when competitive establishments retained the privilege, meant certain failure. Simply put, James Bromley adapted to the demands of his customers and was caught. Two plainclothes deputy sheriffs made the arrest after purchasing "three pints of beer and a half pint of whiskey" at the Elite Restaurant and the proprietor, James Bromley, after being found guilty, paid fines amounting to $87.50. Significantly, in describing the incident, the *Democrat* noted that James was colored.[55] Apparently, James's personal identity was beginning to suffer from the inroads of nonfamiliarity by this time. Suffice it to say, the Elite Restaurant soon folded and James returned to painting and decorating.

Despite the ups and downs of his business ventures, James was able to provide his family with a better-than-average standard of living. Since there was no probate at James's death in 1927, all the family's property was kept in Libbie's name. Their holdings included the home they lived in at 618 Cass Street, assessed at $2,500 in 1927, and a house and lot in the fourth precinct valued at $700 in 1926.[56] By working and living off the accumulated assets from the marriage, Elizabeth was able to survive on her own until 1947, when, at the age of seventy-six, she began to receive old-age assistance under Michigan state law. In 1951 she sold a number of valuable antiques for the sum of one dollar to the Monroe County Historical Museum.[57] At the time of her death, the Monroe County Probate Court revealed that she owned shares of stock in Monroe Paper Products and the Portsmouth Steel Corporation and had cash holdings of $1,274.76. Because Michigan law in 1955 required that the state have first claim on an estate of a person who had been on assistance, there were no monies for dispersal, and over $1,000 was owed after everything was settled.[58]

Ending a life at the age of eighty-four, after being a widow for nearly thirty years, only a bit more than one thousand dollars in arrears, spoke well for Mrs. Bromley's survival capacities. In addition, it reflected Jim Bromley's abilities as a breadwinner. What is also said by this fact is that the community of Monroe allowed James to make a living, not a great one, but one which compared favorably with the majority white population. Since James and the quality of his work were known in Monroe, people hired him for various tasks. A viable personal identity in the community assured not only his survival but a life of some material comfort.

It was through his political activities that James W. Bromley embraced his blackness. Unlike the Fosters, he did not reject his "negritude," and unlike Mrs. Johnson and "Dad" Smith, he did not accept the stereotyped roles for himself. Unfortunately, Jim's earliest efforts in the electoral process on the local level were ridiculed in the press. What was at issue was unknown, but on 31 October 1887 the *Democrat* declared that "Jim Bromley announces himself a candidate for the Fifth ward alderman."[59] This was at a time when there were only four wards in the city! Regardless of whether the comments were made in jest or anger, they conveyed a "whites only" attitude toward Monroe's political preserve. There was little likelihood that Bromley would have an impact on the city's government. Indeed, during his lifetime, he would not emerge as a local "influential."

Political affairs on a higher level, however, provided greener fields for a man of his organizational skills and abilities. A well-read man who had a life-long interest in books and a library of over 500 volumes, James Bromley was very much aware of national trends regarding black leadership and strategy and was keenly conscious of the declining fortunes of the Negro in the Republican party.[60] A Republican, like most Afro-Americans, Jim renewed his political activities in July 1900 as the presidential election approached.

The vehicle for Bromley's efforts was the nationwide black organization, the Afro-American Council. While several authors have discussed the council, no scholarship has connected the efforts of that important organization with Negroes on the state and local level.[61] Usually the treatments have dealt with the various national conventions and the clashes between the "Tuskegee" crowd and more militant blacks. A review of Bromley's activities indicates that the council enjoyed some enthusiasm from its rank-and-file members and some viability on the local level.

Both the *Democrat* and *Record* announced in July 1900 that the colored voters were organizing politically and that James W. Bromley had been "chosen general manager for Michigan, Ohio and Indiana of the Afro-American Lincoln League." The *Democrat* credited Mr. Bromley as "one of the promulgators of the society which is an independent colored organization who are looking for the advancement of their people in the political world independent of party principles." The *Record* noted that the League had local clubs in every Negro settlement and indicated its support for Bromley in the endeavor by commenting that "if pluck and push have anything to do with it, we know Jim will be a leader in the league."[62] The avowed purpose of the League, according to the *Record,* was to unite the forces and resources of the colored voters in the state and nation in order to gain political influence and recognition in the Republican party.[63]

The *Record* continued to follow Bromley's political career among his people in the succeeding months. In August the Republican paper noted with pride that Monroe's leading black citizen had been selected by the National Afro-American League to serve as a representative at its convention in Indianapolis later that month. The purpose of the gathering, the *Record* indicated, was "to consider the advisability of placing a colored candidate in the field for President." James Bromley, the newspaper assured its readers, was "decidedly opposed to putting another ticket in the field" and would continue to support the Republican party's nominees.[64]

Also in August, Bromley began to articulate his views on the nature of the Afro-American's political dilemma in the United States. His initial publishing effort appeared in the *Monroe Democrat* of 2 August 1900. The rival *Record* could not have been pleased with Bromley's essay because it clearly and forcefully delineated his dissatisfaction and bitterness with the Republican Party's treatment of the Negro. The column, which is the only surviving piece of Bromley's writing, is worthy of complete citation.

> Afro American Lincoln League
>
> For the first time in the history of the negro since the emancipation is he beginning to realize that he has a political mission to fill other than to be a shouter and follow the dictates of a chosen few bosses. He realizes that he must, if he is going to be a man and a citizen and would keep pace with his white neighbor, lay aside the prejudices and dead issues of the 60's and take up the live ones of the present, and be as true to his country as he has been in the past to republican bosses, who have held him as a voting chattel. He now observes as he never did before the great duty he owes his country, his family and himself.
>
> He has never received a half representation in office in comparison to the vote cast for that party. Nor can he expect to when they tell us openly and boldly that we have and always will vote with them regardless of men or measures, which has been all true.
>
> But again take fifteen or twenty years ago the negro voted largely

on the issues that brought about the civil war and his freedom and gave him the ballot or, in other words, he was voting the doctrine of Lincoln. Our fathers believed that they were obliged to vote the republican ticket from a motive of principle. Since the party has deviated from the principles enumerated by Lincoln and since the race is not standing still, that notion has been swept away by political intelligence and like his white brother he will cast his ballot where he sees some benefit for his personal and race advancement. We believe also that what benefits the white man, benefits us, that all political questions that are beneficial to one are beneficial to the other.

I believe, judging from the dissatisfaction that exists among our people in regard to the policies of the republican party, that the majority will be perfectly independent of that party this campaign.

The colored race had begun to learn that the republican party of today is not the party of Lincoln, Grant, Sumner and Garfield, that the party has been entirely revolutionized and that a new order of things exists, that the higher we are educated the greater has been the effort to suppress him politically and that he has been and is being used as a cats paw to further the ends of bosses. That we as a race will assert our manhood and show our power will be thoroughly demonstrated from this campaign on.[65]

Jas. Bromley

This essay foreshadowed a more important development in the succeeding months. What role Bromley played at the Indianapolis convention is not known, but soon after he returned to Monroe, Jim turned his writing abilities to publishing a paper of his own. Unfortunately, no copies of the *Black Iconoclast* have survived, but judging from the comments of the Republican *Record,* Bromley drew blood. According to the *Record,* the *Black Iconoclast,* a weekly publication, was "purportedly" issued in the interests of the colored voters of Michigan. In his first number, Bromley advocated the "proper and deserved recognition in the appointive offices of the state and nation." Bromley's goal of putting the Negro on a "equal footing with the white man" in sharing the political plums in proportion to his Republican vote was not a desirable objective for the colored race. Instead the *Record* recommended that Michigan's Negroes follow the example of Booker T. Washington. The Republican editor's interpretation of Washington smacked more of the child-Negro myth than it did the eminent leader's true tactics and goals. The *Record* credited Mr. Washington with keeping "his race out of demoralizing politics" and elevating "his fellowmen by education of the heart and mind." Regardless of what temporary gains the Afro-Americans made as a result of political intrigues, "the great mass of Negroes," in the judgment of the author of the column, "will remain, where they are now, below the ideal of an American Citizen." The writer concluded his criticism by cautioning the "bright and promising" James Bromley to "take council with such men as Booker and other good men who have the true welfare of the negro at heart, and make the *Iconoclast* a medium of education and not of spoils politics."[66]

Apparently feeling threatened by Bromley's prediction of a growing Negro political involvement, the *Record* continued to respond to issues of the *Iconoclast*. When Bromley suggested that Negroes had been treated with cruelty and injustice, the *Record* admitted as much, but then insisted that evil had been committed by both sides. Playing on traditional themes, the white editor of the *Record* observed that with their constitutional rights, Negroes "should not be ambitious to work out their own salvation." Bromley's attempts to attain a higher state of citizenship, by engaging in politics, were misdirected. "The professional politician," the writer asserted, "is not one to be aimed at by one who has the honest intention of elevating his fellow citizens." The critic voiced the hope that Bromley would look "forward to the noblest standard of true citizenship in his efforts for the interest of his colored fellowmen." Citizenship then, at least as far as the *Record* was concerned, did not include meaningful political participation for the Negro.[67]

Significantly, the city's other major newspaper, the *Monroe Democrat*, made no mention of Bromley's *Iconoclast*. This lack of attention, however, should not be regarded as tacit approval of Bromley's message. Instead, it should be viewed as an astute political assessment of the situation. Giving credence to Bromley's ideas would have ensured the loss of many Democratic votes, and agreeing with the Republican press in their evaluation would have been politically pointless when it was in the interest of the Democrats to have the Republicans painted as the undemocratic party. No comment guaranteed the best of all possible worlds: the *Democrat* could not be accused of taking cheap shots at the Republican party, nor could it be attacked for concurring with a Negro. Suffice it to say, the *Black Iconoclast* ceased publication shortly after the election, and the city of Monroe would not have another Negro newspaper.[68]

Bromley's interest in making the Negroes' political presence felt and his commitment to Afro-American causes did not end with the presidential election of 1900. In 1903, when the Negroes of Michigan were forming a mutual cooperation league, Jim Bromley was named the committeeman for Monroe County. This time the organization was geared not only to the political interests of its members but also to their industrial and economic needs.[69]

James Bromley's continuing involvement in black politics in the state of Michigan and his personal identity in Monroe gained him the endorsement of Governor Chase S. Osborn for a federal bureaucratic position in 1910. In May of that year, the manager of the Record Publishing Company of Monroe, A. B. Bragdon, Jr., recommended Bromley for the position of register of the treasury, a position usually held by a colored person.[70] In his letter to Osborn, Bragdon indicated that James had been his schoolmate and was a very capable fellow. In addition to his being trustworthy and active, Bragdon assured the governor that Bromley had "more influence with the colored vote of Mich[igan] than anyone else and he will throw this to Chase S. Osborn at the primary election." Governor Osborn responded by writing a letter to the United States secretary of the treasury endorsing Bromley for the position.[71] Although he never received the appointment, the fact that one of his classmates, a prominent man in Monroe, put his reputation on the line showed the importance of James Bromley's personal identity in the community.

The "Emancipation Day" observances in Monroe in August 1922 demonstrated the ongoing influence of Jim Bromley with the black people of the Midwest and his rather impressive organizational skills. The celebration commemorating the freeing of the slaves in the British West Indies was a three-day affair and included colored people not only from Michigan but also from Ohio, Indiana, and Canada. James Bromley, who was in charge of the affair, told the *Monroe Evening News* that over 8,000 persons were expected to be present. The focal point of the activities was Peltier's Woods, a picnic area about one mile south of the city. Johnson's Band of Detroit provided music for the occasion, and among the speakers were Charles Cotrell, ex-consul to Honolulu, and Dr. Robinson of Detroit. Also planned for the celebration was an all-night breakfast dance on the night and morning of 3 and 4 August.[72]

Even though it rained the first evening and Sheriff Frank Gessner banned the breakfast and closed several concessions at the picnic area, the celebration, on the whole, was successful. *The Monroe Evening News* reported a large Monroe crowd at the bowery dance held the evening of 2 August, and the jazz orchestra which provided the music was thoroughly appreciated. In addition, the promised baseball game between the Pinewood A. C. colored team and Bromley's All Stars of Monroe, which included white players, took place as scheduled and a good time was had by all.[73] Important was the fact that James Bromley's emancipation celebration attracted the participation of many people in the Monroe community, black and white. There could have been no greater testimony to the viability of James's personal identity in the city.

Nothing illustrated the depth of Bromley's character any more than his action in taking Fannie Johnson into his home during the last two months of her life in 1923. Mrs. Johnson, Negro, widowed, and ninety years of age at the time, had no one to turn to for help. When no one else would extend a compassionate hand, Jim Bromley did. For sixty-three days he and his wife nursed their ailing friend. The disposition of Fannie's estate provides some insights into the credibility of James W. Bromley in the community. James received the balance of Mrs. Johnson's holdings after the first-class claims were settled. Mrs. Billie Jenkins of Apalachicola, Florida, Fannie's niece, wrote two bitter letters, one to Jim Bromley and the other to Probate Judge Carl Franke contesting the outcome. She accused Jim of being "nothing but an old black thief" and a liar. She insisted in her correspondence to Judge Franke that "Bromley took her [Fannie] in to get her property, he never would have taken her if she had no home, he played his cards well to win you white people on his side." There may have been some truth to this final allegation because the estate administrator and several of Bromley's white neighbors came to his aid and advised the court that his claims were just.[74]

There would be no probate of James Bromley's estate at his death. Apparently, during a final year of illness, he was able to place all his holdings in Libbie's name. James died at the age of sixty on 15 September 1927. The funeral services were held at St. John's Church, and he was buried in St. Joseph Cemetery.[75] James had led a full life in the space of sixty years. He had spent his entire existence contesting the Negro social identity and had carved out for himself a viable personal identity in Monroe. While everyone knew Jim, he was never completely happy with that fact. He wanted others to know him on his terms. James Bromley's marriage and political activities indicate that his own sense of awareness, his ego identity, demanded an equality with everyone else. A man of more than moderate abilities, Jim knew he was equal to anyone. Indeed, there were few, if any, whites who could measure up to James Bromley in Monroe during the Progressive Era.

The son of James and Elizabeth Bromley, Aaron Alcayde Bromley, also forged a personal identity for himself in Monroe. While in some ways he was similar to his father, the events which are known concerning Alcayde's life tell of a different and in many ways sadder existence in the Monroe community. Born of a mixed marriage, he was forced to suffer not only from the stigma of being black in a white world but also had to face the realization that society regarded his mother as a woman who had made an unforgiveable error. The people of Monroe, as stated before, did not allow Elizabeth to forget her mistake and Alcayde was part of that circumstance.

The second son of the Bromleys and their only child to survive into adulthood, Alcayde was born on 15 April 1890. As with most parents, Jim and Libbie cherished fond hopes for Alcayde. From an early age he was provided with books to read, stories in the Tom Swift and Oliver Optic series.[76] Not insignificant was a volume given to Alcayde by "Aunt Jane" when he was six years of age: *The College of Life or Practical Self Education: A Manual of Self-Improvement for the Colored Race*, an etiquette book, the first 160 pages of which paid exclusive attention to black-related topics and provided the young Alcayde with a "Guide to Success."[77] The importance of the gift does not rest with the actual material or suggestions in the volume but with the fact that the young Bromley was being socially defined as black. There was no ambiguity either in the family or community regarding Alcayde's racial heritage.

An important aspect of Alcayde's life was his apparently thorough integration into the institutional life of the community. Like his parents, Alcayde attended the local high school. While there, he made his mark as an athlete in three sports. Between 1904 and 1910 Alcayde was the best pitcher on a highly successful local nine, and the local press of the era resounded with compliments regarding the youngster's fast ball and base-stealing ability.[78] When the school term ended in the summer, Alcayde continued hurling for the local Orioles and on occasion also pitched for teams in the Monroe factory baseball league. Praises such as the following were rather common: the opposition "crumpled before the mixture of drops, raise balls, spitters, floaters and speedy ones that were served up by the clever Oriole tosser." "Bromley will be handicapped in his work because his team has no catcher to hold him." "Bromley, the local pitcher, complained of a sore arm, but his work did not show it, as he had the Milanites safe at every stage of the game."[79] It is clear that the entire community appreciated the younger Bromley's expertise on the diamond.

Alcayde was also the mainstay of the high school football team. His magic on the football field also won the praise of the community: "Bromley made a touchdown in the first half by speedwork and throughout the game was in evidence." "His catching of punts and dodging runs at once proved features of the game." "Bromley, our star halfback, showed the visitors an assortment of dodging that would have won the game itself." The respect which his teammates and peers held for him was evinced in 1908 and 1909 when Alcayde was elected manager, i.e. captain, of the team.[80]

Bromley's gridiron fortunes, however, did not consist entirely of accolades. Classmates of Alcayde remembered that out-of-town trips, particularly those to Northwestern and to arch-rival Adrian, created very unpleasant situations for all concerned. Adrian students often taunted Alcayde for being a "nigger." In addition, in a day when roads were very poor and the train trips necessitated staying overnight in hotels and taking meals in restaurants, difficult situations resulting from Alcayde's race were inevitable. On more than one occasion, he was refused service in a restaurant or had to eat in the back room. As a result of these extremely unpleasant encounters, Alcayde no longer traveled with the team during his last two years of school.[81]

The speed that Bromley demonstrated on the football field also meant success for him at the high school's annual field day held each May. Alcayde always placed first in the 50-, 100-, and 220-yard dashes and was usually first or second in the running broad jump and the half-mile. So highly respected were Bromley's all-around athletic abilities that he was selected as manager of the school's athletic association during his last year in school.[82]

It would be a mistake, however, to interpret experiences at the Monroe secondary institution as completely positive. In April 1907, for example, the young Bromley and seventeen other students were suspended for rowdyism and Alcayde appears to have been the last one readmitted.[83] Alcayde also experienced rejection on a social level from some of his peers. It was custom in the high school for the students to march in a double file out of the building at dismissal time to the music of a piano. Mr. Ben Poupard, Sr., a classmate of Bromley's, recalled that no one wanted to walk with Alcayde and be his partner, so he assumed the task.[84] Local tradition has it that many of the girls' parents worried about any possible interest between Alcayde and their daughters. He is rumored to have had a romantic interest in one of the Meier girls after high school, but her family broke that up and nothing came of it.

Despite an oral tradition that Alcayde was accepted "the same as everyone else," he does not appear to have shared totally in the life of Monroe High School. Known as a "high yeller," Alcayde was never really part of the group. He did not take part in the senior class play, *Our American Cousin,* and his presiding at the piano rather than walking in at graduation has been attributed to the unwillingness of his classmates to have him for a partner. All the school photographs with Alcayde in them from this time period show him at the fringes of the gathering, mute testimony to his level of acceptance. He did enjoy a measure of respect from his classmates, however, because he "always knew his place." Alcayde was invited to parties and other social events, but it was understood that he would never come. In the eyes of the community, "he was a damn good nigger."[85] Bromley's reaction to his secondary school experiences, as revealed in two quotations in the souvenir book of his graduating class, was not sanguine. In the 1910 publication, both the faculty and students selected their favorite literary passages for inclusion under their names. Alcayde's choices were telling:

> Cultivate forebearance till your heart yields a fine crop of it. Pray for a short memory to all unkindness.
>
> Spurgeon

> They never taste who always drink
> They always talk who never think
>
> Mathew Prive[86]

Without question, his ego identity had suffered grievously at the hands of his peers.

Despite his athletic prowess, the talent which won the most plaudits for Alcayde Bromley from the Monroe community was his musical ability. At an early age, Alcayde showed an interest in music and soon proved himself a more than adequate musician with several instruments. Among the instruments which he played were the mandolin, piano, and cornet. Alcayde had started his training at Austin Gale's Monroe School of Music and by his freshman year was performing admirably in the high school orchestra. The admiration that Monroe citizens had for his musical talents often contrasted sharply with their racist thoughts and behaviors. This ambivalence was exemplified at Alcayde's high school commencement in 1910. Although no student would walk down the aisle as his partner, Monroe teachers thought so highly of his ability that Alcayde was the only musician asked to exhibit his talents at the graduation ceremonies.[87] Excellence merited recognition in Monroe, even if the possessor were black. Intending to make music his career, Alcayde continued to pursue his studies in the field at the Toledo Conservatory of Music after his high school graduation.[88]

In many ways, the young musician remained an integral part of the community of Monroe. When Monroe businessmen under the direction of Dr. Tiffany, a local leader, decided to make a booster trip in automobiles to Tiffin, Fostoria, and Toledo in 1914, Alcayde was invited for the trip. Riding in car number nine, he was just one of more than two hundred male Monroe citizens who made the venture in forty-four cars. For the occasion, all the participants wore "Lady Lee" caps and linen dusters and were instructed to decorate their machines with slogans. "Many autos had catchy mottos on them 'Tiffin or Bust,' 'Get Married in Monroe,' and 'We do it Right in Monroe.'" The main attractions were the sixteen-piece Monroe Cornet Band, which turned out in full regalia, and the showing of a film made in Monroe two years earlier depicting local attractions and industries.[89] The event represented Monroe's most important foray into the outside world during the Progressive Era and was characteristic of the "booster spirit" of the times. A total community event, it was significant that the organizers of the caravan and the town leaders requested Alcayde Bromley to participate. Monroe was not afraid to show other towns that a Negro was, at least on a public level, a bona fide member of its community. There could not have been a greater testimonial to the viability of Alcayde's personal identity in the city.

After three years of intensive preparation at the Toldeo Conservatory of Music, Alcayde embarked on a career as musician, teacher, and piano and organ player in Monroe. At first working out of Mann's Music House and playing the organ during movies at the Family Theatre, Alcayde set up his own Monroe studio in his residence in 1922.[90] From 1921 to 1926, Bromley directed the Monroe High School Orchestra and gained much praise for his efforts. Under his leadership, membership in the orchestra increased from eleven in 1922 to forty-four in 1926. Despite the group's success, Alcayde was not a full-time teacher at the institution.[91] While directing the orchestra, he also retained his private pupils and his position as organist of St. John's Church.

As for Alcayde's personal life, Monroe's parents need not have worried about his mate selection. While he married twice, neither wife was white nor from Monroe. According to his white childhood neighbor, Sabra Opfermann (née Olmsted), Bromley did not marry a Caucasion because he did not "want to disgrace his race." Alcayde wedded his first wife, Florence Woodson of Findlay, Ohio, in his parents' home in 1913. That marriage produced two children but came to a tragic end in 1919 with Florence's unexpected death. He married again in 1924 to Louise Love, also Afro-American, in Montclair, New Jersey. This second union also produced two children and likewise ended tragically with Alcayde's premature death at the age of thirty-seven in 1928.[92]

Unlike his father, Alcayde's choice of profession prevented him from making an adequate living for his family. Often he found it necessary to travel to Toledo to supplement his income tuning pianos. It was revealed at probate that he had failed to make payments on his home at 710 Maple Avenue for some time before his death.[93] Bromley's total estate was found to have more claims against it than it was worth, and his second wife and four children were left without means of support. Suffice it to say, Louise Bromley did not long remain in Monroe. Where she went with her children is not known. In effect, with Alcayde's demise, the city lost its last black representative of the Bromley family. The children returned from time to time to visit their grandmother, but none called Monroe home.

The events surrounding the death of Alcayde as revealed in the *Monroe Evening News* indicated that, for the most part, his personal life had drifted away from Monroe. Although Alcayde was reared a Catholic, his last rites were heard in St. Paul's Methodist Episcopal Church. His pallbearers were the board of directors of the Utopian Club, a black organization from Toledo, and the Abyssinian Quartette of Toledo's Frederick Douglass Community Center sang at the services. No white classmate or friend played a major role in the funeral services.[94]

Alcayde's obituary indicated that although the Bromleys continued to call Monroe their home, their closest associates were Negroes from Toledo. During the 1920s Alcayde appears to have had a particularly strong connection with the Douglass Community Center, a former YMCA, which serviced the black population of Toledo. He served as music director for the organization for several years. While working in that capacity, Alcayde met his future wife, Louise Love, who had been sent to the center by the National Urban League to develop a program for the city's black female children.[95] In any event, it is unlikely that the Bromleys had close social relationships with any Monroe white people.[96]

Aaron Alcayde Bromley is universally remembered in Monroe by his students, his peers, and others as a wonderful person. In fact, in all the oral histories and other local traditions not a single negative reference can be discovered regarding him. Talented, handsome, distinguished, and patient are adjectives which Monroe acquaintances recalled him by. Why such an ending to his life? While it is clear that Alcayde retained a strong personal identity in the city, that recognition did not fulfill his needs. The fact is that few Monroe citizens outside his immediate family could understand his problem. Not many natives of the city, for example, even understood the pain behind the quotations in the 1910 graduation souvenir booklet. In reality, to the community Alcayde might have been a special kind of Negro, but he did not cease being a Negro. It is certain that Bromley found that more of his ego needs were satisfied among black people in Toledo, people who understood the American Negro dilemma.

Having a strong personal identity did not solve the problems of being black. To be sure, being known meant in Monroe that a Negro could pursue an occupation or a profession and survive economically. For the most part, the city assumed some level of responsibility for *its* blacks. But having an identity in Monroe only mollified and did not defuse or nullify the effects of the more powerful social identities. Personal identities themselves are fragile constructions almost by definition. Successful maintenance required reestablishing and renovating them on a daily basis to prevent the brute or child stereotypes from gaining predominance. In addition, if a person himself changed or people who were his knowers migrated or died, the identity vanished. Finally, as has been demonstrated, that identity was unique for each individual and largely dependent upon the characteristics of one's personality. Each Negro who was known in Monroe had his own personal identity. But the crucial difficulty which emerged here was clear: the weak found that their identity tags merged with the social stereotype while the strong found some solace in hard work, athletic, or artistic achievement.

Ray Stannard Baker's contention that Negroes in smaller towns in the North had "come to fit naturally into the life of the communities where they live, and no one thinks especially of their color," was only half true.[97] While known Afro-Americans fitted "naturally" into their environments, they were never allowed to forget the stigma of race. If the talented, resourceful, and gifted Negroes succeeded economically, they did not do so socially or politically and were left with the understanding that there were certain boundaries which could not be crossed. Indeed, a personal identity is at bottom nothing more than an intimate social identity, generated and used by people who know and interact with the person concerned. However, the Bromleys, the Fosters, the Johnsons, and other native Monroe Negroes had to deal with the child-Negro social identity or racial stereotype despite the fact that they were known as real persons. The basic normative and cognitive framework which Monroe whites brought to interactive contexts was racist, and the ego needs of any Afro-American could not possibly have been met within the context of the larger community.

Without laboring the point, it should now be clear that there were as many black personal identities in Monroe as there were black people. Indeed, each Afro-American experienced some freedom in making the force of his or her personality felt on the community. Nonetheless, biography and individual personal identity, no matter how competent, do not tell us the "how" of survival for Negroes in Monroe. Humans do not live as isolated individuals. Rather, they create reciprocity networks with others to meet their economic, social, and psychological needs. They devise adaptive strategies to cope with the exigencies of a demanding world. The black kinship networks developed in Monroe were the most crucial elements in Afro-American survival in that community.

NOTES

1. James Weldon Johnson, *The Autobiography of an Ex-Colored Man* in *Three Negro Classics* (New York: Avon Discus, 1969), p. 486.
2. *Monroe Democrat,* 5 Feb. 1904, p. 8.
3. *Monroe Record,* 4 Feb. 1904, p. 5. The propertyless Smith seems to have wandered around the county for several years, "bumming" food and lodging from acquaintances and friends. He was enumerated in the 1900 census schedules as a "caller" in the home of a Raisinville Township farmer. See *Population Schedule, 1900,* p. 302.
4. Alex Johnson had several children by a previous marriage. *Monroe Democrat,* 28 Aug. 1884, p. 1, 25 Nov. 1904, p. 8.
5. Mrs. Edmund Childs, interview with Mr. and Mrs. Heck, 18 Dec. 1959, in "Recollections of Life in Monroe County, Michigan, 1956–62" (Monroe County Library Board, unpublished), p. 226; interview with Mr. Walter Fragner, n.d., ibid., p. 202. This circumstance was not unusual for Negro women. In fact, advancing age had no impact on the proportion of black women who worked. See Kenneth Kusmer, *A Ghetto Takes Shape: Black Cleveland, 1870–1930* (Urbana: University of Illinois Press, 1976) p. 88.
6. John M. Bulkley, "The Ante-Bellum Auntie Who Is Monroe's Pride . . . Fannie Johnson, Ex-Slave Who Remembers War Times in Old Virginny, Is That Town's Court of Last Resort on Things Cuisine," *Detroit Saturday Night,* 9 Aug. 1913, pp. 4, 9; *Monroe Democrat,* 8 Aug. 1913, p. 7; *Record-Commercial,* 7 Aug. 1913, p. 1.

7. Mrs. Edmund Childs, interview with Walter Fragner, 15 Dec. 1956, in "Recollections," p. 222.

8. "Old Resident Dies," *Monroe Evening News,* 17 Jan. 1923, p. 5.

9. Childs, interview with Walter Fragner, 15 Dec. 1956, in "Recollections," p. 222.

10. *Population Schedule, 1880,* p. 550, *Population Schedule, 1900,* p. 277, and *Population Schedule, 1910,* Monroe Township, sheet 3B; Monroe County Record of Deaths, Book F, 1918–67, p. 83; *Canada West Census Returns, 1861,* Reel C-1020, *Essex County, Colchester County,* p. 42, and ibid., *Amherstburg,* p. 43. The Butlers also appear in the *Canada West Schedules* for *1851* and *1871*. For 1851 see Reel C-953, *Colchester Township,* p. 33, and for 1871 see Reel C-601, *Colchester Township,* p. 21. Levi Foster is in the Amherstburg count for 1871. See Reel C-601, *Amherstburg,* p. 53. Mrs. Rose Ellen Foster Dempsey of Helena, Montana, a great grandaughter of Levi and Elizabeth Waring Foster, has conducted extensive research into her genealogy. Her investigation indicates that Elizabeth Waring's maternal grandmother was a slave, while both of her other grandparents were white—hence the three-fourths judgment.

11. Donald George Simpson, "Negroes in Ontario from Early Times to 1870" (Ph.D. dissertation, University of Western Ontario, 1971), p. 576.

12. *Canada West Census Returns 1861, Amherstburg,* p. 43; *Amherstburg Echo,* 23 Apr. 1875; *Monroe Commercial,* 29 Apr. 1881, p. 1; *Monroe Democrat,* 2 Nov. 1893, p. 1, 16 Sept. 1897, p. 1, 23 Sept. 1897, p. 1, 19 July 1900, p. 1, 26 Sept. 1901, p. 1.

13. *Monroe Democrat,* 26 June 1884, p. 1, 7 May 1885, p. 1, 9 July 1885, p. 1, 1 Oct. 1885, p. 1. The *Democrat* noted the progress in the construction of this home. State of Michigan Monroe County Probate Court, Estate of James W. Foster, 18 July 1900, number 5629.

14. Monroe public schools, Monroe High School collection box 1, Monroe County Archives, Monroe County Historical Museum; *Monroe Democrat,* 19 June 1890, p. 1, 19 Oct. 1899, p. 5, 29 Nov. 1900, pp. 1, 5; *Monroe Record,* 29 Nov. 1900, p. 5, 27 Nov. 1902, p. 5.

15. *Monroe Democrat,* 15 Sept. 1881, p. 1, 4 July 1889, p. 1, 20 Apr. 1893, p. 1, 6 July 1893, p. 1; John Bulkley, *History of Monroe County Michigan,* 2 vols. (Chicago: Lewis, 1913) 2: 942.

16. Minutes and Records of the First Baptist Church 1874–1914, *passim; Monroe Democrat,* 25 Jan. 1894, p. 1, 13 Dec. 1894, p. 1, 16 Apr. 1896, p. 1, 7 May 1896, p. 1, 19 Aug. 1897, p. 1, 11 Jan. 1900, p. 1.

17. Minutes and Records of the First Baptist Church, 15 July 1881, p. 87, 1 May 1890, p. 136.

18. Ibid., 11 July 1900, pp. 213–14; *Monroe Democrat,* 10 Jan. 1901, p. 1.

19. *Monroe Democrat,* 4 May 1899, p. 5, 26 Apr. 1900, 19 July, p. 1; *Monroe Record,* 12 July 1900, p. 1; Bulkley, *History of Monroe County,* 2: 941–42.

20. "Troublesome Crook Gone!" *Monroe Record,* 27 June 1901, p. 1; "Burglar Killed," *Monroe Democrat,* 27 June 1901, p. 1; Childs, interview with Walter Fragner, 15 Dec. 1956, in "Recollections", p. 222. Social class may have had more of a bearing on prosecution and judicial proceeding than race. In an instance involving the peculation of over $20,000 in municipal funds between 1899 and 1902 by city treasurer S. W. Lauer, government officials opted not to prosecute. Apparently, the fact that Lauer made up the shortage from his personal estate and resigned in ignominy was punishment enough. See *Monroe Democrat,* 24 Oct. 1902, p. 4, 31 Oct. 1902, p. 1, 21 Nov. 1902, p. 1, 5 Dec. 1902, p. 1; *Monroe Record,* 30 Oct. 1902, p. 4, 6 Nov. 1902, pp. 5, 8, 20 Nov. 1902, p. 1. Lynott Bloodgood, one of Monroe's prominent wealthy citizens, was accorded special treatment during his trial for the killing of a Toledo man during a mob incident. See "Tea Parties in Bloodgood Murder Trial, Ministers Take Part in the Receptions That Are Held after Court Adjourns," *Toledo Bee,* 11 Feb. 1903, p. 1.

21. *Monroe Evening News,* 12 July 1921, p. 1, 15 July 1921, p. 8. While the Monroe community conferred the status of white on Grace and her child, the racial identities assigned to her siblings are unknown. The 1893 Monroe High School graduation photograph reveals one of her sisters, Ella, as light-complexioned, but another sister, Mae, was very dark. In any event, each of her sisters married early and followed their husbands to other locations, and her brother, Jay, met an untimely end by a gunshot wound while living in Toledo, Ohio. See "Jay W. Foster Murdered Friday the 13th," *Record-Commercial,* 19 Jan. 1911, p. 1, and "Jay Foster Murdered," *Monroe Democrat,* 20 Jan. 1911, p. 1.

22. *Monroe Democrat,* 10 Aug. 1906, p. 1.

23. Civil War military records of Aaron Bromley, National Archives.

24. Monroe County Marriage Record 3, 1852–70, 5 July 1866, p. 105.

25. *Population Schedules 1870,* p. 415.

26. Civil War pension records of Aaron Bromley, National Archives and Joseph R. Smith, GAR Collection, minutes box 4, 15 Apr. 1891, p. 170, Monroe County Archives, Monroe County Historical Museum. Bromley's rejection does not appear to have been a

consequence of Jim Crow attitudes on the part of the membership; indeed, Ellen Bromley's cousin, Joseph Wickliffe, also an Afro-American, became a charter member of the organization in 1882, and another Negro resident of the county, John Williams, joined in 1889. "Comrade Wickliffe" was "appointed janitor at 50 cts per month." Smith Collection, pp. 3, 120.

27. *Monroe Record,* 13 Aug. 1903, p. 4.

28. *Monroe Commercial,* 2 Apr. 1880, p. 1; *Monroe Democrat,* 11 Jan. 1883, p. 1, 8 Feb. 1883, p. 1, 29 May 1884, p. 1, 2 July 1885, p. 1, 4 July 1895, p. 4. James Bromley's autograph book is in the possession of Kenneth Burkey of Monroe.

29. Childs, interview with Kathy Nims, 12 Sept. 1958, in "Recollections," p. 367, and with W. C. Sterling, Jr., 8 Oct. 1956, ibid., p. 27.

30. *Monroe Record,* 13 Aug. 1903, p. 4; *Monroe Democrat,* 14 Aug. 1903, p. 4.

31. *Monroe Democrat,* 10 Aug. 1906, p. 1; *Record-Commercial,* 9 Aug. 1906, p. 8; Childs, interview with Charles Verhoeven, Sr., 24 June 1958, in "Recollections," p. 312.

32. *Monroe Record,* 13 Aug. 1903, p. 4; *Monroe Democrat,* 10 Aug. 1906, p. 1; *Record-Commercial,* 4 Sept. 1913, p. 7.

33. Interview with Mrs. Sabra Opfermann (daughter of Mrs. Olmsted) by telephone, 22 Feb. 1980; Childs, interview with Katherine Nims, 12 Sept. 1958, in "Recollections," p. 367; interview with Miss Elsie Gutman, Monroe County Historical Museum, Monroe, Mich., 2 June 1977; interview with Mrs. Edna Toburen, Monroe County Historical Museum, 2 July 1974.

34. *Monroe Democrat,* 20 Dec. 1888, p. 1; Monroe County Marriage Record 6, 1887–1903, p. 25, 17 Dec. 1888.

35. Both autograph books are in the possession of Kenneth Burkey of Monroe.

36. Monroe County Record of Births, Book D, 1888–97, p. 30, 8 Feb. 1889.

37. Childs, interview with Charles Verhoeven Sr., 24 June 1958, in "Recollections," p. 312; interview with Mrs. Ben Dunlap, 14 July 1959, ibid., p. 556. Mr. Verhoeven owned and operated a well-patronized barbershop during this time period. As a result, he was most certainly at the hub of Monroe's rumor- and myth-producing industry, and his comments reflect a distillation of local opinion. Mr. Verhoeven was Catholic and of Belgian descent. In talking recently with an elderly, life-long Monroe resident, this writer asked if any prejudices existed toward Alcayde, the son of James and

Elizabeth. The answer was a forthright no; but what followed was significant: "We never blamed Alcayde; it was his mother who had lowered herself."

38. *Monroe Democrat,* 1 Mar. 1902, p. 5.

39. Childs, interview with Mrs. Ben Dunlap, 14 July 1959, in "Recollections," p. 556.

40. *Record-Commercial,* 30 Sept. 1915, p. 7.

41. State of Michigan, Monroe County Probate Court, Committal Proceedings of Mrs. James Bromley, 14 May 1917, number 9006. It is unlikely that Mrs. Bromley's infirmity had reached this advance stage because she survived another thirty-eight years.

42. Interview with Mrs. Sabra Opfermann by telephone, 28 Nov. 1979.

43. *Monroe Evening News,* 16 Apr. 1955, p. 11.

44. Interview with Miss Elsie Gutman, 19 Mar. 1977, Monroe County Historical Museum.

45. *Monroe Democrat,* 22 Sept. 1892, p. 1; Monroe County Record of Births, Book D, pp. 30, 68. What is disheartening to note here are the disagreements in the sources over the names of Bromley's first child. In the Record of Births he appears as Leo Noah Bromley, born 8 Feb. 1889; in the *Monroe Democrat* his name is Leo Noel, and finally in the Record of Deaths, Book B, p. 48, he is listed a James Bromley! Since the date of record in the Deaths Book was 12 May 1893, more than six months after Leo died, and the date of death was entered as 29 Sept. 1892, the newspaper in this case was clearly a better source.

46. Childs, interview with Mrs. Ben Dunlap, 14 July 1959, in "Recollections," p. 556.

47. Interview with Miss Elsie Gutman, Monroe County Historical Museum, 2 June 1977.

48. *Monroe Democrat,* 13 Oct. 1892, p. 1, 1 June 1899, p. 5, 6 July 1899, p. 5, 9 Aug. 1900, p. 1; Record Publishing Company business records 1900–1916, in Monroe County Archives, Monroe County Historical Museum, Monroe, Mich., p. 632. See also *City Directory, Monroe, Michigan, 1901,* (Monroe: Record, 1901), p. 11; R. L. Polk, *Michigan State Gazetteer and Business Directory, 1901* (Detroit: R. L. Polk, 1901), p. 1284.

49. *Monroe Democrat,* 5 Oct. 1899, p. 5, 21 Mar. 1901, p. 5, 23 May 1901, p. 5, 26 Sept. 1901, p. 5.

50. *Monroe Record,* 18 Sept. 1902, p. 5; *Monroe Democrat,* 19 Sept. 1902, p. 8. Even after the partnership dissolved, Jim continued to provide some services for the Civic Improvement Society.

The 4 August 1904 entry of the minutes of the Civic Improvement Society (Michigan Historical Collections, Bentley Library, Ann Arbor) shows a payment of $2.23 to Bromley, pp. 44–45.

51. *Monroe Record,* 11 Apr. 1901, p. 5; *Monroe Democrat,* 11 Apr. 1901, p. 5.

52. *Monroe Record,* 30 Oct. 1902, p. 5; *Record-Commercial,* 25 Aug. 1904, p. 5; *Monroe Democrat,* 19 Nov. 1909, p. 7.

53. *Record-Commercial,* 8 Dec. 1904, p. 9, 12 Jan. 1905, p. 5; *Monroe Democrat,* 13 Jan. 1905, p. 5, 20 Jan. 1905, p. 5, 17 Feb. 1905, p. 5.

54. *City Directory, Monroe, Michigan, 1911–12* (Monroe: McMillan, 1911), p. 25; R. L. Polk, *Michigan State Gazetteer and Business Directory, 1913,* Detroit: R. L. Polk, 1913), p. 1009; *Monroe Democrat,* 23 Mar. 1910, p. 7, 24 Mar. 1911, p. 7 advertisement.

55. "Sold Booze—Soaked $87.50," *Monroe Democrat,* 4 Aug. 1911, p. 1; *Record-Commercial,* 3 Aug. 1911, p. 7.

56. Assessment Roll, Monroe City, 2d Precinct for 1927, p. 7; Assessment Roll, Monroe City, 4th Precinct, p. 8, in Monroe County Archives, Monroe County Historical Museum.

57. Donor's agreement, Mrs. Elizabeth Bromley, 30 June 1951, Monroe County Historical Museum, Monroe, Mich.

58. State of Michigan, Monroe County Probate Court, Estate of Elizabeth Bromley, Apr. 27, 1955, number A-2997.

59. *Monroe Democrat,* 31 Mar. 1887, p. 1.

60. Kenneth Burkey of Monroe, Michigan, who possesses over one hundred volumes from the Bromley library, estimates that several hundred more were "tossed" when Mrs. Bromley died. During his childhood, Burkey had mowed the lawn for the aging Mrs. Bromley, and in her final year of life she invited him to take what books he desired from her holdings. It cannot be known what proportion of Jim Bromley's library consisted of Negro topics or black-related books. Judging from what Burkey has retained, however, Jim was a very well-read man. Among the titles were Cooper's *Collected Works,* David Graham Phillip's *The Fashionable Adventures of Joshua Craig,* Jack London's *Smoke Bellow,* Charles Reade's *Collected Works,* Albert Richardson's *Personal History of Ulysses S. Grant,* and Lida Keck Wiggin's *The Life and Work of Paul Laurence Dunbar.* Significantly, several of the volumes were gifts from other Monroe citizens. Dr. Southworth, a prominent local medical practitioner, gave him Octavus Cohen's *The Crimson Alibi.* What that fact communicated was that Jim's love of books and knowledge was a known fact in the community.

did he remain in Monroe? How did he survive? What was the nature of the network system that he must have depended upon?

It is clear that every Afro-American who lived in or passed through Monroe in this time frame often faced a hostile and racist environment. The white populace did not wish to intermingle with blacks on an equal basis. Even for those Negroes who established networks and experienced some advancement, their mobility was not due to any special openness in the community. In Monroe, black individuals belonging to lineages enjoyed an existence with a modicum of rewards; those who were not members of these kinship groups did not. The key ingredients in the creation of these groupings were the timing of arrival and duration of their stay. The Duncansons and Smiths came when the city was first emerging, and the Wickliffes, Bromleys, Millers, and Fosters planted roots in Monroe in the Civil War era, when communities throughout the nation were undergoing vast and rapid transitions. Furthermore, each of these families persisted for several decades in the area. They were well known within the community and occupied the special status of "town folk." Without question, the Afro-American family was the most important ameliorative agency in Monroe. The black kinship networks that evolved in the nineteenth century functioned as mediating structures between their members and the larger community. These support structures cushioned the blows of prejudice and discrimination and devised strategies for success and survival in a difficult milieu.

Extended kinship, augmented households, multiple employment, and hard work spelled occupational and property mobility for many of these people. The Duncansons, Bromleys, Fosters, Millers, and Smiths, if not their brothers' keepers, were one another's keepers. The Duncanson males, most of whom were painters and decorators, had several joint business ventures and certainly aided one another in plying their trade. The Wickliffe-Cox-Bromleys also had arrived at a number of work and living arrangements. There were limits, however, to what a family could provide and the groups themselves were always in a state of transformation.

The Smith and Miller families had vanished from the scene by the 1890s and the Wickliffe-Cox-Bromley network was also in a state of decline. The Cox surname is no longer in the Monroe record after 1870. At some point before 1874, Ellen's three brothers, sister, and mother packed their baggage and left for another location. The Wickliffe line also experienced some losses. Lynden resided with his family in Chicago after 1869. Except for a few years when she served as Wickliffe Fox's guardian, Mary Dickinson (née Wickliffe) claimed Ann Arbor as her home. By 1900, Joseph Wickliffe had removed to Ann Arbor with his family. Death also depleted the ranks of the Wickliffe-Cox-Bromley kinship. Alexander, Minerva, Fannie Wickliffe, and Rebecca (née Wickliffe) and her spouse George Fox died before the turn of the century, and Ellen and Aaron Bromley died shortly thereafter. Noel Bromley, James's younger brother, had left the city permanently by 1889, and after 1912 Wicky Fox was residing in Toledo. Only one core nuclear family, that of James Bromley, remained intact in Monroe in the early twentieth century.[5]

The Foster unit underwent similar changes. Apparently, by the mid-nineties several family members were no longer living at home. Ella and Myrtle do not appear in the 1900 manuscript schedules. James Foster, the household head, died of apoplexy in 1900. In 1911, Ella and Mae resided in Toledo with their mates, Myrtle lived in Oklahoma with her husband, and Jay was dead. Only Grace, the youngest child, remained in Monroetown with her aging mother and a hired man, Carl Schmitt, her future husband.[6]

The largest family, the Duncansons, show a more complex pattern of transition. John and Lucy, the original migrants and family heads, spent their entire lives in Monroe, as did three of their children, Fanny, Simeon, and Nathan. The family of John Deane Duncanson returned to the community from Chicago after his accidental death in 1871. In 1879, Lucius B. Duncanson took up permanent residence in Detroit. He was followed by several Monroe relations. Soon a Duncanson network began taking form in that city as evidenced by Robert W. and Henry appearing in the 1887 *Detroit City Directory,* Louise in the 1889, Andrew in the 1890, and John A. in the 1894 editions. By 1909, there were at least twelve adult Duncansons living in Detroit. A Duncanson kinship satellite was also assuming shape in Toledo, Ohio. Andrew S. moved to that city in 1896 and by the turn of the century was followed by Robert W., Lucius B., and Grace. Duncanson issue, however, continued to comprise an important portion of Monroe's Afro-American contingent in the early twentieth century. John C. and his cousin remained at their Eighth Street address, and Charles Hermann and his wife, Mary (née Duncanson) formed a household that continued to produce children who called Monroe their home.[7]

Why so many of Monroe's "family" Afro-Americans left the community cannot be precisely known. Of course, normal life-cycle events—marriage, birth, and death—took their toll. The time-honored American habit of moving on in search of greener pastures also played some role, as did the relative ease with which a dif-

Wickliffe Fox played on Monroe High School's first football team in 1899 (courtesy Monroe County Historical Museum)

Joseph Holt Wickliffe worked as a chef for the elite "O L Club" in 1898 and was a charter member of the local GAR post (courtesy Monroe County Historical Museum)

,Sept.17,1 am
ept.20,10 am
ia Sept. 24 1 A.M.
ania Oct. 1 1 A.M.
Eastbound.
Service
enoa, Naples,
See Itinerary.
NIA,, Sept. 2
)NIA, Sept. 9
enoa. *Omits
98. Special
China, Japan,
l, South Af-
endent tours
oklet Cunard
R AND OR-
ENT SAIL-
APAN, AND
N. R. Offices,
te Battery.
tte Ave.
Street.
ond Bldg.

—Photo by Gus Beck, Monroe.

to Winc
found th
town wh
manding
quartered
brigade,
nett, enc
ers, com
always "
white to
tinually
and grey
ing and
the old T
decidedly
remained
tragic dr
"Civil
claimed.
it was th
see or h
de Nawt
South d
from ma
misable
every la
carried c
suttinly
days. I
first mea
erates co
and the
vania eve
"Well,
when the
took effe
"De sl
all over
some ma
some cro

Fannie Johnson was famous for her catering (*Detroit Sunday Night*, 9 Aug. 1913, courtesy Detroit Public Library)

The livery of James Foster, 1879–94, was located at 22 Washington Street, adjacent to the Park Hotel (courtesy Monroe County Historical Museum)

The City Livery, owned by James Foster 1879–94 (*Headlight*, July 1896, courtesy Monroe County Historical Museum)

Ella Foster, seated at the far left in the second row, graduated from Monroe High School in 1893 (courtesy Monroe County Historical Museum)

ferent racial identity could be assumed by lighter-complexioned blacks in another community.[8] With Monroe's blacks there was another consideration: the difficulties members of the networks encountered in selecting mates. The community's demographic base precluded black racial endogamy in Monroe. There were few, if any, eligible Negro mates for the city's Afro-American contingent.

To remain and form a family unit in Monroe meant interraial unions for nearly all individuals in these kinships. The marriage of James Bromley and Elizabeth Willetts has already been discussed, as has the 1922 bond formed between Grace Foster and Carl Schmitt. Contrary to what might be expected, race-mixing was not unusual in Monroe in the nineteenth century. Even before Michigan's miscegenation statute was struck down in 1882, the Duncanson family was combining with its white neighbors. The community ignored these transgressions. In 1874, for example, both Robert W. Duncanson and his future wife, Mary S. Dennis, were "conveniently" recorded as white in their marriage application. In 1881, John A. Duncanson and Mary L. Sharlow were white in their marriage record, and in the next year Mary Duncanson and Charles Hermann were designated as white on their license. The technical illegality of the union between Nathaniel Duncanson and Phoebe Grobb was overlooked, as was that of Simeon and his second wife, Mary Louisa. It would seem that interracial unions were the norm in the Duncanson clan.[9]

The racial identity of the Duncansons, Fosters, and Mays, seems to have been ambiguous in the community. The variations in the racial designations of some members of these families in the census manuscript schedules between 1880 and 1910 have been noted earlier. The birth, death, and marriage records also show discrepancies. Mary Hermann (née Duncanson) died white, as did John C. and Eliza Duncanson. Lottie Hermann was born white, and Grace Foster's death record indicates that she was Caucasian. Inconsistencies of this type—or inaccuracies—have been attributed to carelessness on the part of the record-keepers. A more viable hypothesis would be that a mixed background posed uncertainties regarding these questions and perhaps, in the case of vital records where people were known, a degree of complicity. Either way, this phenomenon was indicative of a social process slowly working its way with each succeeding generation through the community—passing.[10]

The descent rule that "requires Americans to believe that anyone who is known to have had a Negro ancestor as a Negro," while an accurate generalization, does not seem to have applied in all instances in Monroe.[11] Passing, it would seem, was an extremely complex mechanism. It does not appear to have been an "either-or" proposition in the community at its inception. It occurred through time and only with certain individuals. Crossing over was not the silent mechanism that some historians have indicated. It involved not only racial heritage but, ironically, family and personal identity. Could an individual known to have an African ancestor be regarded and defined as white? Yes, the interracial backgrounds and unions of the Fosters and Duncansons were matters of public knowledge.[12] Each of the families had a long, continuous heritage in Monroe, and descendants residing in the community today bear no stigma of race and are generally viewed as Caucasian.

Reminiscences of senior citizens in the 1950s indicate that these families were beginning to cross the color line at the turn of the century despite their known ancestry. In 1956, Walter Fragner remembered that "the Fosters weren't really considered as colored people as they were very light colored." Kathy Nims also recalled that the Fosters had "white blood in their veins and that their three daughters were pretty little girls."[13] Miss Nims was somewhat confused as to whether the Duncansons and Hermanns were colored or Indian. Of course, some of the old folks today still suspect that "so-and-so's" grandmother was colored, and there is a strong undercurrent of gossip and speculation on these matters, particularly regarding the Foster descendants. While "whispering" about these things might be popular, it is understood that such knowledge should be kept quiet to allow these people to live as white. This talk rarely has had impact on these people's lives. For Monroe, the matter of passing personified the ambiguity of race.

Apparently there were a variety of complexions among the people of mixed ancestrage. Ben Poupard remembered Mae Foster as "blacker than the ace of spades and a mean one too." Mae moved to Toledo. On the other hand, the 1893 Monroe High School graduation photograph reveals another Foster daughter, Ella, as light-complexioned. Grace Foster Schmitt also had light skin. Even with her, however, citizens continued to look for telltale signs of African heritage. One local tradition is that the Schmitts, who remained farmers, would always show up at the city's public market on weekends to sell eggs and fresh produce. Mrs. Schmitt was always there, and one individual speculated that the reason she wore "gobs of powder" on her face was to mask her racial characteristics. Another citizen recalled that Stella Hermann was very black but that the other girls passed. After Stella married she moved to Toledo.[14]

Today, many of the fifth-generation Fosters and eighth-generation Duncansons have no notion of their genealogical background. Continual intermarriage with white people at each level of descent has erased any of those characteristics generally associated with Negroes, and these individuals lead an unfettered life as white people in Monroe.

Going white did not seem to have been an option for the Wickliffe-Bromleys. Unlike the Fosters or Duncansons, the members of this family groups were all very dark-skinned. If the Duncanson and Foster miscegenation attracted little notice, the union between James and Elizabeth, as has been shown, created a furor. Complexion, rather than reputation, respectability, or middle-class behavior, was the crucial variable in a passing strategy. It is unlikely that the issue of this group could have claimed a white identity without several generations of intermarriage.

While the community was prepared to allow blacks who showed the proper attributes of character some measure of economic and occupational success, it was unwilling to grant them an unrestricted status as full, bona fide citizens. This, it would seem, explains the race activism strategy that evolved in the Bromley family. James Bromley's involvement has already been discussed. Wickliffe Fox, too, was a leader in his own right in Toledo where he was a charter member of the Frederick Douglass Community Center and a leading light in that city's NAACP chapter.[15]

Ironically, race activism also figured prominently in the Foster background; at least one member of the family was an "operator in the underground railroad" in Ohio, and James's father, Levi, is reputed to have been a co-founder with his brothers of the country's first manual training school for black people in Lenawee County, Michigan. An antislavery activist, Levi Foster expatriated to Canada sometime in the 1840s. On at least one occasion he journeyed back across the border to promote black migration to his adopted country. In 1854, he served as a delegate to the "National Emigration Convention" held in Cleveland. Levi sometimes held antislavery meetings in his Amherstburg home to discuss the issue. James's father was familiar with the leading abolitionist figures of the era, and local lore in Ft. Malden, Ontario, has it that he gave up a profitable tavern business in that city after it was determined in a temperance debate that a tavern keeper was worse than a slave owner. Foster, a race militant, "could not let it be said of him that he was worse than a slave holder."[16] There is no evidence that James Foster ever pushed the black cause in Monroe—why should he? He claimed a white identity and the community accepted it. A family tradition of race militancy seems to have had little impact when passing was a viable option.

For "light-skinned" individuals, white Monroe's acceptance of their denial of African identity was illustrative of racism at work. The community obviously believed that it was best to be white. Those who had the physical attributes to pass and who denied their background were permitted to do so and were, in effect, rewarded with the legal appellation "white." Although many in the community might have realized that these people had a "tainted" lineage, the racist ideology allowed the transition as these people were moving in the right direction.

For those caught in the middle of crossing over, life was difficult. Passing was fraught with extreme emotional confusion and tremendous pressure. Often families were divided. Robert S. Duncanson, who was regarded as white in professional circles, received considerable flack from one of his darker-skinned relatives. Apparently in search of some financial assistance, Reuben Graham, a relation by marriage, atttempted to use the issue of race to separate Robert from some of his money. In a letter that has survived in the Duncanson family, Robert upbraided Graham for his narrowness, stating that he cared not for color but only for painting. Eventually Duncanson's demise in 1872 was associated with extreme emotional depression. The conflicts he faced within his family undoubtedly played some role in his mental state.[17]

The transition between races also involved conflicts and tensions for Caucasians who moved into black families. One can only speculate regarding the eventual impact of this decision on the mental decline of Phoebe Grobb Duncanson. Elizabeth Willetts Bromley's traumas have been discussed. The question of identity seemed to plague Elizabeth throughout her lifetime. She enjoyed reading, reciting, and writing verse, and a poem she scribbled out and gave her attorney, George Paxson, sometime in the 1950s, whether her own or imperfectly recalled from some other source, highlighted that concern:

> A little boy who was puzzled—
> He thought the Lord made him brand new.
> He said: "I have eyes of blue like mama's,
> Though I look just like my dad.
> I have red hair like my grandpa's;
> That's the kind he said he had.
> I have aunt Marie's dimples,
> And the chin of cousin Bee's.
> And it starts me sort of wondering:

How much of me is me?
Though I seem to be a jumble
Of the folks of long ago,
Some I've never set my eyes on,
And I guess I'll never know—
Somebody's manners and somebody's wiles,
Somebody's temper, somebody else's smiles.
Now I always had the notion
The Lord made me brand new—
Not of odds and ends left over
Of a family or two.
I'm just like grandma's scrapbook,
Or her crazy quilt, you see:
I'm made up of so many others
That there's none of me is me."[18]

How did blacks evaluate life in Monroe? Unfortunately, the record, in this regard, is almost nonextant. No extensive Negro-generated manuscript exists. Most of what survives must be ferreted out of items in the local press. A careful reading between the lines of a few accounts of incidents involving Afro-Americans can provide some sense of black articulation. It is not complimentary. Anger is a recurring theme.[19] William Stokes, of stabbing fame, had on one occasion threatened to "do up" a local proprietor. Harvey Williams, who had married a white woman, regarded Monroe as wiped off the map. James Bromley's activism and militancy through the years would indicate a more than ephemeral dissatisfaction with Monroe. Finally, the comments of Alcayde in his senior souvenir book tell a tale of much pain and frustration.

What was the black experience in Monroe in the early years of the twentieth century? Undoubtedly the heaviest burdens of racism fell on the shoulders of those Afro-Americans who found themselves living alone, without family in the community and unable to pass into another identity. For those who established family networks, some measure of economic and occupational success was within reach. A level of respect, recognition, and personal identity was also attainable. Ultimately, however, only those who ceased being black could pursue the American Dream. The denial of African ancestry was the price required for less restricted mobility.

On a different level, it is important to ask why a black community failed to take root in Monroe in the late nineteenth century. On the surface, it would seem that conditions were sufficient for such a development. There were always new Negroes moving in, out, or through the town; there was a continuity in family history; several

Afro-Americans embraced their "negritude"; and white racism forced some of Monroe's black citizens to close in among themselves. Yet a genuine black subculture did not evolve. The key ingredient, the presence of an adequate population base, was missing. As such, the primary arena of activity for Monroe's Negroes was the family and not church, neighborhood, or fraternal association. The lives of blacks were family-focused, and, for them, no "subculture orientation of choice" existed. A black community would begin to take form in the city in the 1930s, not as a consequence of conscious planning but rather the result of fortuitous demographic processes—there were simply more Afro-American people.

Monroe was not an atypical situation in the American black experience in the Midwest. The social and structural processes involving Monroe's nineteenth-century Negroes did not differ greatly from those at work in other small midwestern cities. Its experience reflected in microcosm forces and ideas operating throughout the country. The blacks who lived in Monroe during the late nineteenth and early twentieth centuries are most important for the ways in which their existence reified the American dilemma. Certainly each individual citizen and each family were unique, but blacks who achieved some measure of personal identity could be expected to live in most similar midwestern communities in the first decades of the twentieth century. A strong kinship network would most likely underlie each "success" story.

A few token successes were perfectly permissable in this racist milieu. Heavier burdens of prejudice and discrimination would await the great migration North in the late teens and early twenties. Although there was a degree of social and economic mobility for blacks in midwestern nineteenth-century America, the cost was extremely high: the loss of African moorings within the American experience. They were like chaff thrown to the wind. The pervasiveness of racism affected all Monroe Afro-Americans, even when progress was "apparent." Monroe's Negroes were robbed of their cultural and, as time passed, familial base. In the process, an invaluable source of identity was lost—forever.

NOTES

1. *Monroe Democrat,* 14 July 1891, p. 1, 28 July 1898, p. 1, 14 Sept. 1899, p. 8, 23 July 1903, p. 5, 15 Nov. 1912, p. 7, 12 Sept. 1913, p. 7; *Monroe Record,* 23 July 1903, p. 5, 24 Sept. 1903, p. 5, 10 Dec.

1903, p. 5; *Record-Commercial,* 31 Oct. 1912, p. 5, 15 May 1913, p. 7, 11 Sept. 1913, p. 6.

2. *Monroe Democrat,* 6 Feb. 1896, p. 1, 6 June 1901, p. 1, 13 June 1901, p. 5, 16 Sept. 1910, p. 7; *Monroe Record,* 30 May 1901, p. 4, 6 June 1901, p. 1, 13 June 1901, p. 4; *Record-Commercial,* 24 Oct. 1912, p. 7; Monroe City Party Enrollment Register, 1906–10 (race included). An incident involving St. Mary's Church in the Civil War era revealed a great deal about the difficulties faced by blacks who tried to settle in Monroe. "A very respectable colored man had come into the city. He desired a pew in the church; the priest without questioning his color, rented it to him. The following Sunday at Mass he and his family were present. The effect was like an explosion. Never had there been more of a row promised. A prominent Frenchman gathered a gang around him after Mass, and boldly denounced the action, claiming the Negro had no soul, etc. Petitions were circulated, and the priest was told that he [the Negro] was not wanted. Father Frank A. O'Brien, " 'Le Pere Juste,' Right Reverend Joos, V. G.," *Michigan Pioneer and Historical Collections* (Lansing, Mich.: Wynkoop Hallenbeck Crawford, 1906) 30: 271.

3. *United States Twelfth Census of Population, 1900, Michigan* vol. 55 *Monroe (part) and Montcalm (part) Counties,* p. 224A; *United States Thirteenth Census of Population, 1910, Michigan* vol. 62 *Monroe (part) and Menominee Counties,* Monroe City, Third Ward, sheet 21A; *City Directory, Monroe, Michigan 1919–20* (Monroe: McMillan, 1919), p. 111; *Monroe Record,* 3 July 1902, p. 5; *Record-Commercial,* 22 Apr. 1909, p. 7.

4. Monroe City Register of Electors, Fourth Ward, 1900–1904; *Population Schedules, 1910,* Monroe City, Second Ward, sheet 5B; *City Directory, Monroe, Michigan, 1905* (Monroe: Goodrich-McMillan, 1905) p. 87; *City Directory, Monroe, Michigan, 1907–8* (Monroe: McMillan, 1907) p. 103; *Directory of Monroe, 1909–10* (Monroe: McMillan, 1909) p. 123; *Monroe Democrat,* 23 Aug. 1912, p. 7, 30 Aug. 1912, p. 7; *Record-Commercial,* 22 Aug. 1912, p. 1, 19 Nov. 1914, pp. 1, 7; *Monroe Bulletin,* 19 Nov. 1914, p. 1; "Oldest Man In County Dies at 107," *Monroe Evening News,* 29 Apr. 1967, p.1.

5. Monroe County Marriage Record 3, 1852–70, 16 Feb. 1869, p. 200; Glen V. Mills, *Ann Arbor City Directory, 1900* (Ann Arbor: Glen Mills, 1900) pp. 124, 314; R. L. Polk, *Toledo City Directory, 1912* (Toledo: R. L. Polk, 1912), p. 640; *Monroe Democrat,* 5 May 1892, p. 1; "Mortuaries," *Monroe Democrat,* 4 Feb. 1886, p. 8 (Minerva Wickliffe), 4 Apr. 1889, p. 1 (Alexander Wickliffe), 23 Oct. 1890, p. 1 (Fannie Wickliffe), 14 Aug. 1903, p. 4; *Monroe Record,* 13 Aug. 1903,

p. 4 (Ellen Bromley); *Record-Commercial,* 9 Aug. 1906, p. 8; *Monroe Democrat,* 10 Aug. 1900, p. 1 (Aaron Bromley).

6. *Population Schedules, 1900,* p. 277; *Monroe Democrat,* 19 July 1900, p. 1; *Monroe Record,* 12 July 1900, p. 1 (James Foster), *Record-Commercial,* 19 Jan. 1911, p. 1 (Jay Foster); *Population Schedules, 1910,* Monroe Township, sheet 2B.

7. *Monroe Commercial,* 31 Aug. 1854, p. 3 (Lucy Duncanson), DAR cemetery records, Woodland Cemetery, 12 Dec. 1851 (John Duncanson); *Monroe Democrat,* 1 May 1890, pp. 1, 8 (Simeon Duncanson), 3 Dec. 1891, p. 11 (Nathan Duncanson); *Monroe Record,* 1 Nov. 1900, p. 5 (Fannie Duncanson), *Monroe Commercial,* 7 Sept. 1871, p. 3 (John Deane Duncanson); J. W. Weeks, *Detroit City Directory, 1879* (Detroit: J. W. Weeks, 1879), p. 307; R. L. Polk, *Detroit City Directory, 1887* (Detroit: R. L. Polk, 1887) p. 521; *1889,* p. 496; *1890,* p. 537; *1894,* p. 478; *1909,* p. 907; R. L. Polk, *Toledo City Directory, 1896* (Toledo: R. L. Polk, 1896), p. 433; *1900,* p. 496; *Population Schedules, 1900,* p. 232A; *Population Schedules, 1910,* Monroe City, First Ward, sheet 3A.

8. Members of the Duncanson clan who moved to Detroit and Toledo in the nineteenth century apparently "crossed over." The census manuscripts for both cities record each family member enumerated as "white." For Lucius B. Duncanson and family see Mach 102 *Population Schedules of the Tenth Census of the United States, 1880, Michigan* vol. 30 *Wayne County, Detroit City,* p. 390A, and *United States Twelfth Census of Population, 1900, Michigan* vol. 84 *Wayne County, Detroit City,* p. 312B; for Robert W. Duncanson, his son, Andrew, and their families see *United States Twelfth Census of Population, 1900, Ohio* vol. 99 *Lucas County, Toledo City,* pp. 99A, 117A.

9. Monroe County Marriage Record 4, 1867–86, 12 Aug. 1874, p. 108, 13 Apr. 1881, p. 253, 9 Jan. 1882, p. 275. There was at least one additional interracial union between people unconnected to any kinship in this era. Thomas Hayes, black, married Florence George, white, in 1889. See Marriage Record 6, 1887–1903, 31 Oct. 1889, p. 41.

10. Monroe County Record of Deaths, Book D, 1918–32, 21 Nov. 1921, p. 78 (Mary Hermann), 25 Dec. 1926, p. 183 (Eliza Duncanson), 26 Aug. 1931, p. 306 (John Duncanson); Monroe County Record of Births, Book C, 1880–88, 8 May 1884, p. 174 (Charlotte Hermann); Monroe County Record of Deaths, Book F, 1918–67, 30 May 1954, p. 83 (Grace Foster Schmitt).

11. Marvin Harris, *Patterns of Race in the Americas* (New York: Walker, 1964), p. 56.

12. In his recent excellent book *White Supremacy: A Comparative Study in American and South African History* (New York: Oxford University Press, 1981), George Fredrickson has suggested that the South African "social acceptance by the European population of at least some of the offspring of legal interracial unions that were a matter of public knowledge represented a sanctioned form of 'whitening' for which there is virtually no parallel in American history" (p. 120). The experience of the Duncansons and Fosters would seem to contradict this contention. For other discussions of passing and miscegenation see Gary Mills, "Miscegenation and the Free Negro in Antebellum 'Anglo' Alabama: A Reexamination of Southern Race Relations," *Journal of American History* 68 (June 1981): 16–34; David A. Gerber, *Black Ohio and the Color Line 1860–1915* (Urbana: University of Illinois Press, 1976), pp. 128–29, 326–28; Eugene Genovese, *Roll Jordan Roll: The World the Slave Made* (New York: Random House, 1974), pp. 413–31; Ira Berlin, *Slaves Without Masters: The Free Negro in the Antebellum South* (New York: Alfred Knopf, 1974), pp. 161–64. Undoubtedly, the most sensitive treatment of this issue from an autobiographical point of view is Pauli Murray, *Proud Shoes* (New York: Harper and Brothers, 1956), pp. 65–70, 88–91.

13. Mrs. Edmund Childs, interview with Walter Fragner in December 1956, in "Recollections of Life in Monroe County, Michigan, 1956–62" (Monroe: Monroe County Library Board, unpublished), pp. 222; interview with Kathy Nims, 12 Sept. 1958, and ibid., p. 367.

14. Interview with B. J. Poupard, Sr., 28 Dec. 1976, at his home. Interview with Mrs. Sabra Opfermann, 22 Feb. 1980, by telephone.

15. LeRoy T. Williams, "Black Toledo: Afro-Americans In Toledo, Ohio 1890–1930" (Ph.D. dissertation, University of Toledo, 1977), pp. 222, 250–51.

16. Donald George Simpson, "Negroes in Ontario from Early Times to 1870" (Ph.D. dissertation, University of Western Ontario, 1971), pp. 173, 489, 569, 576; Reginald R. Larrie, *Makin' Free: African-Americans in the Northwest Territory* (Detroit: Blaine Ethridge, 1980), pp. 52–57; Wilbur H. Siebert, *The Underground Railroad from Slavery to Freedom* (New York: Russell and Russell, 1898), Appendix E, p. 419; *Proceedings of the National Emigration Convention of Colored People* (Pittsburgh: A. A. Anderson, 1854), p. 18; *Amherstburg Echo,* 23 Apr. 1895; John W. Blassingame, ed. *Slave Testimony: Two Centuries of Letters, Speeches, Interviews, and Autobiographies* (Baton Rouge: Louisiana State University Press, 1977), p. 164; Blanche B. Coggan, *Prior Foster: Pioneer Afro-American Edu-*

cator (Lansing, Mich.: Research Association for Michigan Negro History, 1969), pp. 1, 26; "Slavery Notes" by M. Simpson, North American Black Historical Museum, Amherstburg, Ontario.

17. Letter reprinted in James Dallas Parks, *Robert S. Duncanson: 19th Century Black Romantic Painter* (Washington, D.C.: Association for the Study of Afro-American Life and History, 1980), p. 30. Whether the problem of racial identity played a major role in the difficulties experienced by other Monroe citizens of mixed ancestry is a moot question. Not enough evidence or testimony has survived to allow scholars the opportunity to make reasonable judgments in this regard. In any event, another Duncanson scion, a son of "white" Robert W. and Mary (née Dennis), was emotionally troubled. Born in Monroe in 1886, but residing with his parents in Toledo after the turn of the century, Earl Duncanson had a history of moodiness and despondency. On 21 July 1909 he shot and wounded Mrs. Inez Koester, a friend of several years, and then took his own life. Toledo police reasoned that he "was laboring under a temporary derangement." Another former Monroeite, Mrs. Mae Foster Fields, a daughter of James and Elizabeth Foster, committed suicide at her home in Toledo on 25 May 1913. The *Democrat* reported that she was "suffering from a nervous condition which temporarily unbalanced her mentality, and in the moments of delirium she brought her separation from all things mortal." *Record-Commercial,* 29 July 1909, p. 1, *Toledo Blade,* 22 July 1909, p. 5, *Monroe Democrat,* 30 May 1913, p. 7.

18. This note is in the possession of the author.

19. Some of the most angry verbalizations by Afro-Americans date from an earlier time period. The comments of Mary Belmore, a black woman who lived a few years in Monroe, are especially wrathful. She was bitter about her experience. A pauper in the Monroe Township "poor house" in 1870, she appeared in Toledo two years later under tragic circumstances. She had strangled her newly born son and thrown his body into a privy vault. After being caught, she was questioned as to the reason for her terrible crime. She answered that the child was "better off dead, than to live and be kicked and cuffed through the world." See *Population Schedules, 1870,* p. 381; "Child-Murder," *Toledo Morning Commercial,* 4 June 1872, p. 4; "Infanticide in Toledo," *Monroe Commercial,* 6 June 1872, p. 3. In 1888, Fred Newberg, a "negro giant" threatened to kill his emloyer, Frank Willets, a liveryman. When the police came to pick him up after a warrant had been issued, Newberg cut loose with an "awful string of vulgarity and profanity." He "showered the vilest possible epithets upon the officers and threatened to kill

them." The newspaper judged that "it was one of the most disgraceful disturbances that ever took place in the city." *Monroe Democrat,* 30 Aug. 1888, p. 1. When Newberg ran afoul of the law in Grand Rapids four years later, the *Democrat* rejoiced in the thirty-six year sentence that he received. *Monroe Democrat,* 11 Feb. 1892, p. 1.

APPENDIX

Monroe Afro-American Family Reconstitutions

The symbols in the following family "trees" have been borrowed from the discipline of anthropology. See Alexander Alland, Jr., *To Be Human: An Introduction to Cultural Anthropology* (New York: John Wiley and Sons, 1981), p. 100.

- △ male
- ○ female
- □ individual regardless of sex
- = is married to
- | is descended from
- ⊓ is sibling of
- ⦰ ⚠ individual is deceased

Affines who were not long-time residents or who left from the community shortly after marriage are not documented in any of the genealogies. The genealogy figures are documented as thoroughly as necessary to demonstrate the presence of black kinship networks within the community.

The complete citations for census manuscripts used in the diagrams are Microcopy 704 *Population Schedules of the Sixth Census of the United States, 1840* Roll #208 *Michigan: Livingston, Mackinac, Macomb, and Monroe Counties,* pp. 290–301; Microcopy 432 *Population Schedules of the Seventh Census of the United States, 1850* Roll #359 *Michigan: Monroe and Montcalm Counties,* pp. 691–760; Microcopy 653 *Population Schedules of the Eighth Census of the United States, 1860* Roll #554 *Michigan* vol. 13 *Marquette, Schoolcraft, Mason, Osceola and Monroe Counties,* pp. 521–618: Microcopy 593 *Population Schedules of the Ninth Census of the United States, 1870* Roll #691 *Michigan* vol. 17 *Monroe County,* pp.

394–459; Mach 102 *Population Schedules of the Tenth Census of the United States, 1880* Roll #596 *Michigan* vol. 18 *Monroe (part) and Montcalm (part) Counties,* pp. 503–51; *United States Twelfth Census of Population, 1900* T623 Reel 733 *Michigan* vol. 55 *Monroe (part) and Montcalm (part) Counties,* pp. 221–51; *United States Thirteenth Census of Population, 1910* T624 Reel 664 *Michigan* vol. 62 *Monroe (part) and Menominee Counties.*

The full citations for Monroe City directories are George W. Hawes, *Loomis and Talbott's Monroe, Hillsdale and Coldwater Directory, 1860–61* (Detroit: Hawes, 1860); *Monroe City Directory, 1874–75* (Detroit: Burch, Montgomery, 1874); *Monroe City Directory, 1892–93* (Monroe: Frank Wilder, 1892) (pages unnumbered); *Monroe City Directory, 1896–97* (Monroe: Billmire and Kiley, 1896) (pages unnumbered); *City Directory, Monroe, Michigan, 1901* (Monroe: Record, 1901); *City Directory of Monroe, Michigan, 1904* (Monroe: Goodrich, 1904); *City Directory, Monroe, Michigan, 1905* (Monroe: Goodrich-McMillan, 1905); *City Directory, Monroe, Michigan, 1907–8* (Monroe: McMillan, 1907); *Directory of Monroe, 1909–10* (Monroe: McMillan, 1909); *City Directory, Monroe, Michigan, 1911–12* (Monroe: McMillan, 1911); *City Directory, Monroe, Michigan 1913–14* (Monroe: McMillan, 1913); *City Directory, Monroe, Michigan, 1915–16* (Monroe: McMillan, 1915).

Numerous references are also from newspapers: the *Monroe Commercial,* the Monroe *Record-Commercial,* the *Monroe Record,* the *Monroe Democrat,* and the *Monroe Evening News.* Much statistical information was taken from the official Monroe County vital records: the Record of Deaths, Record of Births, and Marriage Records. All the probate proceedings took place in Monroe County. Also cited extensively were the Minutes and Records of the First Baptist Church of Monroe, Michigan, 1874–1914, and Polk's *Michigan State Gazetteer and Business Directory,* various years.

Citations for the sources to the family diagrams were often shortened. The appearance of an individual in the federal population schedules is simply indicated by a decennial date. An underlined date indicates that a person was in the Monroe city directory for that year. Presence in a local news item is shown by an italicized abbreviation of the newspaper's name. The Monroe County Record of Deaths was reduced to ROD, Record of Births to ROB, and Marriage Records to MR. Probate citations were condensed after an initial reference in a family reconstitution. Finally, Polk's *Michigan Gazetteer and Business Directory* was reduced to *MSG & BD.*

Family Reconstitutions

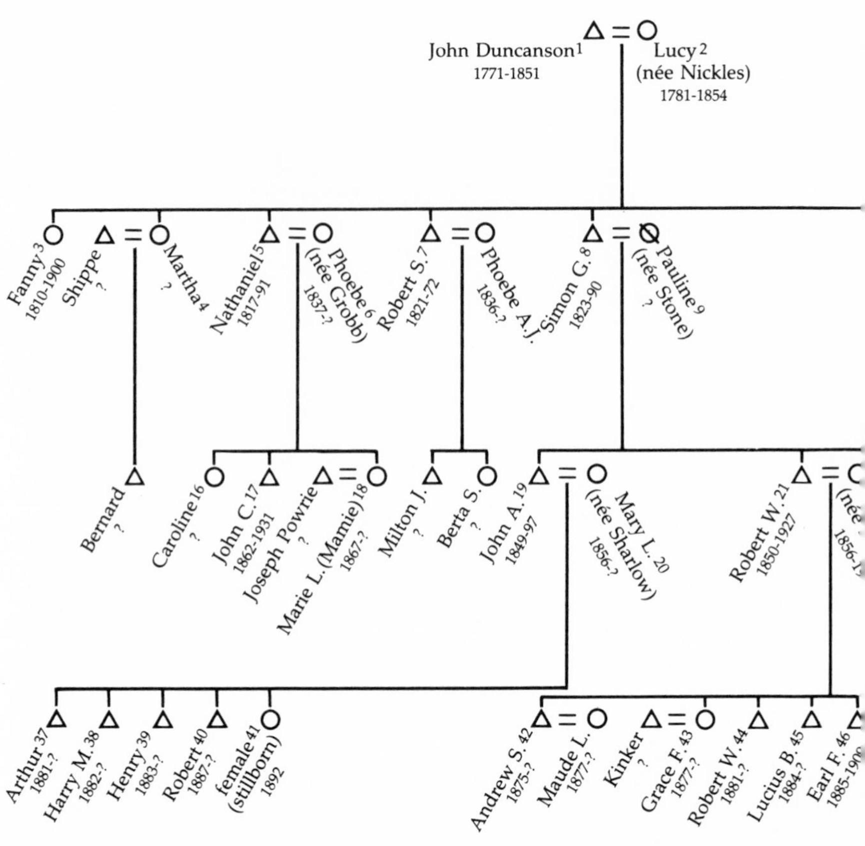

Figure 1. Duncanson Family Reconstitution, 1836–Present*

(*notes on page 166*)

*descendants of John and Lucy Duncanson currently reside in Monroe

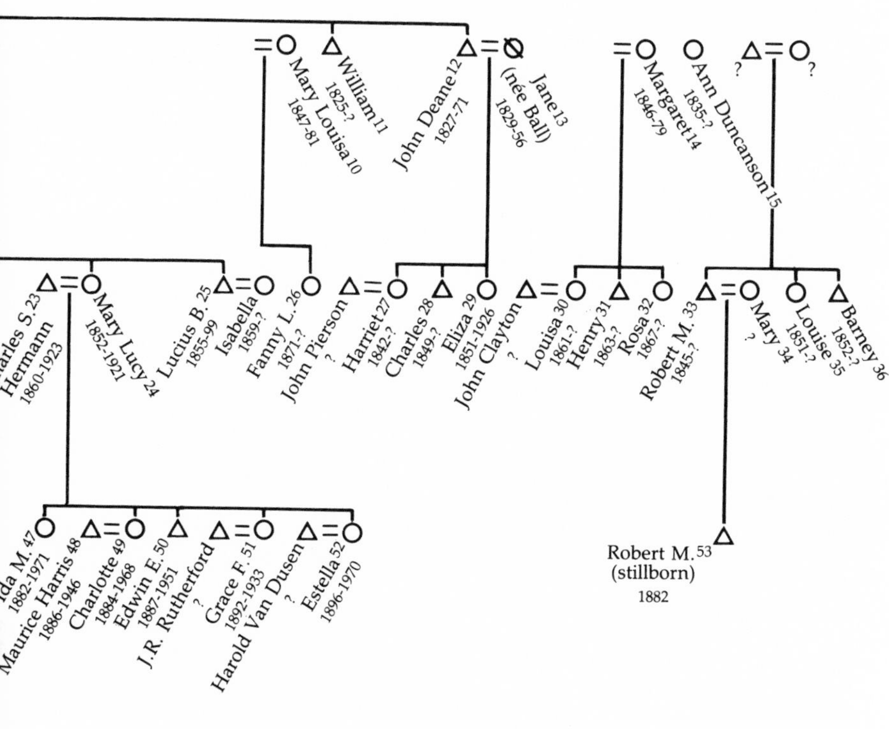

Mary Louisa 10
1847-81
William 11
1825-?
John Deane 12
1827-71
Jane 13
(née Ball)
1829-56
Margaret 14
1846-79
Ann Duncanson 15
1835-?
?
?
...arles S. 23
Hermann
1860-1923
Mary Lucy 24
1852-1921
Lucius B. 25
1855-99
Isabella
1859-?
Fanny L. 26
1871-?
John Pierson
?
Harriet 27
1842-?
Charles 28
1849-?
Eliza 29
1851-1926
John Clayton
?
Louisa 30
1861-?
Henry 31
1863-?
Rosa 32
1867-?
Robert M. 33
1845-?
Mary 34
?
Louise 35
1851-?
Barney 36
1852-?
...da M. 47
1882-1971
Maurice Harris 48
1886-1946
Charlotte 49
1884-1968
Edwin E. 50
1887-1951
J.R. Rutherford
?
Grace F. 51
1892-1933
Harold Van Dusen
?
Estella 52
1896-1970
Robert M. 53
(stillborn)
1882

Notes to Figure 1, Duncanson Family Reconstitution:

[1] 1840, 1850; Monroe County Deed Record 1836–37, Liber Z, p. 56, 8 Sept. 1836; City of Monroe Assessment Rolls 1840–46, *passim;* DAR cemetery listings, Woodland Cemetery, 12 Dec. 1851.

[2] 1850; DAR cemetery listings, Woodland Cemetery, 12 Aug. 1854; obit: *MC,* 31 Aug. 1854, p. 3.

[3] 1850, 1860, 1870, 1880, 1900; Wing, *History of Monroe County,* p. 509; Monroe City Library Register of Books, 1849–58, p. 176, March 12-June 19, 1855; *1860–61,* p. 19; *1874–75;* p. 30, *1896–97; 1901,* p. 19; Minutes and Records Baptist church, *passim;* ROD Book B 1888–1906, p. 171, 29 Oct. 1900, obits: *MD,* 1 Nov. 1900, p. 5; *MR,* 1 Nov. 1900, p. 5.

[4] Monroe County Probate 12842, Estate of John Duncanson, 1928.

[5] 1860, 1870, 1880; *1860–61,* p. 19; Chapin and Brother, *Michigan State Gazetteer and Business Directory 1867–68* (Detroit: Detroit Post, 1867), p. 304; City of Monroe Register of Electors, Ward 1, 1859–70, 1872–80, 1880–84, 1888–92; *MD,* 16 Apr. 1885, p. 1; Probate 4104, Commitment Proceedings Phoebe Duncanson, 1890; ROD Book B 1888–1906, p. 28, 25 Nov. 1891; Steiner Hardware customers account book 1865–71; obit: *MD,* 3 Dec. 1891, p. 1.

[6] 1860; Probate 4104

[7] *Monroe Gazette,* 17 Apr. 1838 to Apr. 1839; *MC,* 14 Sept. 1871, p. 3, 26 Dec. 1872, p. 3.

[8] 1850, 1860, 1870, 1880; *1874–75,* p. 30; James Sutherland, comp., *State of Michigan Gazetteer and Business Directory for 1856–57* (Detroit: H. Huntington Lee, 1856), p. 158; Hawes, *Michigan State Gazetteer 1860,* p. 247; Chapin and Brother, *Michigan State Gazetteer, 1867–68,* p. 304; R. L. Polk, *Michigan State Gazetteer and Business Directory 1875* (Detroit: Tribune, 1875), p. 556; City of Monroe Assessment Rolls 1846, pp. 115, 151; City of Monroe Highway Tax Roll List 1854–59, 1860–61, *passim;* City of Monroe Register of Electors, Ward 1, 1859–70, 1872–80, 1888–92; G. F. Grant Jewelry Store records 1855–65; Steiner Hardware daybook 1868; "Early Marriage Records of Monroe County, Michigan," p. 162, 12 Feb. 1841 (witness); Probate 1994, Estate of John Deane Duncanson, 1871; Probate 2025, Simeon Duncanson Guardian, 1872; Probate 4095, Estate of Simeon Duncanson, 1890; *MC,* 12 July 1855, p. 2, 26 Mar. 1868, p. 3; ROD Book B 1888–1906, p. 17, 25 Apr. 1890; obit: *MD,* 1 May 1890, p. 1.

[9] 1850

[10] 1860, 1870, 1880; ROD Book A 1867–88, p. 165, 11 May 1881; obit: *MD,* 28 Apr. 1881, p. 1.

[11] 1850

[12] 1850, City of Monroe Assessment Rolls 1840–46, *passim;* Probate 1994, Estate of John Deane Duncanson, 1871; obit: *MC,* 7 Sept. 1871, p. 3.

[13] 1880; obit: *MC,* 10 Apr. 1856, p. 3.

[14] *1874–75,* p. 30; DAR cemetery listings, Woodland Cemetery; Probate 1994; Probate 2025.

(*notes continue on page 171*)

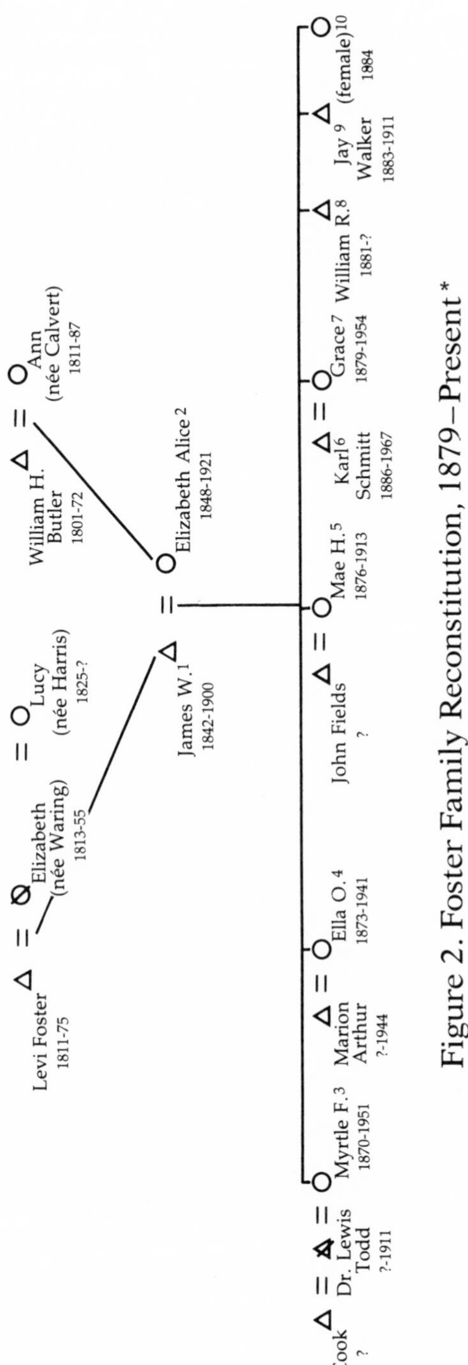

Figure 2. Foster Family Reconstitution, 1879–Present*

(*notes on page 173*)

*descendants of James and Elizabeth Foster currently reside in Monroe

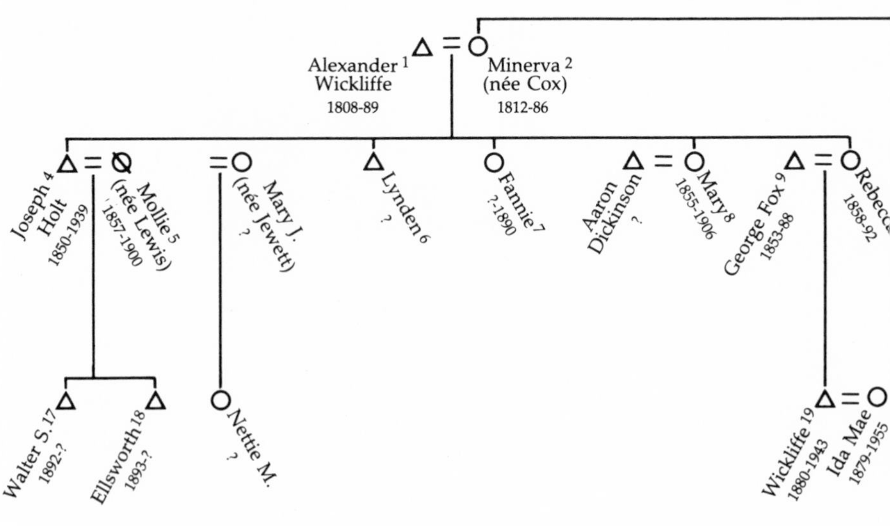

Figure 3. Wickliffe-Cox-Bromley Reconstitution, 1864–1955

(*notes on page 174*)

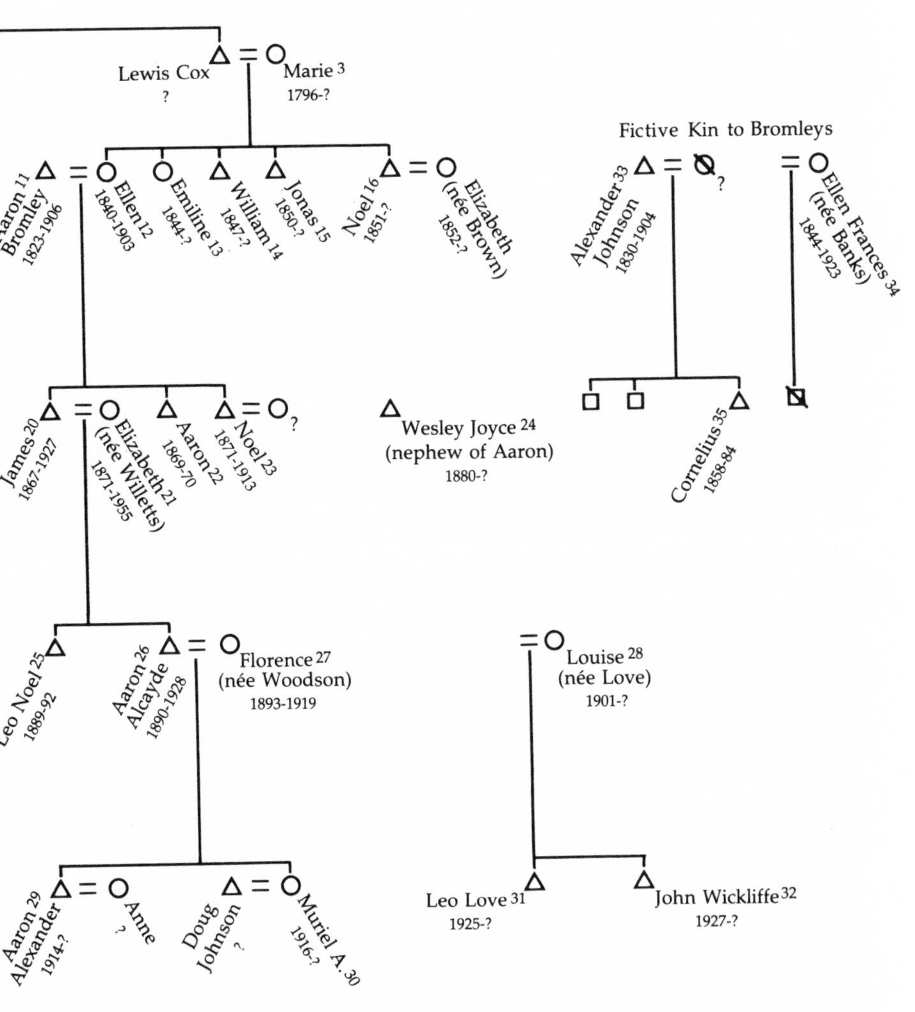

Lewis Cox
?
Marie 3
1796-?
Fictive Kin to Bromleys
Aaron 11 Bromley 1823-1906
Ellen 12 1840-1903
Emiline 13 1844-?
William 14 1847-?
Jonas 15 1850-?
Noel 16 1851-?
Elizabeth (née Brown) 1852-?
Alexander 33 Johnson 1830-1904
?
Ellen Frances 34 (née Banks) 1844-1923
James 20 1867-1927
Elizabeth 21 (née Willetts) 1871-1955
Aaron 22 1869-70
Noel 23 1871-1913
?
Wesley Joyce 24
(nephew of Aaron)
1880-?
Cornelius 35 1858-84
Leo Noel 25 1889-92
Aaron 26 Alcayde 1890-1928
Florence 27
(née Woodson)
1893-1919
Louise 28
(née Love)
1901-?
Aaron 29 Alexander 1914-?
Anne ?
Doug Johnson ?
Muriel A. 30 1916-?
Leo Love 31
1925-?
John Wickliffe 32
1927-?

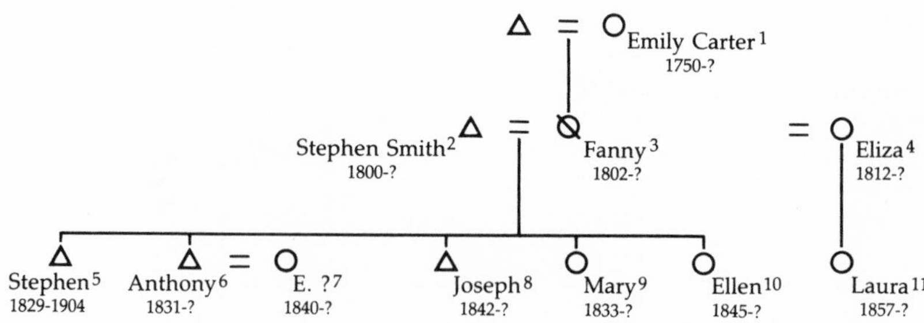

Figure 4. Smith Family Reconstitution, 1830–1904

(*notes on page 176*)

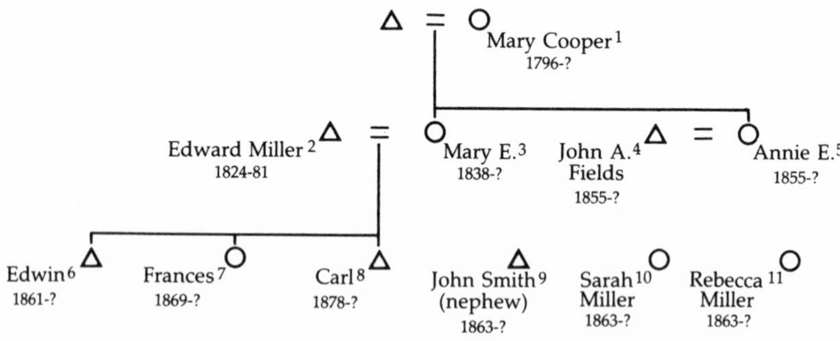

Figure 5. Miller Family Reconstitution, 1860–90

(*notes on page 176*)

[15] 1870

[16] Probate 14046, Estate of John C. Duncanson, 1931

[17] 1870, 1880, 1900, 1910; *1892–93; 1896–97; 1901*, p. 19; *1904*, p. 25; *1905*, p. 27; *1907–8*, p. 27; *1909–10*, p. 33; *1911–12*, p. 37; *1913–14*, p. 43; *1915–16*, p. 49; City of Monroe Assessment Rolls, 1903–13, 1914–15; City of Monroe Register of Electors 1880–84, 1888–92, 1892–96, 1896–1900, 1900–1904, 1904–8, 1908–12, 1912–13; Probate 4104; Probate 12842; Probate 14046; ROD Book D 1918–32, p. 306, 26 Aug. 1931; obits: *MEN*, 27 Aug. 1931, p. 1, 28 Aug. 1931, p. 10.

[18] 1870, 1880; *1892–93; 1896–97;* Probate 12842; Probate 14046; Minutes and Records Baptist church, p. 286.

[19] 1850, 1860, 1870; *1892–93;* Probate 4095, Estate of Simeon Duncanson, 1890; City of Monroe Register of Electors 1872–80, 1880–84; MR 4 1867–86, p. 253, 13 Apr. 1881; *MD*, 1 Dec. 1892, p. 1.

[20] Minutes and Records Baptist church, *passim;* MR 4 1867–86, p. 253, 13 Apr. 1881; *MC*, 15 Apr. 1881, p. 1.

[21] 1850, 1860, 1880; Minutes and Records Baptist church, *passim;* Probate 4095; MR 4 1867–86, p. 108, 12 August 1874; *Monroe Evening Commercial*, 11 June 1886; *MD*, 14 Aug. 1884, p. 1, 21 Aug. 1884, p. 1, 18 Mar. 1886, p. 1.

[22] 1880; Minutes and Records Baptist church, *passim;* MR 4 1867–86, p. 108, 12 Aug. 1874.

[23] 1900, 1910; *1896–97; 1901*, p. 31; *1904*, p. 39; *1905*, p. 43; *1907–8*, p. 43; *1909–10*, p. 53; *1911–12*, p. 59; *1913–14*, p. 65; *1915–16*, p. 89; Minutes and Records of Baptist church, *passim;* MR 4 1867–86, p. 275, 9 Jan. 1882; City of Monroe Assessment Rolls, 1910–15; DAR cemetery listings, Woodland Cemetery; Probate 10654; Probate 10698, Estate of Charles Hermann, 1923, p. 3; obit: *MEN*, 29 Jan. 1923, p. 3.

[24] 1860, 1870, 1880, 1900, 1910; *1904*, p. 39; *1905*, p. 43; *1907–8*, p. 43; *1909–10*, p. 53; *1911–12*, p. 59; *1913–14*, p. 65; *1915–16*, p. 89; Minutes and Records Baptist church, *passim;* MR 4, 1867–86, p. 275, 9 Jan. 1882; DAR cemetery listings, Woodland Cemetery; City of Monroe Assessment Rolls, 1910–15; Probate 4095; Probate 10654, Estate of Mary Lucy Hermann, 1922; ROD Book D, 1918–32, p. 78, 21 Nov. 1921; obit: *MEN*, 22 Nov. 1921, p. 1.

[25] 1860, 1870; *1874–75*, p. 30; R. L. Polk, *Michigan State Gazetteer and Business Directory, 1875* (Detroit: Tribune, 1875), p. 556; Polk, *Michigan State Gazetteer and Business Directory, 1877* (Detroit: R. L. Polk, 1877), p. 634; City of Monroe Register of Electors, 1872–80, 1880–84; Minutes and Records of Baptist church, *passim;* Probate 4095; Probate 12842; *MC*, 15 Apr. 1881, p. 1.

[26] 1880; Probate 4095.

[27] 1850; MR 2 1853–64, p. 207, 27 Nov. 1860.

[28] 1850

[29] 1870, 1880, 1900, 1910; *1874–75*, p. 30; *1904*, p. 25; *1905*, p. 27; 1907–8, p. 27; *1909–10*, p. 33; *1911–12*, p. 37; *1913–14*, p. 43; *1915–16*,

p. 49; Probate 1994; Probate 2025; ROD Book D 1918–32, p. 183, 25 Dec. 1926; obit: *MEN,* 27 Dec. 1926, p. 4, 28 Dec. 1926, p. 8.

[30] 1880; Probate 1994; Probate 2025; Probate 12842; Minutes and Records Baptist church, *passim.*

[31] 1880; Probate 1994; Probate 2025.

[32] 1880; Probate 1994; Probate 2025; *MC,* 25 June 1880, p. 1.

[33] 1860, 1870

[34] ROB Book C 1880–88, p. 93, 25 Dec. 1882; ROD Book A 1867–88, p. 190, 25 Dec. 1882.

[35] 1860

[36] 1860

[37] ROB Book C 1880–88, p. 16, 21 September 1881.

[38] Ibid., p. 75, 24 Sept. 1882.

[39] Ibid., p. 119, 24 Nov. 1883.

[40] Ibid., p. 357, 30 Jan. 1887.

[41] ROB Book D 1888–97, p. 145, 27 Jan. 1892.

[42] 1880; *RC,* 29 July 1909, p. 1.

[43] Ibid.

[44] ROB Book C, 1880–88, p. 19, 1 Dec. 1881.

[45] Lucius B. is recorded in the 1900 manuscript schedules for Toledo with Michigan as his state of birth and an April 1884 birthdate. His parents resided in Monroe at that time but his birth was not recorded. *United States Twelfth Census of Population, 1900, Ohio* vol. 99 *Lucas County, Toledo City,* p. 99A.

[46] *RC,* 29 July 1909, p. 1.

[47] 1900; *1905,* p. 43; *1907–8,* p. 43; *1909–10,* p. 53; *1911–12,* p. 59; *1913–14,* p. 65; Minutes and Records Baptist church, *passim;* Probate 10654 and 10698; *MD,* 27 June 1901, p.1.

[48] 1910; *1911–12,* p. 59; *1913–14,* p. 63; *1915–16,* p. 87; MR 7 1903–10, p. 224, 25 Nov. 1909; ROD Book F 1918–67, Monroe City, p. 267, 22 Nov. 1946; Probate 24625, Estate of Maurice Harris, 1946; obit: *MEN,* 22 Nov. 1946, p. 3.

[49] 1900, 1910; *1905,* p. 43; *1907–8,* p. 43; *1909–10,* p. 53; *1911–12,* p. 59; *1913–14,* p. 63; *1915–16,* p. 87; MR 7 1903–10, p. 224, 25 Nov. 1909; ROB Book C 1880–88, p. 174, 8 May 1884; Minutes and Records Baptist church, *passim;* Probate 10654; Probate 10698; Probate 24625, Estate of Maurice Harris 1946; obit: *MEN,* 12 Feb. 1968, pp. 11–12.

[50] 1900, 1910; *1905,* p. 43; *1907–8,* p. 43; *1909–10,* p. 53; *1911–12,* p. 61; *1913–14,* p. 65; *1915–16,* p. 87; Minutes and Records Baptist church, *passim;* Probate 10654; Probate 10698; obit: *MEN,* 17 Oct. 1951, p. 19.

[51] 1900, 1910; *1909–10,* p. 53; *1911–12,* p. 59; *1913–14,* p. 65; Probate 10654; Probate 10698; Probate 14046.

[52] 1900, 1910; Minutes and Records Baptist church, *passim;* Probate 10654; Probate 10698.

[53] ROB Book C, 1880–88, p. 93, 25 Dec. 1882; ROD Book A, 1867–88, p. 190, 25 Dec. 1882.

Notes to Figure 2, Foster Family Reconstitution:

[1] 1880, 1900; *1892–93;* Monroe County Liber 105, p. 34, 18 Oct. 1881; Polk, *MSG & BD 1881*, p. 838; *1883*, p. 1118; *1885*, p. 1192; *1887*, p. 1254; *1889*, p. 1396; *1891*, p. 1142; *1893*, p. 1157; Minutes and Records Baptist church, *passim;* Probate 5629, Estate of James W. Foster, 1900; Monroe City Register of Electors, 1888–96; Munch's Cigar Store records, 1884–97; DAR cemetery listings, Woodland Cemetery; ROD Book B 1888–1906, p. 165, 11 July 1900. James W. Foster's name appears many times in the Monroe press between 1880 and his death in 1900; obits: *MD*, 12 July 1900, p. 5, 19 July 1900, p. 1; *MR*, 12 July 1900, p. 1.

[2] 1880, 1900, 1910; John Bulkley, *History of Monroe County Michigan*, 2 vols. (Chicago: Lewis, 1913), 2: 941–42; Minutes and Records Baptist church, *passim;* Probate 10134, Estate of Elizabeth A. Foster, 1921; DAR cemetery listings, Woodland Cemetery; ROD Book D 1918–32, p. 86, 12 July 1921; obits: *MEN*, 12 July 1921, p. 1, 15 July 1921, p. 8.

[3] 1880; Minutes and Records Baptist church, *passim; MD*, 4 July 1889, p. 1; Probate 5629; Probate 10134; Probate A2467, Estate of Grace Schmitt, 1954; Dr. Ames Long, dental register, 1893–95; obit: *MEN*, 11 Sept. 1951, p. 16.

[4] 1880; *1901* ad; Minutes and Records Baptist church, *passim; MD*, 20 Apr. 1893, p. 1, 6 July 1893, p. 1, 19 Oct. 1899, p. 5; *MR*, 27 Nov. 1902, p. 5; Probate 5629; Probate 10134; Record Publishing Co. records 1900–1906, p. 641; Dr. Amos Long, dental register, 1893–95; obit: *MEN*, 26 Nov. 1941, p. 9.

[5] 1880, 1900, *1901* ad; Minutes and Records Baptist church, *passim; MD*, 19 June 1890, p. 1, 7 May 1896, p. 1; *MR*, 11 Jan. 1900, p. 1, 29 Nov. 1900, p. 5; Record Publishing Co. records 1900–1906, p. 641; Probate 5629; Dr. Amos Long, dental register, 1893–95; obits: *MD*, 30 May 1913, p. 7; *RC*, 29 May 1913, p. 7.

[6] 1910; Minutes and Records Baptist church, *passim;* Probate 5629; Probate 10134; Probate A2467; obit: *MEN*, 27 Mar. 1967, p. 24.

[7] 1880, 1900, 1910; Minutes and Records Baptist church, *passim; MD*, 19 June 1890, p. 1, 30 June 1898, pp. 1, 4; Probate 5629; Probate 10134; Probate A2467; ROD Book F 1918–67, p. 83; Dr. Amos Long, dental register 1892–93; obit: *MEN*, 31 May 1954, p. 9.

[8] ROB, Book C 1880–88, p. 18, 22 Apr. 1881; DAR cemetery listings, Woodland Cemetery.

[9] 1900, 1910; ROB Book C 1880–88, p. 119, 12 Mar. 1883; Minutes and Records Baptist church, *passim; MD*, 27 June 1901, p. 1; *MR*, 27 June 1901, p. 1; Probate 5629; DAR cemetery listings, Woodland Cemetery; obits: *MD*, 20 Jan. 1911, p. 1; *RC*, 19 Jan. 1911, p. 1; *Toledo Blade*, 13 Jan. 1911, p. 1.

[10] ROD Book A 1867–88, p. 214, 1 Aug. 1884.

Notes to Figure 3, Wickliffe-Cox-Bromley Reconstitution:

[1] 1870, 1880; *1874–75,* p. 70; Monroe County Liber 73, p. 623, 11 Mar. 1871; City of Monroe Register of Electors, 1859–70, 1872–80, 1880–84, 1888–92; Record of Monroe First M. E. Church, 1867–94, p. 32; obit: *MD,* 4 Apr. 1889, p. 1.

[2] 1870, 1880; *1874–75,* p. 70; Record of Monroe First M. E. Church, 1867–94, p. 32; obit: *MD,* 4 Feb. 1886, p. 8.

[3] 1870

[4] 1870, 1880; *1874–75,* p. 70; *1892–93; 1896–97;* MR 6 1887–1903, p. 37, 24 Aug. 1889; *MD,* 27 Aug. 1889, p. 1, 31 Jan. 1889, pp. 1, 4; United States military and pension records of Joseph Holt, 1864–1939; Probate 4431; Probate 8273; Joseph R. Smith GAR Post 76 collection, box 4; City of Monroe Register of Electors, 1872–80, 1880–84, 1888–92, 1892–96, 1896–1900; obit: *MEN,* 10 Oct. 1939, p. 9.

[5] MR 6 1887–1903, p. 37, 24 Aug. 1889; *MD,* 27 Aug. 1889, p. 1; Dr. Amos Long, dental register, 1892–94; obit: *MD,* 22 Mar. 1900, p. 8.

[6] MR 3 1852–70, p. 200, 10 Feb. 1868; Probate 4431, (witness); Probate 8273.

[7] Obit: *MD,* 23 Oct. 1890, p. 1; ROD Book B 1888–1906, p. 18, 16 Oct. 1890.

[8] *1892–93; 1896–97;* Probate 4386, Estate of Rebecca Fox, 1892; Probate 4431, Guardian Proceedings Wickliffe Fox, 1892; Probate 8273, Estate of Mary Dickinson, 1914; Minutes and Records Baptist church, *passim;* City of Monroe Assessment Rolls, 1903–20.

[9] United States military and pension records of George Fox, 1865–91; DAR cemetery listings, Woodland Cemetery; ROB Book B 1874–80, p. 302, July 1880 (father).

[10] 1870, 1880; Probate 4386; Probate 4431; obit: *MD,* 19 May 1892, p. 4.

[11] 1870, 1880, 1900; *1874–75,* p. 20; *1892–93; 1896–97; 1901,* p. 11; *1904,* p. 17; *1905,* p. 17; City of Monroe Register of Electors, 1880–84, 1888–92, 1892–96, 1896–1900, 1900–1904, 1904–8; Monroe County Liber 61, pp. 577–78, 19 Oct. 1864; City of Monroe Assessment Rolls, 1903–4; Record of First M. E. Church, 1867–94, 1896–1924; United States military and pension records of Aaron Bromley, 1864–96; Joseph R. Smith GAR Post 76 collection, box 4; ROD Book C, 1906–17, p. 217, 4 Aug. 1906; *MD,* 7 Sept. 1893, p. 1, 16 Jan. 1896, p. 1, 27 Feb. 1896, p. 1, 1 Feb. 1900, p. 5; obits: *RC,* 9 Aug. 1906, p. 8; *MD,* 10 Aug. 1906, p. 1.

[12] 1870, 1880, 1900; MR 3 1852–70, p. 105, 5 July 1866; Record of Monroe First M. E. Church, 1867–94, 1896–1924; ROD Book B, 1888–1906, p. 221, 8 Aug. 1903; obits: *MR,* 13 Aug. 1903, p. 4; *MD,* 14 Aug. 1903, p. 4.

[13] 1870

[14] 1870; MR 3 1852–70, p. 200, 10 Feb. 1868 (witness); MR 4, 1867–86, p. 18, 13 Jan. 1869 (witness).

[15] 1870

[16] MR 3 1852–70, p. 200, 10 Feb. 1868.

[17] ROB Book D 1888–97, p. 161, 15 Jan. 1892.

[18] ROB Book D 1888–97, p. 241, 21 Aug. 1894. The date of record for Ellsworth Wickliffe's birth is 26 Oct. 1940. He appears in the 1900 population schedules for Ann Arbor with a birth date of Aug. 1893. *United States Twelfth Census of Population, 1900* T623 Reel 746 *Michigan Volume 75 Washtenaw County,* p. 51A.

[19] 1900; ROB Book B 1874–80, p. 302, 1 July 1880; Monroe City Register of Electors 1900–1904; Probate 4386; Probate 4431; Probate 8273. There are many references in the local newspapers between 1899 and 1902 about Fox's athletic ability; obit: *MEN,* 9 Oct. 1943, p. 6.

[20] 1870, 1880, 1900, 1910; *1892–93; 1896–97; 1901,* p. 11; *1904,* p. 17; *1905,* p. 17; *1907–8,* p. 17; *1909–10,* p. 23; *1911–12,* p. 25; *1913–14,* p. 27; *1915–16,* p. 32; Polk, *MSG & BD 1895,* p. 1240; *1897,* p. 1235; *1899,* p. 1249; *1901,* p. 1284; *1903,* p. 1310; *1905–6,* p. 1510; *1907–8,* p. 1479; *1909,* p. 1331; *1911,* p. 1297; *1913,* p. 1009. Jim Bromley's name appears frequently in the Monroe newspapers for the early twentieth century. *MD,* 20 Dec. 1888, p. 1 (marriage); City of Monroe Register of Electors, 1888–92, 1892–96, 1896–1900, 1900–1904, 1904–8, 1908–12, 1912–13; City of Monroe Assessment Rolls, 1908–27; Record of First M. E. Church, 1867–94; Death Records, St. Johns Catholic Church, p. 16; Probate 9006, Commitment Proceedings Elizabeth Bromley 1917; Probate 10687, Estate of Ellen Francis Johnson, 1923; DAR cemetery listings, St. Joseph; ROD Book D, 1918–32, p. 197, 15 Sept. 1927; MR 6, 1887–1903, p. 25, 17 Dec. 1888; Dr. Amos Long, dental register, 1892; John A. Kirschner business records, 1912–15; Record Publishing Company records 1900–1905, p. 632; obit: *MEN,* 15 Sept. 1927, p. 7, 12 Sept. 1927, p. 9.

[21] 1900, 1910; *1904,* p. 17; *1905,* p. 17; *1907–8,* p. 17; *1909–10,* p. 23; *1911–12,* p. 25; *1913–14,* p. 27; *1915–16,* p. 32; Dr. Amos Long, dental register, 1892; *MD,* 20 Dec. 1888, p. 1; MR 6 1887–1903, p. 25, 17 Dec. 1868; Probate 9006; Probate 12854, Estate of Aaron Alcayde Bromley, 1928; Probate A2997, Estate of Elizabeth Bromley, 1955; obit: *MEN,* 16 Apr. 1955, p. 11.

[22] ROD Book A 1867–88, p. 30, 2 Mar. 1870.

[23] 1880; *MD,* 2 July 1885, p. 1; *MD,* 5 May 1892, p. 1, 10 Aug. 1906, p. 1; *MR,* 13 Aug. 1903, p. 4; *RC,* 4 Sept. 1913, p. 7.

[24] 1900; *1901,* p. 37; City of Monroe Register of Electors 1900–1904.

[25] *MD,* 22 Sept. 1892, p. 1; ROB Book D 1888–97, p. 30, 8 Feb. 1889; ROD Book B 1888–1906, p. 48, 29 Sept. 1892.

[26] 1900, 1910; *1905,* p. 17; *1907–8,* p. 17; *1909–10,* p. 23; *1911–12,* p. 25; *1913–14,* p. 27; *1915–16,* p. 32; ROB Book D 1888–97, p. 68, 15 Apr. 1890. Aaron Alcayde appears in many local news items between 1900 and his death. *RC,* 28 Aug. 1913, p. 7 (marriage); Probate 9006; Probate 12854; Baptism Records, St. Johns Catholic Church, p. 45; City of Monroe Register of Electors, 1912–13; obit: *MEN,* 14 May 1928, pp. 1, 6, 15 May 1928, p. 7, 16 May 1928, p. 9.

[27] *1913–14*, p. 27; *1915–16*, p. 32; *RC*, 28 Aug. 1913, p. 7.

[28] Probate 12854.

[29] ROB Book F 1906–17, p. 394, 20 May 1914; *RC*, 28 May 1914, p. 7; Probate 12854; Probate A2997.

[30] ROB Book F 1906–17, p. 415, 22 Mar. 1916, p. 415; Probate 12854; Probate A2997.

[31] ROB Book G 1918–25, p. 275, 25 July 1925; Probate 12854; Probate A2997.

[32] ROB Book H 1926–33, p. 56, 24 Oct. 1927; Probate 12854; Probate A2997.

[33] 1900; *1892–93; 1904*, p. 45; City of Monroe Register of Electors, 1888–92, 1892–96, 1896–1900, 1900–1904; City of Monroe Assessment Rolls, 1903–23; Record of Monroe First M. E. Church, p. 16; Minutes and Records Baptist church, p. 190, 3 Apr. 1897; ROD Book B 1888–1906, p. 246, 20 Nov. 1904; obit: *MD*, 25 Nov. 1904, p. 8.

[34] 1900, 1910; *1904*, p. 45; *1905*, p. 47; *1907–8*, p. 47; *1909–10*, p. 57; *1911–12*, p. 65; *1913–14*, p. 71; *1915–16*, p. 77; *Detroit Saturday Night*, 9 Aug. 1913, pp. 4, 9; *MD*, 9 Aug. 1913, p. 7; *RC*, 7 Aug. 1913, p. 1; ROD Book D 1918–32, p. 100, 16 Jan. 1923; Probate 10687; Records of First M. E. Church, p. 16; obit: *MEN*, 17 Jan. 1923, p. 5, 18 Jan. 1923, p. 2.

[35] *MD*, 28 Aug. 1884, p. 1.

Notes to Figure 4, Smith Family Reconstitution:

[1] 1850

[2] 1830, 1840, 1850, 1870; City of Monroe Register of Electors, 1859–70; MR 4 1867–86, p. 18, 13 Jan. 1869 (witness); *1874–75*, p. 64.

[3] 1850

[4] 1870

[5] 1850, 1860, 1900; ROD Book B 1888–1906, p. 228, 3 Jan. 1904; obits: *MR*, 4 Feb. 1904, p. 5; *MD*, 5 Feb. 1904, p. 8.

[6] 1850, 1860

[7] 1860

[8] 1850

[9] 1850

[10] 1850

[11] 1870

Notes to Figure 5, Miller Family Reconstitution:

[1] 1870; *1874–75*, p. 24.

[2] 1860, 1870, 1880; *1860–61*, p. 33; *1874–75*, p. 52; ROD Book A 1867–88, p. 164, 14 Apr. 1881; MR 4 1867–86, p. 91, 11 Nov. 1873 (witness); Clark, *Michigan State Gazetteer and Business Directory 1863–64*, p. 408; Chapin and Brother, *Michigan State Gazetteer and Business Directory 1867–68*, p. 305; Burley and Platt, *Lake Shore Gazetteer and Business Di-*

rectory 1868–69 (Buffalo, N.Y.: Sage, Sons, 1868), p. 208; J. E. Scripps and R. L. Polk, comps., *Michigan State Gazetteer and Business Directory for 1873* (Detroit: Tribune, 1873), p. 464; R. L. Polk, comp., *Michigan State Gazetteer and Business Directory for 1875* (Detroit: Tribune, 1875), p. 557; *1877*, p. 636; *1879*, p. 812; *1881*, p. 839; City of Monroe Register of Electors 1859–70, 1872–80; obits: *MD*, 14 Apr. 1881, p. 1, 21 Apr. 1881, p. 1; *MC*, 15 Apr. 1881, p. 1, 22 Apr. 1881, p. 1.

[3] 1860, 1870, 1880; MR 4 1867–86, p. 91, 11 Nov. 1873 (witness); Polk, *MSG & BD 1883*, p. 1118; *1885*, p. 1194; *1887–88*, p. 1256; *1889–90*, p. 1398.

[4] MR 4 1867–87, p. 91, 11 Nov. 1873.

[5] 1870; MR 4 1867–86, p. 91, 11 Nov. 1873.

[6] 1870

[7] 1870, 1880

[8] 1880

[9] 1880; *MD*, 23 Sept. 1880, p. 1.

[10] 1880

[11] 1880

Index

A Note on the Author

James DeVries is a native of Indiana and graduated from Hope College in 1964. He earned his M.A. (1968) and Ed.D. (1978) from Ball State University. He is presently professor of history, Monroe County Community College, Monroe, Michigan.

BOOKS IN THE SERIES

Before the Ghetto: Black Detroit in the Nineteenth Century *David M. Katzman*

Black Business in the New South: A Social History of the North Carolina Mutual Life Insurance Company *Walter B. Weare*

The Search for a Black Nationality: Black Colonization and Emigration, 1787-1863 *Floyd J. Miller*

Black Americans and the White Man's Burden, 1898-1903 *Willard B. Gatewood, Jr.*

Slavery and the Numbers Game: A Critique of *Time on the Cross* *Herbert G. Gutman*

A Ghetto Takes Shape: Black Cleveland, 1870-1930 *Kenneth L. Kusmer*

Freedmen, Philanthropy, and Fraud: A History of the Freedman's Savings Bank *Carl R. Osthaus*

The Democratic Party and the Negro: Northern and National Politics, 1868-92 *Lawrence Grossman*

Black Ohio and the Color Line, 1860-1915 *David A. Gerber*

Along the Color Line: Explorations in the Black Experience *August Meier and Elliott Rudwick*

Black over White: Negro Political Leadership in South Carolina during Reconstruction *Thomas Holt*

Keeping the Faith: A. Philip Randolph, Milton P. Webster, and the Brotherhood of Sleeping Car Porters, 1925-37 *William H. Harris*

Abolitionism: The Brazilian Antislavery Struggle *Joaquim Nabuco, translated and edited by Robert Conrad*

Black Georgia in the Progressive Era, 1900-1920 *John Dittmer*

Medicine and Slavery: Health Care of Blacks in Antebellum Virginia *Todd L. Savitt*

Alley Life in Washington: Family, Community, Religion, and Folklife in the City, 1850-1970 *James Borchert*

Human Cargoes: The British Slave Trade to Spanish America, 1700-1739 *Colin A. Palmer*

Southern Black Leaders of the Reconstruction Era *Edited by Howard N. Rabinowitz*

Black Leaders of the Twentieth Century *Edited by John Hope Franklin and August Meier*

Slaves and Missionaries: The Disintegration of Jamaican Slave Society, 1787-1834 *Mary Turner*

Father Divine and the Struggle for Racial Equality *Robert Weisbrot*

Communists in Harlem during the Depression *Mark Naison*

Down from Equality: Black Chicagoans and the Public Schools, 1920-41 *Michael W. Homel*

Race, Kinship, and Community in a Midwestern Town: The Black Experience in Monroe, Michigan, 1900-1915 *James E. DeVries*

Down by the Riverside: A South Carolina Slave Community *Charles Joyner*

Reprint Editions

King: A Biography *David Levering Lewis* Second edition

The Death and Life of Malcolm X *Peter Goldman* Second edition

Race Relations in the Urban South, 1865-1890 *Howard N. Rabinowitz, with a Foreword by C. Vann Woodward*

Race Riot at East St. Louis, July 2, 1917 *Elliott Rudwick*

W. E. B. Du Bois: Voice of the Black Protest Movement *Elliott Rudwick*

The Negro's Civil War: How American Negroes Felt and Acted during the War for the Union *James M. McPherson*